"Heroes come in different shapes and sizes, but what they all have in common is a big heart. Nobody I know has a bigger heart than Nick Scott. (His biceps aren't too shabby either—do NOT arm-wrestle this man!) The other thing all heroes have is an unshakeable desire to reach their goal and in that respect, Nick has risen to the rank of super hero. Not a fictional movie character, but a real live super hero. Somebody we can all believe in."

—Barry Morrow,
Academy Award-winning screenwriter, *Rain Man*

"Nick is one of the nearly thousand youth with spinal cord injuries who I have cared for during the past 25 years. Nick is particularly noteworthy because of his energy, ingenuity and resilience that guided him through the trials and tribulations of such a severe event as a spinal cord injury. He is a soft-spoken advocate with a very powerful and clear message articulated in words and by example. He inspires all of those around him, both those with and without special needs, to have the vision to dream and courage to pursue them."

—Lawrence C Vogel, MD, professor of pediatrics,
Rush University, assistant chief of staff, medicine,
chief of pediatrics, Shriners Hospitals for Children, Chicago

"As the Director of the Spinal Cord Injury Program at Shriners Hospital for Children in Chicago, I have known Nick Scott since shortly after he sustained his traumatic spinal cord injury. Nick's charismatic personality has shown through since day one. He has taken a tragic life event and turned it into an opportunity both for himself and for others. I know Nick as a patient, an athlete, a scuba diver, and now as a colleague in our ventures with the world's only Wheelchair Bodybuilding Camp for teenage boys with SCI. Nick has given much of himself to be a leader and mentor for those young men and women with disabilities. Nick inspires, Nick motivates, Nick encourages, Nick listens, Nick cares!!! When I think of the quote by Marshal Ferdinand Foch, 'the most powerful weapon on earth is the human soul on fire'…I think of Nick Scott!!!"

—Sara J. Klaas, MSW, C-ASWCM, director;
Spinal Cord Injury Service, project coordinator;
corporate development, Shriners Hospital for Children

JOURNEY

NICK SCOTT

9.25.21

NickFitness.com

nickscott@nickfitness.com

Book design by:
Arbor Books, Inc.
www.arborbooks.com

Printed in the United States of America

Journey
Nick Scott

1. Title 2. Author 3. Memoir

Library of Congress Control Number: 2010902662

ISBN 13: 978-0-615-35739-3

I would like to dedicate this book to my mother, father, brother Raymond, uncle Tom and other family and friends who are parts of my life through my journey. For years I felt lost, but over time you all have made an impact on my life and I will never forget it. Thank you so much!

Mother and Father,
I love you more then you will ever know, and, you mean the world to me. You gave me strength when I hit rock bottom. A part of me died the day of the accident, but a new part of me was born and you helped me see the light in the darkest part of my life. I thank you from the bottom of my heart. I love you both and I am blessed that you are my parents.

Raymond,
I can never thank you enough for being there for me. Many people gave up on me and didn't believe in me. You were one of the few who were there for me no matter what. You are dear to my heart, brother, and I love you. I will always be there for you, brother.

Uncle Tom,
I love you and thank you for always being there for me.

TABLE OF CONTENTS

CHAPTER 1
Awake

As I gratefully opened my eyes, I saw the vivid blue sky with a couple of clouds, and felt a gentle breeze on my face that had the scent of fall. It was the kind of beautiful autumn day that you wish came all year round.

I was peaceful, just lying on the ground staring into the ocean of sky, as if I were in heaven. Suddenly, I heard voices. A man was kneeling on my right side, talking to me persistently to ensure that I remained awake. I must have been unconscious. Could this be real or was I in a dream?

I remembered crashing into the ditch and rolling the car, but afterward the world had gone black. How did I get on the ground, though, and how long had I been lying there?

Other louder, shriller voices could be heard, all coming from the general direction of my feet. A girl's voice called out in horror, "Oh, my god! That's my brother." Then a man's voice said, "No, that's not Josh."

Everything was blurry, but I recognized the man's voice. It was my best friend, Lucas, standing with a girl from school. I managed to call out, "Luuuuuuuke." Instantly he responded, "My god! That's Nick!"

Chills went down my spine upon hearing the fear in his voice. They did not recognize me.

I understood that I had been in an accident, but I did not know how awful it was; I couldn't even think about that. I just lay there, not even trying to get up. Thoughts of dying or being severely injured never crossed my mind. I was at peace and felt no pain.

In the distance I heard sirens getting louder and louder. Soon, more people surrounded me, but now they were moving faster and asking me questions. A man asked if I knew my name, age, and where I was; I politely answered. Afterward, he touched my arm and asked if I could feel it; I did. He moved his hand to my leg and asked me the same question; I couldn't feel a thing. Next, he told me to move my foot, so I did. He repeated himself, asking me again to move my foot. I told him that I was.

Soon, a snug brace was carefully placed around my neck, and I was moved side to side so that a hard board could be placed under my body. Then I was lifted up and put into the ambulance.

It was cold in the rear of that ambulance. EMTs talked to me, keeping me conscious while they fixed the oxygen mask on my face. They turned on the siren and we headed to Ottawa.

CHAPTER 2

Ransom Memorial Hospital

It seemed like a very fast ride. The whole way I really did not think of anything, and I was out of the ambulance in no time.

I ended up at Ottawa Ransom Memorial Hospital, where a lot of medical staff surrounded me. I had no idea what was going on or what would take place next, but a male doctor came over and told me that they would take good care of me.

Bright lights shone in my face as the doctors immediately began cutting off all my clothes. Lying there totally nude, I felt so uncomfortable and helpless with everyone all around me. A nurse told me that she needed to put a tube in to suck out my stomach. I didn't know why they specifically needed to suck out my stomach; I just did what they asked.

The tube was the approximate size of an air tube from a fish tank. The nurse also had a little disposable cup with a straw ready for me. She instructed me to drink when I felt the tube at the back of my throat, but as soon as I felt it in my nose, I started drinking. What I did not immediately grasp was that she was going to stick the tube all the way *down* my nose, and she just kept shoving it in at a quick pace. The feeling of that tube creeping down my nose to my stomach was a horrible experience. I was so relived when it was over.

They began sucking the fluids from my stomach; since the deep cylinder was in my nose and in my view, I saw everything that was being sucked out of me. There were all types of things going through that tube, especially a lot of dark black chunks. It was too much to grasp all at once. They then finally covered me up and began sticking me with a needle to insert an IV.

My mother appeared by my side and I was delighted to see her, but I simultaneously felt awful; I was concerned that she would be furious with me. The first thing I said to her was how sorry I was for wrecking the car. She told me the car could be replaced, but my life could not. We didn't have any more time to talk because I was getting ready to get X-rayed.

The tube from my nose was pretty long and hanging over the side of the bed; as they were moving me around, my mother bumped the tube. She did not realize that she had bumped it, but that was the least of my concerns. As I was going down the hallways on my way to be X-rayed, the lights I saw were like those in a horror movie, heightening my level of anxiety.

When I got to the X-ray room, my mother waited outside. They transferred me to the X-ray table, along with the medical board that was keeping me straight. Then they took what seemed like masses of X-rays. The pain never seriously bothered me until then. It crept up on me, though I didn't complain that much.

After the X-rays were finished, my mother came in and asked the nurses to give me some pain medicine, which they put in my IV. Still, from the pain I was feeling in my back, I knew something bad had happened.

The doctor carefully examined the X-rays and told my mother that I should be transported to a facility that specialized in back and spinal conditions. She already knew specifically where she wanted me to go. At the time, the only hospitals that dealt with spinal conditions were KU Medical Center in Kansas City, Missouri, or one in Wichita, Kansas. My loving, affectionate mom chose for me to be transported to KU by life flight. She had heard good things about that hospital, and it was close to home.

When they loaded me in the helicopter, my mother wanted to

ride by my side, but the hospital staff would not allow it. By then, the pain in my back had gotten worse and my left arm was starting to hurt excruciatingly.

Unknowingly, I was having an allergic reaction to the morphine they had given me in the hospital. Although this was my first time ever in a helicopter, I was dozing in and out.

CHAPTER 3

KU Medical Center

The helicopter ride felt even shorter than the one in the ambulance, though we covered about fifty miles. I don't recall landing or going into KU, although, upon my arrival, they evaluated me further.

My mother arrived shortly before I went in for testing; Mark, a friend and coworker, had driven her. I underwent everything from a CAT scan, an MRI, and a sonogram to lab work. After the full review, the doctor informed my mother that I had broken my back and could have spinal cord damage. He explained that they needed the swelling in my back to go down before they could perform surgery and made it evident to her that there were serious risks, including bleeding, infection, a bad reaction to anesthesia, numbness, paralysis and even death. At that time, I was dozing in and out; all I knew is that I required surgery. I still had no idea what was wrong with me.

I waited a long time for my operation. I had arrived at KU Med Center the night of August 17, and it wasn't until the morning of the nineteenth that I went in for surgery. It actually went quickly for me since I was out almost the whole time, and I don't even remember going in for the operation. I woke up the evening of the nineteenth in the intensive care unit.

There was a throbbing pain in my back, but all I urgently wanted was to see my mother. I called for her and she came quickly. I was thrilled to see her and that the operation was over. We got to spend some time together, but it wasn't too long before one of the physicians who had performed my surgery came in to see me. He said there were no complications and that the operation was a success—then stated bluntly that my football days were over.

He went on to say that I was paralyzed from the waist down and that I would never walk again. I was utterly destroyed and instantly burst in tears; the news was absolutely devastating. I was only sixteen years old, a junior in high school, and felt as if my life were over.

My mother was furious about the way in which the doctor had informed me. She told me not to listen to him, and that we'd take it day by day. But the physical pain was nothing compared to the mental pain of knowing what had happened. The doctor left us as I cried.

I had a hard time accepting what he'd said, and all I could think of was that I'd never play football again. Football was my life-breath; I played it with passion. That sport meant the world to me—and now it was gone. Something so precious had been taken away from me…then it hit me that I wasn't going to be able to walk anymore.

When that sunk in, it hit me hard, and I cried even more. It was just too much for me to handle all at once. I had a million things going through my mind—and they all somehow involved walking and football. I kept asking, "Why me? Why did this happen to me? What did I do to deserve this?"

My mother and I cried for some time together. Then she told me that my dad was waiting outside the room to see me. Only one parent could visit me at a time so he couldn't be in there with us.

My dad was employed out of town hundreds of miles away. My mother had called him the night of my wreck and told him that I had been in an accident; he had left the hotel where he was staying soon after he got the call and traveled day and night to be by my side. A day and a half later, he met up with my mother at the hospital. She told him how severe the accident was, and he instantly fell to his knees and broke down. A man with such pride instantly crumbled.

My mother left the room and my father came in. I hadn't seen him in months and here he was, seeing his baby boy like this. I told him how sorry I was; he just told me how much he loved me and how grateful he was that I was alive. We cried together, maybe for the first time in our lives.

CHAPTER 4

The Wreck— Paralyzed

I had broken my back and severely damaged my spinal cord at T-12 L-1. The break was incomplete and they found glass all over my back and in the undersides of my arms. I had horrific bruising on my sides, arms and parts of my back. They also found bone splinters in my spinal cord.

During surgery, they performed a posterior fusion on T-11 through L-2 with iliac crest bone graft and synthetic fixation rods. They shaved the bone from my hip in order to graft it in my spine. It took over seventy staples to close my wounds: more than sixty for the one over my spine and about ten more for the wound where they shaved my hip.

The nights were miserable, full of fierce, tormenting pain, loneliness, and grief. When I did fall asleep, I would wake up off and on in excruciating pain or in a cold sweat. Everything was blurry since my glasses had been broken in the wreck. I would cry for hours and relive the accident, frequently seeing and hearing in slow motion the unique sounds of broken glass and crushing metal that had surrounded me—the reason I was lying in that bed in the first place. I would think of what I could have done differently so that I wouldn't have wrecked the car in the first place. The mental images I saw and the sounds I heard scarred me for life.

I sorted out what had happened as I lay there alone: It had been a Monday—August 17, 1998. I was sixteen and it was the week before I started my first day as a junior at Pomona High in Pomona, Kansas. I had just gotten off work at the Country Kitchen in Ottawa, Kansas, and was headed to get my car out of the mechanic shop, where it had a rebuilt transmission put in. The plan was to then head to football practice that afternoon at Pomona High.

As I was driving from Ottawa to Pomona, I felt like I was on top of the world. I was cruising down the highway alone in my white '84 Buick Skylark, with a red interior, a hula girl on my dash, white fuzzy dice on my rearview mirror, and a white fuzzy steering wheel cover. The look was for the girls, but it also made me feel cool.

I had the music turned way up so that my seat was vibrating from two twelve-inch JL Audio subwoofers in the trunk, powered by a Rockford Fosgate amplifier. The hula girl danced for me when I had the music playing that loud—but I loved the sound of bass in my car and could never have it loud enough.

I was sticking to the speed limit and as I drove onto a bridge, my left front tire blew out and jerked my car to the right. The bridge had side rails, so I pulled to the left to avoid hitting them. That's when I lost control of the car and it went into the other lane, where a truck was coming directly at me.

I could see the woman in the truck and did not want to hit her; reflexively, I pulled to the right, preventing a head-on collision. When I got off the bridge, my car skidded to the right as the tires spun. I headed toward the ditch on the left: a medium slant with crisp green grass.

It all happened so quickly, but it felt like slow motion as I headed into the ditch. I realized what was going to happen next and that there wasn't anything I could do. I wasn't scared about what was coming next; I just held the steering wheel, loosened my grip, closed my eyes and said to the Lord, "I'm in your hands now."

The car hit the ditch and immediately began to roll onto its right side. Everything was dark but I felt myself rolling as well, and heard the sound of glass shattering. That's when I saw the sky.

Witnesses reported to the police that I had rolled my car five and a half times. No one saw me thrown from the vehicle. They believed I had been ejected from the driver's side window and, as I was thrown, my car struck me in the back as it was rolling. The significant impact from the hit I took was enough to break my back. The sides of the car were caved in. I wasn't wearing my seatbelt, but the police strongly believed that if I were, it would have killed me.

CHAPTER 5

Recovery and Friends

The endless night of August 19 was the worst for me. On the twentieth, I was sleeping on and off, recuperating from my surgery. When I was awake, all I could think about was what had recently taken place; vivid images always came to mind, especially since the surroundings in the room was blurry.

Straight in front of my bed hung the kind of calendar that you rip off day by day. The digits were blurry but they were so enormous that I could still see them, for the most part. Yet what was there to see? It was just another long, miserable day that seemed like it would never end. When the night came around, it was almost an exact repetition of the night before, except I knew by then that I was paralyzed.

The next day, I was fitted for a TLSO brace: a hard, white plastic brace that came in two pieces that fitted together. The brace covered my back, abdomen, and trunk. It had six Velcro strips, three on each side; the straps were attached to the backside and could be tightened to the front. The harder you pulled the straps, the tighter the brace got, which held the body and pieces of the back together.

Occupational therapists wanted to see if the brace fit, but first they had to assist me in getting dressed: putting on a simple shirt and pants. They then gradually rolled me from side to side as they slipped the brace under my back, attached the front chest piece and tightened the Velcro straps. As I lay there, they adjusted the brace to make sure it aligned in a certain position, not too high or low, so it wouldn't put unnecessary pressure on my legs since I wasn't able to feel them. After seeing that the brace fit, they removed it and I returned to resting.

On the twenty-second, I began seeing people other than my mother, father, nurses, and physicians. My football coach, Ed Ramsey, and some of my teammates came to visit me, including my close friend Rocky. They were all seeing me in my worst state.

The lights were dim as they walked in, and I was lying in the bed, nothing but tubes coming from my torso. I had oxygen tubes in my nose, a tube coming from my mouth, a tube stitched in my neck, wires monitoring my heart, an IV in my arm, a machine monitoring and injecting my pain medication, and a catheter bag that was full of a mixture of urine and blood. They looked at me as if I were in a horror scene from the *X-Files*.

Ed Ramsey is a great coach, leader and friend. He was the one who taught me to love football and weightlifting. Rocky and I have been going to school together since my freshman year. We played football side by side for the previous two years and got along great on and off the field. I was overwhelmed with their presence, as well as that of the team. They remained as long as they were permitted, but just seeing them for that short time meant the world to me.

However, when they left, I felt miserable, alone, and as if I weren't part of the team anymore since I couldn't play football. My pillow dampened with tears.

Of course, I was grateful to be alive, but I couldn't do anything except lay there, torching myself with my thoughts. I tried to suppress my emotions, but they were too strong to hide. The emotional and physical pain was evident in my bloodshot eyes.

The medical staff had brought in a machine with which, by simply pressing a button, I could manually inject myself with pain medicine every thirty minutes. I had used it once or twice before I found out that the less I utilized it, the better off I'd be and the faster

I'd heal. As soon as I heard that, I didn't want to use it anymore. I decided that I'd rather suffer then press that button. Getting better and going home was all that mattered.

During the remainder of my stay at KU Medical Center, my brothers and sister came to see me, as well as my grandparents, uncles, aunts, and various friends, including my two close friends, Lucus and Zack.

My mother also found my old pair of glasses so I could actually see everybody and watch some TV, too. My classmates, teachers, school officials, and neighbors, as well as my friends and family, sent me cards, balloons, flowers, candy, and stuffed animals. It was great receiving so many wonderful things. That really got to me, knowing how many people cared and were concerned for me. Reading what they wrote helped take my mind off many negative and depressing thoughts. It relieved the pain more than any medication could.

CHAPTER 6

Occupational Therapy

I underwent occupational therapy from August 22 until I was released. The occupational therapists helped me relearn how to get dressed and put on the TLSO brace.

Once they were satisfied with where the brace was on me, ensuring that it was aligned on my hips, they then raised the top portion of my electronic bed with the remote control. I could only be raised to a certain angle or it would make me dizzy and nauseated. But once I was used to sitting like that, an occupational therapist (OT) helped me move my legs off the bed to sit in an upright position. This was a huge step.

As I held on to the bed, the OTs gave me temporary additional support by holding on to me as I struggled to sit up. After only a couple of seconds, I began to feel lightheaded and sickish again, so they placed me back down with my head throbbing.

A moment or two later we were at it again; this time, I could sit longer but the nausea was still too strong and restricted the amount of time I could stay in that position. After a while, my tolerance increased and I managed to sit for longer periods.

The OTs wanted me to begin to move around, even though I felt helpless. Their main goal was to get me in a wheelchair so I would have back support while sitting in an upright position.

The wheelchair was a basic hospital model, except it had a special gel pad cushion for me to sit on. Since I couldn't feel my butt, the cushion reduced the probable chance of my getting pressure sores.

But how I supposed to get in the wheelchair remained a mystery to me. The bed was up pretty high and I didn't have the use of my legs. The OT had the answer: a smooth rectangle board, called a transfer board, to help successfully transfer patients. I learned to simply stick it under one butt cheek, angle it in the direction I wanted to go and just slide.

However, this was much more complicated than it sounds when the OTs tried to get me ready to get in the wheelchair. There were at least seven steps to take and the OTs were telling me things I needed to watch out for. They had to put the wheelchair at just the right angle, remove the armrest, and lock the brakes. Placing the transfer board just right, they angled it toward the wheelchair; I was ready to slide. They put a rehab belt around the middle of the TLSO brace and told each other to pay careful attention to where my feet were and how I was angled.

With one OT in front of me and another by the wheelchair, they instructed me to lean forward as they slid me along. They managed to get me in the wheelchair, but it was so much work for something so simple. Still, I felt good sitting in that chair. I had a sense of freedom and I did not experience dizziness or nausea.

Once I was sitting comfortably, the OTs replaced the armrest and adjusted my legs on the leg rest. They told me to do pressure releases every three to five minutes, but I had no idea what they were talking about. They explained that it meant simply lifting my butt off the cushion for a couple of seconds by holding on to the armrest and pulling my body up. Doing pressure releases would relieve the pressure on my butt (which I was unaware of) to ultimately reduce the possibility of developing an ulcer.

It was so hard to do a pressure release in the beginning, and later I discovered why. I had not considered leaning forward a little while pushing myself up. So the whole time I was leaning back and every time I lifted myself up, my TLSO brace dragged on the backside of the wheelchair, which added resistance. Believe me, it was a workout.

Overall, though, it was breathtaking to be able to get out of bed. Despite all the negative things I was going through, that one step caused me to immediately brighten up.

However, sitting fatigued me and I wore out easily; it was as if the accident and surgery took all my energy just so I could survive. When I would grow tired, the hospital staff would either help me transfer to bed or someone would just lift me onto it. Later, though, I'd be expected to do that whole transfer thing over again when I wanted to get out of bed.

After a few times, I could stay out of bed for longer—sometimes up to one hour—so my body must have been adapting very quickly to the situation. My family would push me around the hospital just to get me out of my room, and sometimes when my friends visited me, I would be out of bed and we could go for a stroll.

I did not have too many days left before I was transferred from KU Medical Center, but I did learn a lot in the brief time I was there. The OTs' job was to get me back to doing essential things for survival, and that they did.

When they came to get me for rehab, they started by teaching me to get dressed in my bed. I began by trying to put on a shirt by moving side to side. It was very tough to dress myself, as I was stiff and had limited movement, but I always did my best. After getting my shirt on, they helped me with my TLSO brace. But putting on pants and socks was the hardest thing to do; I couldn't just hop out of bed like I used to and pull them on really quickly. First, I had to raise the top portion of the bed to a certain angle then grab my leg and try to drag it up toward me. I never got very far with that at KU, so the OT would graciously assist me—that or my family assisted me before the OT arrived. The OT eventually brought a hooked rod to try to help me put on my socks, but that never worked for me, either.

After I was dressed, the OT would focus on my balance, which was horrible. Without holding on to something, I could easily fall to one side or off the bed, as if I were an infant. However, the OT instructed me to let go of the bed and try to hold myself up as long as I could. We practiced that for some time.

Time passed quickly, even though the nights were endless. My day of discharge, August 28, 1998, came around and a van was set to take me to Topeka. My family and I said our goodbyes to the hospital staff before heading to the lobby. As I was wheeled to the front of the hospital, despite not actually knowing what lay ahead, I was prepared and willing to move on.

The van was wheelchair-accessible, with a special opening on one side that folded down to the ground so I could roll my wheelchair on. As I got on the lift, orderlies strapped my wheels with belts so I would not roll off as it was moving. The lift was interesting in how effectively it worked; it was pleasant and easy, though it took at least five minutes to get me into the van and for them to secure me inside.

There was a specific spot in the vehicle where my wheelchair was supposed to stay and there were belts and locks made just for wheelchairs so I wouldn't roll or move when the vehicle was in motion. My dad rode with me in the van and my mother followed with her friend Mark.

I'll always remember what a beautiful day it was when I was transferred to the rehab center in Topeka.

CHAPTER 7

Topeka Rehab

I was admitted to Topeka Rehab on August 28, 1998, and upon arriving, I was fatigued. The trip seemed to take forever and it was the first time I had been in a wheelchair for that long.

When we got to the facility, I was just looking forward to lying down, but instead we looked around to check the place out. There was nobody around my age; all the patients were fifty to eighty years old and they all looked so miserable. Their attitudes were so depressing, as if they could care less about being there and getting better.

When I went to my room, my name and age were written above my bed. My mother had arranged for me to have a private room so my father could stay with me at all times while my mother got things prepared for me to come home. Yet, despite her work and renovations to the home, she still came to see me every day.

My first day there, the nurses, who attended to all my needs, showed me where everything was, including where I would do my daily rehab. The nurses' station was just outside my room and behind it was a posted schedule of which therapist I would be working with at what time; all of the patients' names and appointment times were written on this big board in magic marker.

The nurses also served breakfast, lunch and supper in my room around the same time every day. During each breakfast, I had to circle my food choices for the next day's meals. It was your basic rehab facility with everything run in a precise and orderly fashion.

What never seemed to become routine for me, however, was

being paralyzed. That consistently got worse. I had lost function of my bladder and bowel control, and since the wreck I was forced to wear a catheter at all times in my penis to drain my urine into a bag that was always by my side.

A day after I got to Topeka, one of the main nurses, nicknamed Goldfinger, came to talk to me about the self-catheter and bowel program, which would require me to catheter myself at a specific time and schedule. To begin the catheter program, she would have to watch me do it the first time to make sure I was applying it correctly.

First, she took out the catheter that had been in me since the wreck. After that, I had to wait one to two hours since the catheter had drained all the urine out of my bladder. She brought me plenty of water and juice to drink in order to ensure that some urine was produced. When Goldfinger returned, she brought me all sorts of things: latex-free gloves, iodine swabs, numbing gel packets, red bags, a urinal, and a sixteen-inch catheter tube sealed in sterile plastic bag. She stood right beside me like a drill sergeant, giving me commands about what to do.

She told me to put on the gloves—which needed to be latex-free because all spinal cord injury patients become sensitive to latex after their accidents. Then I opened and set the numbing gel packets to the side. Next, she made me clean myself with an iodine swab to prevent infection. Then I placed the urinal in front of me and grabbed the catheter. All I could think of was how long the tube looked and how much it was going to hurt; my hands actually shook as I opened the sealed bag that held the catheter.

As I pulled the tube out, I thought to myself that I had no choice—or someone would be doing this for me all the time. That eased my mind about what I was about to go through. So I grabbed that numbing packet and put the gel all over the front of the catheter tube and the rest on myself, until I used it all up. All I had to do now was stick the tube in my pee hole.

I asked the nurse how far I had to stick it in and she told me to keep going until pee started coming out; she was a real help. That freaked me out even more, as I was holding that long damn tube in my hand. But it had to be done, so I went for it. As I inserted the catheter, it hurt like hell, but I gently kept going. Then I put the end of the tube in the urinal. Most of the catheter was in me, however, and when pee started to come out, I can't explain how happy I was to see it in the urinal!

After I was done, I pulled the tube out and put everything I'd used in the red bag. The nurse recorded how many cc's I peed. From then on, I'd have to catheter every three hours and log how much I peed. Peeing every three hours reduced the possibility that I would pee on myself and recording how much I peed let them know that I was drinking enough fluids and regularly keeping myself hydrated.

A nutritionist also came to advise me, telling me how important it was to have proper nutrition and giving me a pyramid chart to follow. I was to try to get eleven servings of carbohydrates a day, as well as enough of the other servings listed on the chart. That wasn't a problem. But the bladder program was something else!

The bowel program required me to visit the toilet on a regular schedule, using suppositories to stimulate and force bowel movements. They were going to start me in the next couple of days, but they first needed me to have a bowel movement since I hadn't had one since my wreck. The same nurse, Goldfinger, got out a blue plastic sheet with cotton on one side and put it under me; the point was to have me go to the bathroom in my bed. As I turned to my right side, I saw that she had gloves on and was holding a packet of KY gel and suppositories. All I could think was how messed up this was!

She stuck the suppository in me and left afterward. I, on the other hand, was a sitting time bomb just waiting to go off. After about an hour, I started to feel weird and my stomach was turning;

I knew I had to go to the bathroom. Soon, I felt relief as the smell permeated the air.

I paged the nurse with the button on my bed and found that she had been waiting for me. My self-esteem was so low as she cleaned me up, but I had to think of it as one of those things that needed to be done or it would have made me even more depressed. Later, I found out that that one nurse did all the dirty work—hence, her nickname, Goldfinger.

■ ■ ■

A couple of days later, Goldfinger returned and gave me a choice of routines: every second day either in the morning or in the evening. So I chose the evening and she was planning to return the next night to get this program started.

When she returned, I was ready. I had it set in my mind that this had to be done; I had no alternative. As she came into the room, I knew it was time. She helped me get in the wheelchair and head into the big bathroom. They had a toilet chair above the toilet, a good foot and a half high. The seat looked like a wider version of a toilet seat with armrests on each side.

The nurse assisted in transferring me to the seat and then pulled down my pants. She wanted me to use the suppositories myself, so I did. At a moment like that, I just kept going back to the thought that it had to be done and that was it.

So every second night, I used the restroom at a specific time and afterward thought about all the things the wreck had taken from me, forcing me to do things against my will. Think about it: If something like that were ever to happen to you, you'd be doing the same thing...

■ ■ ■

I spent most of the time in my room. The life-threatening operation I had and the medications I was taking made me constantly hot, so I asked to have the AC on the highest it could go. It was like my body was going through different stages; despite the room being so cold, I would wake up at night in a sweat, with only a sheet covering me. Later I found out that my family, friends and hospital staff always talked about how cold my room was. They said that they froze every time they entered.

In the beginning, occupational and physical therapists met with me anywhere from once to a couple of times daily. I was still badly off but recovering. When I had occupational therapy, we performed the basics in life, like getting dressed—a continuation of what I had done in KU's rehab. Putting on a shirt was still so tough, especially when lying down with limited mobility, and I could never manage to put the brace on by myself.

But what still got me the most frustrated was putting on my sweatpants. The OT would stand by and try to give me advice, but I felt so worthless not being able to do such a simple thing. Regardless of how hard it was for me, though, I would never let myself get pessimistic or give the therapist a tough time. Their job was to help me improve and I did not see any point in not cooperating. After all, I wanted more than anything to move on and eventually recover.

After I was dressed, the OTs helped me get in my wheelchair and found other challenges for me to do. They took me to a kitchen area for rehab and had me try turning on water in a sink, or open and close cabinets. For the top cabinets, they gave me a claw-gripper device to help me grab glasses and objects that I couldn't reach from a considerable distance. I had to repeat some of these actions to make sure I could do them, and all of the tasks were much more difficult when I wore the TLSO brace.

The physical therapist, on the other hand, worked with me to improve my balance, flexibility, wheelchair skills, and everyday

encounters. Since I would have physical therapy right after occupational, I was already dressed and would sometimes be in my
wheelchair.

The PT would oftentimes wheel me to the rehab training area
until I could wheel myself. Once I was there, they had me transfer
myself with the sliding board to a padded table with dark yellow
mats that had an inch and a half of padding. I had to lie down so
they could stretch me out, but before they could do that, I had to
get my legs on the table. My legs were dead weight, and I wasn't a
little guy, either.

I had to hold on to the table as I tried to bend forward to grab
my leg. Well, I didn't get too far…and the whole time I was trying
to grab my leg, two therapists were standing beside me. One held
me from the back with a belt while the other stood in front to
catch me if I started to fall.

After a couple of failed attempts, the therapists would help me
get my legs up and I would lie down for my stretching. They would
stretch me out on my back, sides, and stomach. After ten minutes
or so of stretching, I sat back up on the edge of the table with my
feet and calves hanging off. The first time I moved my legs off the
table, they just slid off and I saw and heard my bone and flesh
grind against the wood. It didn't look too pleasant, but I didn't feel
anything. Still, it made me pay more attention to details. Seeing
that was kind of freaky and didn't look right.

As I was sitting in that position, the therapists worked on my
balance and wanted me to let go of the padded table so I would not
use my arms as a support. I let go of the table and quickly started
to fall to the side, as if I had no abdominal muscles or lower back
muscles at all. They had me try over and over, even though I fell
every time.

The therapist in front of me was sitting on a small stool with
a black cushion and wheels. She would move all around, making
sure I would not fall. I felt so worthless in the beginning, but there

was nothing I could do except try my best. The therapist behind me held me up while I tried to sit. Eventually, I could sit up and keep my balance without holding on to the table or having the therapist hold on to me, but if I moved too far to the side, front or back, I would fall over. Even still, the littlest improvements meant the world to me. Never before had something so simple made me so happy.

■ ■ ■

When I could sit up without support, the therapists and I started playing catch with a tennis ball. It was easy when they threw it at my chest or stomach, but when they threw it to the side and above my head, where I had to reach for it, it became difficult. How far I had to reach to the side would determine if I would fall over.

Even with a new task, however, I knew over time I could do it. If the therapist threw the ball way to the side, I would fall a bit but would catch it as I fell, then catch myself with my arm and pull myself back up to a certain degree. I was thrilled to be doing anything that related to sports, and it showed!

I always liked to have a good time with whatever I was doing and the therapists and I would talk and laugh every time I was in rehab. Even so, I did everything they asked and put forth all my effort. Every once in a while when we were playing catch and they would throw the ball too far to the side, I would act like I was falling off the front of the table while I was reaching for it and they would both instantly grab me. After I sat up, I would tell them that I had just been playing and they would freak out. Not only would they feel bad for dropping a patient on the floor, but they would have to fill out a ton of paper work for an accident report also. I only did things like that when they would least expect it since that was the only way to get the full shock factor out of them. It was great.

After rehab, I would lie back in bed and take off my TLSO brace, which made me sweat a lot. In the beginning, blood oozed out of my back and my staples left blood spots on my shirts; about halfway through rehab, though, they removed the staples from my back. I could feel them being pulled out, except for the lower ones. Some hurt worse than others, but I just had to tough it out.

■ ■ ■

While all of this physical rehab was going on, I also had to undergo mental rehab as well. I had to go through all sorts of psychiatrist testing to see if I was mentally normal. I would be on an old computer and had to press the enter key every time I saw a certain type of shape. The psychiatrist also had different cards that he showed me and I would have to tell him what I saw. Then he would give me two different things and I would have to tell him what they had in common. He once asked me, "What do a fly and a tree have in common?" Well, I did not know what to say to that, so I answered, "I don't know…they're both alive."

I constantly joked around and he did not like that at all. I could tell that he thought I behaved immaturely, but I didn't care. I had a good time.

So I asked him, "What *do* a fly and tree have in common?" He wouldn't tell me because it was confidential.

Every time I saw him after that in the lobby area or just walking around, I went up to him and asked, "So what do a fly and tree have in common?" I could tell I got to him, but he never would give me the answer. I went around and asked some nurses and other staff the same question, but no one knew. The whole time I was at rehab, I never found out the answer…and to this day I don't know.

CHAPTER 8

Wheelchair Skills— and Social Skills

In physical therapy, I also had to work on my wheelchair skills. Learning to maneuver a wheelchair is pretty tough in the beginning, and being able to turn corners is especially confusing at first.

When you want to turn a corner, you basically have to hold one tire or slow one tire down while you move the other one faster. So if you want to go around in circles to your right, you would hold the right tire still and push the left one forward.

Nothing compares to opening doors, though; that's one of the most difficult and complicated things to do when you're sitting in a wheelchair. A lot of people don't realize how many different types of doors are out there!

The difficulty of a door all depends on how broad or heavy it is, its resistance factor, and if it is a push or pull. Pushing a door open is pretty easy, unless it is a heavy or hydraulic door; then, you basically have to use brute force to try to push it open. If you have to pull open a door, you must grab it with some force with one hand while you hold on the tire with your other hand so you could pull back on your wheelchair and open the door at the same time (this is especially hard if a person doesn't have good balance). When you have the door open enough, you can move the wheelchair and start going through the door then use the front of the wheelchair to hold it open—but, partway through, you have to push the door so it doesn't drag on your tire. If this all sounds complex, it is, because opening a heavy, hydraulic, resistant door is complicated.

However, with all of the wheelchair skills training going on, nothing fascinated me more than popping wheelies!

My wheelchair had bars close to the ground that extended from the bottom out to the rear; they were anti-tip bars, designed so people in wheelchairs would not fall backwards. Despite these anti-tip bars, I got really good at popping wheelies—and they even made it easier to stay in a wheelie position by leaning back and resting on them.

To pop a wheelie, I simply had to lean back in the wheelchair and push myself forward. The more I leaned backwards, pulled, and pushed, the bigger and quicker my wheelie would be. (Without anti-tip bars, you'd have to lean your head forward when you fell so you wouldn't crack it open on the floor.)

In the beginning, I practiced my wheelie skills, thinking I was cool. But I trusted in the anti-tip bars more than I should have because they didn't always work.

One day, I had just finished rehab and went back to my room, feeling hungry. I asked my father to get me something to eat from the McDonalds or Burger King about a block away. When he was gone, I began popping wheelies.

After a few minutes, I decided to lean back and rest in the wheelie position by keeping my weight on the anti-tip bars. It was nice just relaxing at that angle, sitting with my TLSO brace on as if I were in a recliner. A couple of minutes later, however, I felt myself slowly going back even more. I was falling, and I tried to go forward but it was too late.

I was falling in slow motion, with my only thought being to lean my head forward before I hit the floor. The fall turned out not to do any damage; it was more of a rush than anything! I didn't yell or call for help—I just lay there laughing!

I was on the ground for a minute or two before my father came back with my double cheeseburger; he just about had a heart attack seeing me on the ground. He quickly helped me up while I laughed at the whole thing. I told my dad that the anti-tip bars didn't work, but he didn't think it was that funny.

I also practiced transferring to places other than my bed. When I got home, I might want to sit on the couch, recliner or floor, so I practiced transferring with the sliding board to the rehab's recliner and back to my wheelchair. Then I tried transferring to the couch, and from there my therapist had me slide down to the floor.

Everything was fine going down, but getting back in my wheelchair was a problem. To sit back in it, the therapist wanted me to lock the wheelchair right behind me and, as I was about to sit with my back facing the wheelchair, put my arms behind me high on the cushion and lift myself in. It was impossible to get up in the chair like that, but I tried anyway. My arms were too short and I was too weak to lift my heavy self up at that angle. So instead I rolled on my knees, kneeling in front of the chair, and lifted myself up. It may not have been as graceful, but it was a lot easier than what she wanted me to do.

■ ■ ■

Being around people during the day kept my mind occupied a lot of the time; I was always resting, having rehab, or talking to someone. All the nurses and therapists liked me and I made them laugh whenever they were around me. I always tried to have a good time with whatever I was doing, but night was the worst for me. I would cry for hours and try to deal with all that had happened.

At night, thoughts of dances, sports, and the simplest things that I could never do again went through my mind as tears rolled down my cheeks. It was hard on my father to see me like that; he would cry along with me, trying to understand my pain. But no one could know what I was going through.

Most of the time, I tried to kept my emotions inside and dealt with what had happened as best I could. I could have given up and gone into a state of depression, or turned violent and not cared about life, but I wanted to get better. I wanted to go home and see my friends. That is what drove me to work as hard as I did during each day.

And what great friends I had! My close friend Rocky did one of the greatest things someone could do for me during that time. Even though he had school, football, and other things going on in his life, he came to visit me a few times in Topeka, as well as in KU, and one time, I asked him if he could get this particular girl to come see me. She had been going to school with Rocky and me since our freshmen year, and I had the biggest crush on her.

Rocky is a good friend. That weekend, he came back with her and three of her friends and we all talked and hung out for a while. I didn't think she would actually come! She knew that I had a crush on her but didn't like me in that way. It was nice seeing her, though.

After they left, something weird happened. I never thought of looking at myself until then. In fact, since my accident, I hadn't so much as glanced in a mirror. But when I was alone in my room after their visit, I looked for a mirror and found one in a drawer near my bed.

When I picked it up and looked at myself for the first time, I was shocked! I looked awful. My hair had grown into a mini-Afro and I had a spotted beard with no mustache. I wore an older pair of glasses (since my other ones were lost in my accident), and they were pretty big and square. The worst was that I had gained a lot of weight, which you could see in my face. I was disgusted with myself; I couldn't believe that was me in the mirror.

At that moment, I swore to myself that I would never look like that again. I never imagined that in such a short time, I could change so much. I hated the thought that the girls had seen me like this, but there was nothing I could do about that. From then on, though, I was more driven and focused. Deep down a fire had been lit, and a couple of minutes later, I was shaving my face.

CHAPTER 9

Home

My time had come; I was finally being discharged after a month, and was so excited to finally be going home. Nothing meant more or was sweeter than knowing that I was leaving the hospital after weeks of surgery and rehab. But I had to admit that being away from home helped push me through some tough times; all the rehab I had done prepared me to be on my own and helped me mentally and physically. I had a long way to go, but I was moving forward.

I had never been away from home that long at any time. While I was in rehab, my mother told me that we were moving to a house in Ottawa. At the time of my accident we lived in Pomona. My mother had found a house to rent and my relatives that were carpenters remolded it, making the necessary changes for it to be handicap accessible. They constructed a ramp up to the porch and made some of the door openings and walls wider. (My mother's friend Mark was the owner; he was a great guy who didn't care what changes had to be made and let my mother do what she needed.)

■ ■ ■

With my new skills, getting into a car was pretty easy, especially with the help of the sliding board. I traveled home with my mother and Mark as my father followed us in his truck. As we were heading home, we passed through the town of Pomona and I saw my high school with all the cars in the parking lot. Seeing all the auto-mobiles automatically made me want to see everybody so badly and to let them know that I was out.

As we continued on to Ottawa, we passed the spot where I had my wreck and I got flashbacks. I could see and feel everything as if the accident had just happened. Seeing the bridge didn't make me feel uneasy, though, and I wasn't scared—just wondering what was going to happen next.

We finally made it to the house. The drive took a lot out of me; all the excitement and the hour-and-a-half ride drained me mentally and physically. Soon after arriving, my brothers, sister, and uncle came out to greet me. They showed me all the work they had been doing to get the home ready for me. It was so thrilling and honestly meant so much to me that my family had done all that for me.

It was a nice, small house that had everything you could need. They ended up making the dining room into my room for easy access, and my mother bought me one of those remote control beds like the ones in the hospital, so I did not have to lay flat when I wanted to relax.

As soon as I toured the house, I could see what they done. The smell of newly cut wood and fresh paint filled the air. It still blows my mind how much stuff they finished, and I am so grateful to those who helped make it all come together.

It was nice being home; the atmosphere was totally different than being in the hospital and I was at peace. Just lying in bed with my family so close comforted me and started healing the broken pieces inside. It had been a tough journey but, little by little, things were starting to change.

■ ■ ■

Later that week, I ended up going to school. There was a pep rally taking place in the afternoon since we had a football game that Friday night. I thought that would be the perfect time for me to go back and see everyone.

My mother and Mark took me to school and as we approached, I was so nervous that my hands got cold and sweaty. We ended up getting there an hour before the pep rally began.

A couple of teachers and classmates saw me and were shocked. They couldn't believe that I was out so soon after hearing how severe my wreck was. After talking for a while, we headed down the halls and managed to get to the gym early, before the other students began coming in for the pep rally.

I sat in the wheelchair off to the side of the basketball court. When the students began coming in, they saw me sitting there and immediately surrounded me, asking how I was. The look on their faces, upon seeing me for the first time, is something I will never forget. As the gym filled up, all eyes were on me.

The pep rally started typically, until one of the football players took the microphone and began speaking. He got the football team to line up on the court and a couple of the players came to the side and pushed me in front and center of the team. The player at the mic made a few comments about how the team was going to perform and how they were going to dominate the game that night, and the coach began telling the school how we had a tremendous team. Then he expressed how glad the team was to have me back as well, saying a few words to honor me.

Everyone stood up and started clapping, yelling and whistling. The chills I felt at that time were overwhelming; it was one of the greatest feelings in the world.

After talking to my classmates and teammates after the pep rally, I went back home to get some rest since I still got tired fairly quickly. A couple of days later, a newspaper reporter from Ottawa came to visit me. He had come to do an article on me and take some pictures. It was weird seeing myself in the paper for the first time.

But it wasn't all excitement. That coming week, I had a serious choice to make: I could either take a year off school or get a tutor and graduate with my class. Without hesitation, I chose to be tutored. Graduating with my class meant a lot to me. Their support during that crucial month following my accident gave me strength and kept me sane.

That following Monday, I immediately began being tutored by my fourth grade teacher. She was an older woman but very delightful and passionate. She eased me into what we would be doing and was very sympathetic; all she wanted was to help me any way that she could.

The school provided some assignments but I was so far behind after a month away. We tried to touch on different subjects, but the time I could actually spend with a tutor was an hour to an hour and a half, max. The mental concentration drained so much of my energy that I practically had to take a nap every time she left.

The following Monday, on September 28, I also started physical therapy at Ransom Memorial Hospital. My schedule was tutoring in the morning and physical therapy in the afternoon. It was hard but after about a month of getting tutored, I ended up going back to school in the mornings. For the remainder of my junior year of high school, I went to class from 8 a.m. until noon, when my father would pick me up and take me to McDonald's, where I would get two or three cheeseburgers or double cheeseburgers. After that, I'd head to therapy full.

CHAPTER 10
School

Once I was back at school, I switched my bowel program to the mornings and I consistently "cathed" (used the catheter) before going to school, which was perfect because I did not have to cath again until I came home. That way, I was eliminating any possible accidents…and embarrassment.

Going back to school was a difficult time for me, but thrilling. Everything I had ever known felt different—and, in fact, it *was* different. I was like everybody else but I did not feel the same—I *wasn't* the same. I had limited mobility and abilities, but I was not helpless. However, with a part of me gone, I began to notice everything more closely and was more aware of my surroundings. It was as if I had gained a sixth sense.

Everyone in school was so compassionate. They wanted to help me out in every way possible, particularly my friends. They opened doors, pushed my wheelchair, and always asked me if I needed assistance. It was heartwarming that they cared that much, but I could also tell they felt sorry for me.

■ ■ ■

Another big change was that I had no need for a locker; I just carried all my books and everything I needed in my bag on the back of my wheelchair. That saved me time and energy. But every time I went to class, I felt like an outsider. There was no spot for my wheelchair so I would sit at the side of the room. While all my classmates faced the teacher, I always faced halfway toward the teacher and halfway toward my fellow students.

I also had no desk; all the desks were single seats with tables attached at an angle, so I balanced my books on my legs. The school asked if I wanted a special desk, but I chose not to have one because I felt out of place enough as it was. Having a "special" desk would have just made it that much worse for me.

Another disappointment was weightlifting, one of the four classes I had. I thought it would be the one comforting class, but I was wrong. It turned out to be the toughest one. I just had to sit and watch everyone else do the things that I loved to do. It was hell. Watching other students lift weights was bad enough, but watching them play kickball, dodgeball, softball, volleyball or any of those activities crushed me mentally.

I loved the competitiveness of sports and loved to win. There were times during that class when I wanted to cry so badly, but I didn't. I kept my feelings hidden. After a couple of weeks, I couldn't take it any longer. Being limited was one thing; not doing anything was another.

The doctors had limited me to lifting no more than five pounds. Keeping that in mind, I started doing bench presses with my TLSO brace on. I started light, paying close attention to my body and my back to see if I was injuring myself. After a couple of months, though, I wanted to lift more, so I began working out and doing more and more bench presses. That really got me focused. Instead of having thoughts about what I couldn't do, I significantly altered my focus to what I *could* do.

I thought that even if I couldn't play sports, I could become very powerful. As time went on, I worked out harder, learning different exercises and adapting them to my limitations. I felt that I had a purpose, a goal, something for which to strive. Even though watching others participate in physical activities was still hard, I had bench pressing.

What was especially great was that the football coach/PE teacher wanted students to get involved in powerlifting and competitions. He had been doing that with the school for a few years, and I had participated before my crash. Our school just had a couple of hundred students, but there were quite a few competitors, primarily from my class.

At the time, I went to all the powerlifting meets to be encouraging, yelling and cheering for my friends. I wanted to compete so badly, but it was too soon to put that type of pressure on my body. Besides, if I were to compete, I wanted people to remember who I was.

There were three lifting categories to compete in: squats, bench presses, and power clean. To win a medal, someone would have to finish among the top three elite participants in the weight class in each lift (each school awarded differently; some acknowledged only first place, while others recognized total or best lifter). All of my close friends were competing and I just sat in my wheelchair with my TLSO brace on. Finally, there was a sport that I could actually do, but I couldn't fully participate because I was still healing.

It was also weird in the beginning to go to different schools in my wheelchair. This was the first time I had been around different people my age, other than my friends and classmates. It was an odd feeling when someone looked at me then quickly looked away. People stared, trying not to make it obvious by looking at me from the corner of their eye, but I didn't care that much. Being around my friends and classmates helped me get over people's looks. Besides, even at my school, there were new faces in the freshmen class and, for some reason, it didn't bother me that they looked at me. In fact, everyone had to glance at me for a slight second as I was going though the halls; they had no choice but to look at me because they had to try to avoid my wheelchair.

So at powerlifting meets, I yelled and screamed loudly for my friends and team; it pumped them up as well as the crowd. Hearing people cheer for you while you lift gets your adrenaline pumping and makes you not want to fail since all eyes are on you. Once I initially began yelling like crazy, it was easier for others to join in because they did not feel odd for being loud. When I screamed like that, the attention was off me and on the individual who was lifting because it automatically made others wonder who that person was and how much weight was on the bar. Personally, I didn't care if they were lifting 135 pounds or 500 pounds; I yelled the same for squats, bench presses, and power clean. In the end, our school ended up placing third at state.

Even though I did not participate in the meets, I went to every one and kept lifting for the rest of my junior year. I benched heavier and heavier, trying to make up for the time I'd missed because of my wreck. My freshmen year bench press max was 175 pounds and sophomore year was 275. My final max on the bench in my junior year was 325 pounds.

CHAPTER 11

Prom

One of the toughest and most emotional times for me was the prom. I did not ask anyone because I didn't think any girl would want to go with me since I was in a wheelchair. How was I supposed to dance with anyone while sitting in a wheelchair? I just felt weird and did not care to go with anyone, but I still wanted to go.

I felt strange going into the prom by myself so I hurried inside without stopping to take pictures. When I got in, I started talking to people right away to get my mind off the fact that I was alone. I ended up sitting with a group of friends who had all brought dates. No matter what I did, I just could not deny the fact that I was…alone.

I had a good time during fast songs. I would go out on the dance floor and the girls would surround me, but I dreaded the slow songs. When one played, I felt so alone, sitting by myself at the table. I didn't want to ask anyone to dance because it just felt awkward. I couldn't hold them close like I used to and if I did dance with a girl, I couldn't actually move.

It wouldn't be so dreadful when there was someone at the table with me, but when everyone got up to dance to the love songs, it hit me hard. Some of my friends' girlfriends did ask me to dance, and I complied, but I didn't want to. The girl would just stand beside me, holding both of my hands and pacing left and right as I moved my upper body. I wasn't comfortable, but I did it nonetheless. However, it didn't help my confidence at all. I strongly believed that no girl would ever like me because I was in a wheelchair.

After prom, all of my friends went to party while I waited for my dad to pick me up. I felt like a loser who had no life. That night, I lay in bed wishing and praying to be able to walk again. Tears ran down my face as I stared at the ceiling, thinking that I would have been better off if I died in the wreck. But I concluded—as always—that everything happens for a purpose, which seemed to ease the pain.

CHAPTER 12
Rehab

Rehab was something I had to do, but I wanted to do it, too. It enhanced my strength, mobility, and abilities more than I ever thought possible—and those things made me feel better about myself.

When I arrived at the rehab facility in Ransom Memorial Hospital, I would sit in the waiting area for my name to be called or my therapist to come and get me. The first time I met my main therapist, Meg, I thought she was delightful, had a great personality and was cute. We got along well from the beginning. The first session I had, she took me to the furthest room in the back, where I would ultimately end up having almost all of my rehab sessions. The area had the same kind of padded table I'd used at Topeka and, on our way there, I saw many different exercise stations, including free weights, multi-colored ankle weights, sand weights, bands, medicine balls, stationary bikes and much more. It looked like a place to be tortured, but the machines and weights were fascinating to me.

Rehab was a long process. I spent over a year and a half healing, going to rehab, and exceeding all of my expectations—more than I thought possible. Going to rehab was the best thing that ever happened to me.

In the beginning, we discussed the many factors that affected me and what sort of progress could be made. Meg tested my flexibility, strength, and reaction sensors in my lower body so she could monitor and record my progress to see how much I improved, if at all. After transferring me to the padded table with my sliding board, she would stretch my legs out while I lay on my back, sides, and stomach. For the most part I was flexible, except for my quadriceps. They always seemed to be tight when she stretched my feet to my butt; my foot did not even come close to touching its target.

When Meg performed the reaction sensors test, she tested my legs for my sense of feeling. There were two separate aspects to consider: hot or cold and sharp or dull. She tested my quadriceps first, working down to my toes. As she touched my quadriceps, I could tell I had regained some feeling in them since my previous rehab at Topeka. I could feel a dull touch in their upper three-quarters. If she poked me with a dull object or a sharp one, it felt the same, but I could still feel something! Any other place on my legs was numb, however, and I could not even tell if she was touching me at all.

The hot or cold test was quick; it felt just like the dull test on my upper quadriceps. I could not tell if she was touching me with a hot or cold object, but I could feel a dull touch. (People always wonder what it's like to not be able to feel your legs or feet. Well, you know when your hand falls asleep and you get the tingles? It feels as if my legs fell asleep, to a certain extent, and instead of a sharp needle, I feel dull needle pokes. If you have ever tried to move your hand when it was asleep, but you barely could, well, it's just like that except my legs don't move when I try to move them. It's as if they are dead weight. What is bizarre is that I know where my legs are, and sometimes I try to move them, but they just don't move.)

Anyway, pretty much all the strength in my legs was gone, except for a little in my quadriceps. If I let my legs hang off a table, I could extend them both as if I were kicking a ball. It wasn't much, but I was happy, considering that they told me I was paralyzed from the waist down.

All the rehab I'd done at Topeka had obviously paid off.

However, while sitting on the padded table, my balance was still bad. Even though I worked at it a lot, I had a long way to go before I would be able to sit on my own.

Knowing what I could do and what my limits were was the first hurdle. Getting stronger and more stable was the next challenge, so that's what we did. Meg had me doing exercises against gravity, such as sitting on the edge of the table and kicking my leg out for a couple of sets of ten or fifteen repetitions. She gave me resistance with her hands as well; when I kicked a leg out, she would push down on my ankle, making it harder on me and stimulating my muscles. She didn't have to give much resistance, though, because my legs were so weak. There were some exercises I couldn't do at all, but we still went through the motions while I concentrated on my muscle and the movement.

My hamstring muscles were worthless. Every time Meg had me lie on my stomach and try to bring my foot to my butt, I couldn't do it, but we worked it anyway and she would lift my leg for me. Abduction muscles are what you use to spread your legs open, and I did not have those muscles, either. I would lie on my sides and try to lift a leg up toward the ceiling, but, again, it was something I couldn't do. Meg would lift my leg for me and I'd concentrate and focus as if I were lifting it myself.

For my balance, Meg had me do similar training to what I'd done at Topeka—but my balance had improved a bit from all the weight training I'd done at school. They strengthened my core without me focusing on working my abs or back, and my body began adapting as if its upper half was compensating for the loss of my legs.

As I became more and more addicted to upper body exercises at school, especially the bench press, I began to have more upper body strength—and everything became much easier.

Transferring was totally different once I was able to handle my own weight. I could almost lean all the way forward and sideways then sit straight back up without holding on to the table, wheel-chair, or some sort of support. When transferring now, I locked my brakes, removed the armrest and got close to the table, then grabbed the table with one hand and the wheelchair with the other and lifted up my butt without the sliding board. It was so nice, and so much easier. I didn't have to worry if the sliding board was placed at the right angle. I could just lift and sit.

On top of that, my lower body grew stronger to the point where I could extend my legs straight out. Meg could actually add ankle weights and I could extend them unfazed. I also gained more sensation in my quadriceps and could feel all the way down to the top of my knee, though the touch test remained the same. My adduction, abduction, and hamstring muscles were starting to function a little, too. All the rehab strengthened my legs, and my exercise at school so early in the stages of healing played a vital role in my improvement.

Since I moved so much getting on and off benches as I was transferring, as well as lifting, this stimulated my lower back muscles, nerves, and circulation. I could have just sat around and done nothing and felt sorry for myself, but I consciously chose to proceed. I gained all this strength over many months of hard work, dedication and will power. There were still some unforeseen problems, though.

People who are paralyzed (myself included) have problems with their toes curling in. Since we can't move our toes, any type of pressure can accelerate the curl. Just sitting in the wheelchair, gravity can push the toes down, and so can a blanket when you rest, spasms in the toes, feet and legs, and many other factors. So physical therapists and doctors advised that I wear an ankle-foot orthosis (AFO) at night while I rested to help straighten my toes as well as prevent curls from developing. Meg recommended a place for me in Topeka, and we had her schedule an appointment to get me fitted.

When my parents and I went to get my AFOs fitted, the man wrapped both of my legs from the knees down and wet the wraps as if I were going to get a cast. The wraps looked like a muddy, putty bandage when wet. When my leg was wrapped down to the toes, he applied more water then supported my ankle and foot at a ninety-degree angle, ensuring it was going to remain like that. After the material dried, he cut it off and I was free to go.

After about ten days, the AFOs were ready. They looked like clear plastic casts of my legs that started from about four inches below my knee; they were open at the front, surrounded the back and sides of my legs, came up to about three-quarters of my calves, and had a Velcro strap to hold them in place. The foot piece extended out about three-quarters of the length of my foot, so it did not go all the way to the tips of my toes. The bottom did come up on the sides of my foot a little, but did not cover the top portion of my foot, and there was padding where the arches of my foot would be.

The braces fit at a ninety-degree angle. The man had me wear them barefoot to see if the plastic fit too snugly or if the edges put any pressure on my feet. There were a few spots that curved in too much but he quickly fixed them by sanding them down. Since I couldn't feel the lower parts of my legs, there was no way to tell if they were injuring or irritating my skin; I would just have to wear them at home for thirty minutes to an hour and check my legs for redness or any sort of skin irritation. If any spots occurred, the braces would have to be adjusted or they could cause me to have skin breakdown, which could lead to ulcers.

I wore the braces home, and when we arrived, I checked my legs and feet to see if there was any redness. Oh, yeah…there were a few spots on both of my feet and ankles. The next day we returned and told him where the redness occurred; he made the adjustments and after that I had no problems.

The braces were meant for me to wear when I slept at night,

but that's not what ended up happening. Since I moved around so often, I wore the braces while I transferred, which made it a lot easier and ensured that I wouldn't roll my feet. So I wore the braces during the day and took them off at night.

My therapist liked how the braces turned out and I figured, *Whatever works!*

CHAPTER 13
The Miracle

Rehab continued as always, and we kept moving forward. Since getting the braces, my balance and transferring skills had increased even more. My quadriceps had gotten extremely strong and overpowered my legwork. When doing adduction and abduction movements, my quadriceps did all the work, rather than my inner and outer thighs. With all that improvement, the next thing we spoke about was walking. Could I possibly walk again?

Many months had passed since my accident and the doctors had clearly stated that I was never going to be able to walk again; I was paralyzed. However, my quadriceps might have the strength to hold me up. Meg told me there were parallel bars in the back if I wanted to stand up and try to take a step. She adjusted the bars to the height of my hips. Still wearing my TLSO brace and AFOs, she wrapped the rehab belt around me. With the wheelchair brakes locked, I sat between the parallel bars and she stood in front of me, holding me with the belt.

This was it! I grabbed the bars and lifted myself up. I was standing! My legs were shaking and unstable, but happiness and excitement overcame me. Despite what the doctors had told me, here I stood! In my mind I knew I was going to walk again; I always believed I was going to.

As Meg held me, I went for it. I dragged my right foot forward as I lifted it a little, then I dragged the other leg. I did it! Even though I held onto the bars the entire time, I had taken my first steps! All the months of pain, suffering, and hard work were for this one moment. It was the greatest feeling in the world, and chills and goosebumps traveled through my whole body.

Deep inside, I desired more. It was a miracle and I felt so blessed to have come so far, but I knew I could do a lot better. Now I had another challenge to overcome: to develop enough strength and endurance to be able to stand up for longer periods and to be able to walk more smoothly.

■ ■ ■

From then on, Meg would include the parallel bars in my routine for standing and walking. For my training with standing, they had this big rectangular box with a hole in the top for me to stand in. It came up under my armpits when I stood (I am 5'10"), and the front door had a little lever so the box could open and I could get in. I called it "the coffin," because that's what it reminded me of. The purpose of the coffin was to lock my knees while I stood up so I would not have to hold on to anything to constantly maintain my balance. Doing that really helped to build my endurance. There were instances when I would be able to stand for over twenty minutes at a time. After getting out of the box, my legs would be fatigued but, after a while, it made standing with the parallel bars much easier.

When I stood between the parallel bars, the shakiness and unstableness was significantly reduced and I could stand longer with ease. I did not have my legs locked, and my strength and balance kept improving. Standing became a more natural feeling.

As time went on, Meg did not have to hold the belt anymore. My balance was good, but if I moved slightly forward, backward, or sideways, I could fall easily, so I held the bars the whole time to figure out my limits with how far I could move from front-to-back and side-to-side. That's where having upper body strength benefited me a lot.

Shortly afterward, I began to push my limits by taking my hands away from the parallel bars and trying to stand while holding on to nothing. I could do it for a few seconds but then I began to tilt forward and had to catch myself by grabbing the bars and pushing myself back up. I repeated this over and over. During nights at home, I found any place I could hold on to—a wall, bed, dresser or something high enough to grab—and practiced standing. I locked my wheelchair behind me just in case I fell backwards and couldn't catch myself, but I had a definite goal: to stand for fifteen minutes straight without holding on to anything. If I fell, I would simply start over.

I practiced every day, standing longer each time. I got to thirty seconds, then one minute, and three minutes—but then I would lose my balance and have to start over. I always had a clock in my view to watch the time. It was tedious and hard work, but I didn't care. The longer I stood, the more my lower back ached and the pain would intensify, but I just kept pushing my body to the limit.

My father built me parallel bars out of pipe so I could walk in the backyard at our house. With stronger quadriceps and better balance, my steps looked a lot better, but they still did not look normal. When taking steps, I could now lift my feet up so they wouldn't drag, but when I took a step forward, my legs wanted to move to the outside rather than to the inside when I stepped down, similar to the movements in the movie *The Karate Kid* when he is waxing the car. There was nothing I could do to improve my steps more except to just keep training.

At rehab, Meg had me walk sideways and backwards on top of all my other standing and walking. One time she had me take off my AFOs to see how well I could stand and walk without them. Without them, I had to hold the bars the whole time; if I let go, I would lose my balance instantly. Since I couldn't control or move my feet or calves, my legs bent forward easily, which automatically made me lose my balance and fall forward. The AFOs kept my feet and calves at a ninety-degree angle, held in place by the Velcro strap at the top, and my quadriceps muscles constantly maintained my balance. However, the muscles in my legs had shrunk significantly since my wreck. The saying is true: "If you don't use it, you lose it."

■ ■ ■

Meg put gel pads on me and hooked me up to a machine that stimulated and contracted my muscles through electric current. With the turn of a knob, it efficiently controlled the length and pressure used to stimulate the muscle. When she hooked up my hamstring or calves, I couldn't feel any shock, but my toes and calves would move without my trying.

Standing in the box also started to become easier, as did my movements in the parallel bars. Next, Meg brought me forearm crutches. They were two separate aluminum rods that were adjustable in length with rubber grips at the bottom and rubber handles at the top, along with forearm supports. The crutches were so I could walk anywhere, without being limited to the parallel bars.

The only crutches I knew of before went under your armpit. This was something I never knew existed and they totally caught me off guard; I wasn't too sure about them at first. When I stood up by a wall, dresser or parallel bars, I could catch myself if I fell. These crutches surrounded my forearms (with an opening in the front, just in case I needed to get my forearms out), but what if I fell? There was no wall, dresser or parallel bars for me to catch myself on.

Meg demonstrated how to use the forearm crutches two different ways. First was the hop method: It was the movement you do with regular crutches. Then there was the walking method, which was slower. For that, she moved the right forearm forward then took a step with her left foot, then moved the left forearm forward and took a step with the right foot. After her demonstration, it was my turn, but I still wasn't confident. Using these crutches would take me outside my comfort zone…yet I wanted to try them.

Meg wrapped the rehab belt around me and gave me the forearm crutches. I tried to grab the handle but my forearms did not fit through the support even though there was an open gap. My forearms were too big! She had to stretch them out quite a bit so they could go through. I was prepared after that. Trying to figure out how to properly direct them just right felt like the first time I tried to stand up. I angled the forearm crutches out in front of me and leaned forward. As I tried to push myself up, Meg aided me by pulling on the belt.

I did not like the feel of the forearm crutches; I was unstable and uncomfortable. The parallel bars were solid and did not move, but the forearm crutches made me feel unbalanced. Meg wanted me to try the hop movement, though, and I wanted to try it, too, but I didn't. Fear overcame me. I felt like I would fall and that just scared me.

After a minute or so, I tried to do just a little hop, but I almost fell. We then tried the walking version. It felt strange and I still did not feel safe. I took a few steps then moved the right crutch in too far and tried to step. I immediately began to fall, but Meg caught me. This was too much to handle. I had to get used to the feeling first to build up my confidence. So Meg had me practice just standing there with the crutches.

Just lifting them up and moving them around built up my confidence. I was getting the feeling through my hands where my limits were regarding where I could place the crutches and where I couldn't. It was as if I were becoming one with the crutches and they were an extension of my arm.

I still didn't like the hop-scoot version, so I tried the walking version again. I moved the crutch then took a step. I moved the other crutch and took a step with the other foot. It felt smooth and I did not feel like I was going to fall. So I took more steps, becoming increasingly confident with every second I stood.

Then I took a wrong step and down I went. Meg tried to catch me by pulling back on the belt but that did not help. It was kind of hard for her to stop me from falling when I weighed 200-plus pounds and she weighed around 130. So I fell down forward to the right and caught myself with my hand before I hit the ground.

After *actually* falling, my fear of falling wasn't so bad anymore. I just sat there for a second and laughed. Then Meg helped me get back up and I kept going. The first day I took a few steps just to get used to the crutches. Then I began going a few feet, then ten feet, just walking and then turning around and walking back. Meg had me slowly build up my endurance by walking more and more.

The parallel bars were so easy when I went back to them. There, I worked on my *walking form* rather than just walking. Meg told me to follow through with each step, ensuring my step was straightforward rather than out to the side. She had me walking around the hospital, going further and further each time to push my limits. When I was walking with the forearm crutches, people were so excited to see how I was progressing. Many of the different people I saw day in and day out knew my situation and were surprised by how far I had come; they were amazed at my dedication and drive. Sometimes people would come up to me and compliment me on my progress, while others would smile and stare.

Meg always had something challenging for me to do; next, she would have me fall. Yes, she wanted me to FALL! I was like, "*What?*" She wanted me to learn how to fall correctly, so that if I did fall, I would be less likely to injure myself. So we went to an open area and she put pads on the floor. As I sat, she demonstrated how to fall with the forearm crutches. Basically, if I fell, I was to push the forearm crutches away from me and fall forward and to my side, catching myself with my hands without my elbows extended and locked so that I wouldn't break my bones.

I stood up with the crutches and the pads right in front of me. When I tried to fall, it just did not feel natural. I started to lean forward and went down fast. I threw my crutches to the side and caught myself before hitting the pad. Now, that was freaky!

Next, I learned to open doors while I was walking. That wasn't too hard, though; it just took some getting used to. I opened the door and then put the bottom of my crutch as a doorstop to keep it from closing.

We went outside as well and walked on different surfaces. Grass and gravel weren't any big deal, but I still had to be cautious around loose gravel or dips in the ground, which could make me easily fall. Another thing that was hard was going up any type of hill or slope. Since my AFO was set at a ninety-degree angle, going uphill always pivoted my foot and I would have to walk on the inside of my shoes. Other than that, it was easy, and I assumed that was about it concerning the different things to learn about walking.

However, there were a few steps in the hospital, and I never even thought about going up or down stairs. Going up them was easy if I held on to the railing and used one crutch on the opposite side's rail. I just took it one step at a time. That wasn't good enough for Meg, though. She wanted me to use only the forearm crutches to go up the steps without using the side railing. Some places didn't have railing, and that was the whole point of this training. She wanted me to be prepared.

Going up stairs with only forearm crutches was the hardest thing yet and extremely terrifying. This time, if I fell, it could lead to some serious injury. Just trying to go up one single stair was tough enough, but there were two flights of five to seven steps.

First I put my crutches on the steps then I stepped up with

my feet. I fell so many times trying to go up the stairs, catching myself with the railing. Meg was prepared to grab and catch me, but it was so aggravating not being able to climb one step without struggling. Going up those stairs took everything out of me; sweat dripped off my face and a pattern of sweat appeared on my shirt and darkened as we kept going. But I did ultimately end up getting up both flights of stairs! It may have taken me a couple of weeks, but I successfully achieved it without falling.

With Meg's help, I had accomplished more than I ever dreamed possible. I was satisfied where I was and there wasn't any more she could teach me, but there was still more I could do.

I was done with rehab at Ransom Memorial Hospital and I was discharged. After over a year and a half, I was finally finished! I went from being wheelchair-bound to walking with forearm crutches; I was so grateful and blessed.

I never imagined that I could have made such progress and I was actually sad to leave. I had spent so much time with Meg (and the rest of the staff0, and she helped me out more than she will ever know. I am so thankful that I had her to push me as hard as she did—and to always be there when I fell.

CHAPTER 14

Shriners

Shriners Hospitals for Children is a network of twenty-two pediatric hospitals in the U.S., Canada, and Mexico that provide specialized care for orthopaedic conditions, burns, spinal cord injuries and cleft lip and palate. All services are provided at no charge. Eligibility for care is not based on financial need or relationship to a Shriner.

— www.shrinershq.org/Hospitals

Shriners are distinguished by an enjoyment of life and a commitment to philanthropy. They enjoy parades, trips, dances, dinners, sporting events and other social occasions. They support what has been called the 'World's Greatest Philanthropy.' Shriners Hospitals for Children are operated and maintained by the Shrine. All children, up to eighteen years old, may be eligible for treatment at Shriners Hospitals if they, in the opinion of the hospital's chief of staff, could benefit from the specialized care available at Shriners Hospitals.

— www.shrinershq.org/Shrine/Membership/

About a month after I began walking with forearm crutches, I ended up going to The Shriners Hospital in Chicago, where I was scheduled for a one-day evaluation. It was to take me through a series of tests and examinations, and to see what my current condition was.

My family and I were excited to see if they could help me any further. At the time, it was snowing pretty badly in Kansas, as well as in Chicago, so we decided to arrive there a day early to ensure we made it on time.

When the time came for me to leave for Chicago, my mom and uncle came with me but my dad was on a job and couldn't come. The snow was thick on the ground as we headed to the airport. Once we got there, I felt weird because people glanced or stared at me. This was a completely different feeling than at school because I wasn't around my peers but others who were older and younger than me. Some was trying not to stare but I could frequently see them looking at me from the corners of their eyes.

I was different to them and I felt different. Mainly I thought that the reactions I got from people were fascinating, though some made me feel uneasy. The children did not bother me because they didn't know differently and spoke what was on their mind; some children, for example, asked their mother or father what was wrong with me. The parents would quickly try to stop the kid from talking or would respond to them quietly. But I could tell that the parents felt embarrassed and they would sometimes apologize to me.

A security person patted me down before entering the terminal since I couldn't fit through the metal detectors. I couldn't just get up and walk though them and even if I could, my rods would set off the alarm no matter how little clothing I wore. As we waited at the gate, my mother had us pre-boarded so we would get the closest seats to the front. When they were ready for us, the individual in charge took us through the long, sloping hallway.

Getting on the plane was interesting; it wasn't wide enough for my wheelchair, nor could I fit down the aisle. Instead, the airline provided a special tiny transporter chair with roller wheels at the bottom that fit down the aisle; it looked like an old 1800s torture device.

I decided not to use the chair; instead, I just got close enough to the plane and stood up. I held on to whatever I could and walked to the front seat and my mom and uncle sat beside me. As I entered the plane, some people looked at me like I was faking being in the wheelchair. Most people are quick to judge and don't realize or understand what is wrong or the things that are going on in your life, and so they assume whatever they want to.

It didn't bother me, though. This was the first time I had ever been on an airplane, and it was my first trip to Chicago! The flight was awesome and the takeoff and landing were exciting. Once we arrived, we got our belongings and took a taxi to a hotel that was close the Shriners Hospital since my appointment was first thing in the morning.

When morning came and we approached the hospital, I noticed it was a nice, big facility located next to a chocolate factory, so it smelled good, too. We went into the lobby area, which was filled with colorful and bright seats, and the woman at the desk checked me in and was so welcoming.

I waited to be called among all the other kids. When it was my turn, they took us in the back to a huge area filled with many rooms and it wasn't long before some medical staff came to see us. We ended up talking to various therapists, nutritionists, urologists, and doctors—there were so many others that I can't remember them all! They were all caring, friendly, and yet so professional—and they all asked so many questions specifically relating to their field.

Dr. Vogal was my main doctor and he was tremendous. Thanks to him, I had been accepted into the Children Shriners Hospital in Chicago in the first place. He had an awesome personality and was very compassionate about everything we discussed.

After the evaluation, they had me go through different tests and by late afternoon, I was done. We ended up spending another night at the hotel before flying back to Kansas because my mother was worried that, after everything I had gone through, flying would be too much for me. But flying back felt good. I had gone to another state and I had a great feeling that so much more lay ahead of me.

CHAPTER 15

Gym

After my junior year of high school, I was still doing rehab when the summer arrived. Before my wreck, I weighed close to 190 pounds but, since then, I had gained a lot of weight and excess fat. Since I was curious, my brother helped me weigh myself. There was no way I could really weigh myself so I just sat on the scale with my legs hanging off. It said 250 pounds. I was shocked! I knew I had gained some weight, but I did not know I gained that much!

I usually ate a couple of cheeseburgers after school but, before my accident, I did the same thing and stayed slim. My body had gone through some significant changes and it was as if I were a completely different person physically and mentally.

One of my friends had given me a coupon for a free three-month membership at the local gym in Ottawa. He knew that I loved lifting weights. So Lucus, my older brother Raymond, and I thought we would lift at the Ottawa Nautilus over the summer. The gym was only about five minutes away from our house. Moreover, Lucus' older brother had been lifting off and on there for a while.

When we went down to the gym to sign up, the woman was very friendly—and we were excited and pumped that we were all doing this together to get ready for next year's weight meets. They showed us around a bit and then we were on our own. Leo was there and showed us some of the equipment and the things he had been doing. He had a good build, so we listened to him.

The weight room was never intimidating to me, even in the

wheelchair. With all the rehab and getting adjusted to my surroundings, I was very mobile and could transfer easily from one machine to another. Some machines were difficult to get on because they were too high or at an awkward angle, but that did not stop me. I never let failure overcome me by feeling as if I couldn't do something. Instead, I tried to get on those machines with brute force, using my upper body strength to handle my own bodyweight.

■ ■ ■

Going to the gym was interesting compared to lifting at school. At school, there were only students around my age and a lot of them weren't too serious about lifting; they just wanted to get credit for the class. Most of the time, they would be fooling around and talking, except the ones that competed—and a lot of them took weightlifting at different hours.

At the gym in Ottawa, however, most of the members were serious about lifting. I was among others who had the same drive as me and they were all older. Being in the wheelchair at the gym was weird at first. It's one thing to see someone in a wheelchair and another to see someone lifting in one, but everybody was so friendly and helpful. As Leo had been lifting there for a while, he introduced us to many of his friends, who would help correct our form when we tried doing exercises we had never performed before.

We all talked in between lifts about the different exercises, forms, our goals, and all sorts of different things; we also cracked a lot of jokes. It was a good time and the workouts always went by fast.

Since Coach Ramsey had us on strength workouts at school, we lifted heavy and benched often. We were some of the heaviest benchers at the gym, as well as at school. There were only a few people benching 315 pounds or more at Ottawa Nautilus.

We did all sorts of weights on the bench and eventually worked up to 315 pounds or higher. When benching the heavier weight, I made all kinds of noises, such as yelling loudly to psych myself up, as well as to draw people's attention to me. When they watched me, it gave me a rush. My energy levels went up just knowing I had an audience. But I would only do that if I was about to bench my max or really close to it.

■ ■ ■

Over that summer, I learned so much and could never get enough of working out; even at the end of one workout, I would get excited and look forward to the next day's session. I loved the feeling of soreness, of consistently having my muscles throbbing; the constant pain felt good. Eventually, I began doing some research on supports for a bigger bench press.

■ ■ ■

During my sophomore year, we had begun using wraps. The wraps were solid white with red stripes down the center; they were about seven to eight feet long by four inches wide. We wrapped our knees when we did squats and our elbows when we benched. The wraps supported your knees and elbows by keeping them tight. It not only felt good on the knees and elbows when we lifted, but we could push more weight up when doing a squat or bench.

At school, Ramsey showed us how to wrap, and he would wrap it snug. Well, after a few times of using the wraps on my elbows, it seemed that the tighter the wraps were, the more weight I could push up. I also found that the solid white wraps did not have as much elasticity as the white ones with red stripes—and the more elasticity the wraps had, the tighter they got.

Ramsey did not like my theory on the wraps, which was that the tighter you wrapped, the more weight you could push up. Still, I had my friends wrap my elbows insanely tight, so that my hands and forearms turned purple and white as they cut the blood circulation off in my arms. As soon as they finished wrapping me, I would bench and then take them off. Many of the guys liked my theory and ended up getting wrapped extremely tight as well and pushing up even more weight.

During my research, I also found that there were better wraps than what we were using. They were called the Iron Wrap Z, and they had a lot more elasticity and felt a lot snugger when you wore them. So over the summer, we trained with the Iron Wrap Z and benched even more weight.

But summer passed fast; I was still doing rehab in the afternoons and lifting in the mornings. When school started, my brother and I slowed down going to the Nautilus because I ended up going to school full-time and still had rehab in the afternoons. I still lifted at school and on the days when I did not have rehab or anything else going on. My mother also bought me a home gym so I could lift at nights.

Once school started, Leo and Lucus did not lift together anymore. Leo went to college and Lucus had football practice, so Raymond and I were on our own. It was about this time that I decided I really wanted to lose some weight. I looked for guidance and got started on the Body for Life program. They were giving away an awesome to the person who improved most over so many weeks, and my brother and I signed up for it. We took multiple pictures holding up the newspaper showing proof of the date. Well, the program did motivate me, but I did not read or follow it to the letter because I couldn't. I couldn't do cardio and many of the exercises because I was wheelchair-bound and there weren't any instructions for people in wheelchairs.

So I did my own thing, reading and studying material and watching videos on bodybuilding. I wasn't about to let anything slow me down.

CHAPTER 16

Senior Year

Going back to school, I was stronger and more comfortable being around other people. Meeting and talking to a lot of new people at the Ottawa Nautilus helped me a lot in that department.

But since I was going to school full-time now, I had to worry about when I was going to cath. I never talked about cathing or told anyone that I had to do it, except my family. It was such a personal thing to me and it would have bothered me if anyone knew.

Trying to figure out where I was going to use the bathroom was a problem. In the men's bathroom, the stalls were not wide enough for my wheelchair to fit, nor were the men's stalls in the locker room. I could have approached the principal and had the school widen the stalls, but I did not want to draw that type of attention to myself. If I didn't want a "special desk" in the classroom, I *definitely* didn't want them to change the bathroom.

I had no clue what I was going to do until I finally saw that Mr. Ramsey had a cubical bathroom that was just big enough to fit my wheelchair…but I couldn't close the door. The bathroom was in his office, though, and all I had to do was close and lock his office to make it private. It was the perfect solution.

So I talked to the coach about my situation and explained to him what I had to do. He had no problem allowing me to use his bathroom and his office. Lunch was after my fourth class and weightlifting was my fifth, so after my fourth class I always went over to his office to cath.

After cathing, I was supposed to eat the school's lunch, but I thought I would feel weird putting the tray on my lap as I got the food, or that the teachers would have to help me get my food. I didn't want people to see me struggle or need assistance when it came to the basic things.

Even if I did have a tray of food, I actually wouldn't have a place to sit. I could sit alone eating with the tray on my lap or at the edge of the tables where the bench was connected, but it wasn't the same as sitting with a group. So instead of eating lunch with everyone, I regularly brought my own lunch: a couple of Slim Fast drinks or Boosts, as well as a couple of protein bars. For the remainder of my senior year, I did the same thing every day: eat that food alone.

I would head to the weight room after my quick lunch and begin warming up and lifting alone before the rest of the class and Ramsey would show up. I wasn't supposed to, but I did it anyway. Once everybody began coming in, we started lifting heavy. On Monday, Wednesday, and Friday we lifted weights and on Tuesday and Thursday, the rest of the class played games like volleyball, soccer, and other activities that I couldn't. It still bothered me deep down, so I would just go lift weights—and some of my friends would, too, sometimes.

Lifting was the best way to keep my spirits up in spite of all the other struggles.

CHAPTER 17
Chess

I discovered the chess club at school around the same time football started. The chess club had been around since my junior year and now I thought I would give it a shot. I had played chess off and on since the eighth grade at Pomona. Chess had always fascinated me, even though I lost a lot of the time.

The chess club was meeting to draw names out of a hat to see who played whom and set it up as a tournament. When I showed up, there were approximately sixteen to twenty students there. I was shocked since I didn't think that many people were into playing chess. There were a lot of athletes and my friends there, which was a nice surprise.

As they drew names, we began setting up and playing on the basic kind of chessboards you could get from Wal-mart. The winners played the winners and the losers played the losers to determine their spots on the ladder.

Finishing the initial tournament took a couple of days because some games lasted an hour or more. There was no timer involved; we just played until someone lost. Once the tournament ended, a student's position on the ladder was determined depending on where he or she had placed. I ended up placing first or second (can't remember which). Once the ladder was arranged, the only way to move up was to challenge someone and win. The only catch was that you couldn't challenge anyone more than two places higher than you.

Regardless, I remember becoming number one on the ladder within that first week, and once I became number one, I stayed there for the entire school year. Many challenged me, but they all failed in getting my coveted spot.

As I continued my chess instruction, I learned one of the most fascinating moves, which not many people know of: en passant. I liked this move and properly used it every time I had the opportunity. The reason? To mess with my opponent's head, since most people will argue that there is no such move in chess.

The English teacher was in charge of the chess club and we met twice a week in the mornings to go over strategies and learn how to write down our moves, as well as our opponents' moves. He needed us to learn this if we wanted to compete against other schools in tournaments. I was thrilled; I hadn't known such competitions existed—and, as I've said, I loved to compete!

The tournaments were normally held on Saturdays and only six students from each school could participate, but hundreds of students were there. We just sat around talking and waiting for the tournament to begin, and when it did, they posted a sheet on the wall with a number by your name, as well as your opponent's. The number indicated where you would sit.

When the first round was about to begin, you headed to your seat. There were an endless number of nice, big chessboards lined up on all the tables. The squares were blue and white, and each one was about two inches by two inches; the king and queen pieces were almost five inches tall. The whole setup was impressive, but intimidating.

As I found my place, I noticed a card on which to write our moves and one timer with two separate clocks set up next to the board. We each got a total of thirty minutes. When it was your turn to move, your timer was ticking. After your move, you pressed the button on your clock to start your opponent's timer. If your time expired, you lost the match.

We were required to write down the moves so that the match could be replayed later for others to see how you played the game;

also, if you lost, you could go back and learn what went wrong or, if a dispute occurred during the game, the officials could determine what was actually going on.

As I sat at my table, my hands were cold and sweaty from nerves. I had played everybody from seventh graders to seniors—but the ones that would beat me were usually the seventh and eighth graders. They were especially good.

If had a chance to perform en passant, I would do so even if it did not help me. As I moved, I would actually say, "En passant." Most of the players had never seen that move before and would throw a fit because they believed I had performed something illegal. Then we would get one of the judges, who would tell my opponent that it was a move and that I was right.

That was my way of psyching out my opponents to make them believe I studied all the time and knew a lot about chess. It made them think I was smarter than they were and that gave me confidence. When I played the same opponents time and time again (since only the number two and three spots could challenge me), it became easy to anticipate their next moves so I would talk trash and mess with their heads by saying things like, "Checkmate in four moves," meaning I would win the game in four moves. It freaked the other person out because I could actually make my predictions come true. I would win my tournament most of the time, but sometimes my lack of knowledge got the best of me.

One time my opponent had only a king and I had my king and a rook but I did not know how to put him in checkmate. After so many moves, the game ended up as a tie. That made me mad, so afterwards I practiced putting a king in checkmate with just a king and rook until I excelled at it.

During another match, I played a guy my age who made me really angry. His time was running out; I had almost won the match and I was so excited that I could hear my heart beating. Then I castled through a check and made an illegal move. Well, once I did that, the guy threw a big fit and said that since I moved illegally, he should have time added on his clock. I argued that he shouldn't, so we got the judge over and he agreed with my opponent, who ended up winning the match. Playing in tournaments was always intense for me and I hated to lose.

Of the three or so tournaments I did in my senior year, I generally won four or five games. At Paola, I placed fourteenth out of around two hundred students, and I usually did the best of the six students from my school. Our school ended up taking second place at the state level, but I couldn't compete because I chose to go to the Shriners' Hospital at that time.

However, I did study books on moves and strategies to get an edge and I did take the game of chess very seriously. But I also really enjoyed playing, and would take on anyone who challenged me. The teacher who had taught us the moves had been playing for many years, yet I beat him fifty percent of the time. My friends and I played for hours while saying very little to each other; we just concentrated and strategized the next move. Brandon was a good friend of mine with whom I began playing chess at lunchtime. Once, the bell rang for class but we wanted to finish the game because it was such an intense and even match. So we decided to skip the next class. We ended up finishing the game about an hour and a half later, barely even talking to each other because we were both so focused. One wrong move could have given the other person an edge. I ended up winning the match and I can now say that it was the best game I have ever played—most definitely worth missing class for!

I had some good times playing chess and won an award at the end of the year for being the best player at my school. I had tried so hard so that I could win a trophy, but it turned out to be just a piece of paper: a certificate of achievement. Better than nothing, though.

CHAPTER 18

Football—
My Senior Year

Football was another big part of my life during senior year. Coach Ramsey put the number 62—my number—on the back of the team's jerseys and all of the helmets. I was so honored, but could never go to any of the practices because I had rehab most of the time and it was always too hot at that time of the day anyway. Sitting in that heat made me sweaty and miserable, but I made sure I went to every single game, home or away, and I was always on the sideline with my team wearing my number 62 jersey.

To show my support, I rode the bus with the football team—always in the back because that was the cool thing to do. As we traveled to different schools, we were usually quiet, focusing on what lay ahead. Sometimes, though, I would start different chants, such as "The ants go marching…" but would replace "ants" with "Indians" because we were the Pomona Indians. I'd also change any "little kid" words with my own version to make it sound manly and tough as we sang in deepened voices.

■ ■ ■

Being in the wheelchair at away-games in other schools felt no different than being at home, except regarding accessibility. There were times I couldn't fit into doorways because my wheelchair was too wide, or there would be steps to go down or fences to squeeze through. I couldn't always go where the other players went, so some of them would help me find a different way around. When the coach gave some of his speeches in the locker rooms, I couldn't usually be there because there were too many stairs, so I would have to wait outside. But sometimes I would be there when Coach Ramsey told the players that I'd give anything to be in their spots, to be given the chance to play one more game. I got chills when he talked like that. It gave them a reality check and opened their eyes to the opportunity they had in front of them. After that, I could tell they were all fired up.

At home games, I always came early and set up my stereo to play music beforehand when the team was warming up and at half-time for the dance team. My stereo was huge with massive wattage; I hooked up six subwoofers, a couple of 6 x 9s and one or two other speakers to it. That was the first time music was properly played at the games at Pomona, and it made me feel good that I could help pump up my team and our supporters. It made me feel like a part of it again.

During the games, I'd yell and scream and really get into it. This was the first season since my wreck that I was able to watch my teammates play. It was great to be there to see my fellow class-mates play their last year of high school football.

Sometimes, though, I'd almost get involved in the action myself. As I was on the sidelines, there were instances when I was almost tackled. If the play was to the outside, every once in a while I had to move quickly or someone moved me out of the way. My team-mates, primarily Lucus, would push me up and down the sideline during the game and any time I needed to be moved around on the field. It was extremely hard to push myself around on the grass; that wheelchair was not made to go off-roading.

After the game, the players, cheerleaders, and fans always went by the goal to listen to the coaches speak. Losses were always a silent time as the players would kneel and listen. But when we won, everyone would go wild, yelling and cheering, and Ramsey always had a specific chant when we'd win.

We won our first home game of senior year, and everyone was

pumped and ecstatic! As the coach spoke, he told the team how proud he was and gave them the glory they deserved. Then he wanted me to come up there with him.

Some of my fellow teammates helped me get beside him, then Ramsey put his hand on my shoulder. He began saying he wanted to dedicate this win to me and his eyes became filled with tears. When he started getting emotional, tears rolled down my cheeks as well. After he finished, he leaned in to give me a hug. Everyone clapped and cheered, and, for me, the moment was priceless. It was such an honor and I couldn't ask for better teammates, friends, or a coach that cared as much as he did.

That season, the team started winning game after game and clinched the district championship, which was significant for Pomona since our football teams hadn't won districts in many years. The championship was held at another stadium, and on the bus ride home after the victory everyone was quiet. One of my teammates asked me about the trapezium muscle, since he couldn't seem to develop his. I went into a discussion on that particular muscle, explaining different ways of working it and how to make it look bigger by flexing it a certain way.

Soon I had my shirt off, showing him how to flex it and he did the same thing. Others wondered what we were doing and, before long, they started comparing their trapezium muscles, too. What was funny about the whole thing was that everyone took off their shirts—though most of them had no clue how it got started in the first place. Even Ramsey took his shirt off.

The only person left with a shirt on was the bus driver. Everyone chanted for him to take it off and, a few seconds later, he did. The bus driver was hairy like a gorilla, and the whole incident was so funny. It was certainly a memorable way to celebrate our victory in the last game of the season.

CHAPTER 19
Weight Meets

After football games, I would lie in bed at night when everybody was asleep and think what I could have done if I were able to play football again. In my sophomore year, I had played varsity as the starting offensive guard or offensive tackle and defensive tackle. Playing offense and defense non-stop is tiring after a while but I would have given anything to be in that situation again.

Thoughts of football would keep me awake for a long time, but all I could try to do was focus on things that I could participate and compete in, which were primarily powerlifting and chess. Lifting weights kept me sane. Reliving the old football days was touchier; reality was hard to cope with but the weight meets would help.

With my first weightlifting meet approaching, I was ready. My father drove me to Williamsburg High School and was concerned because I was sick, but I didn't care. I went anyway. I wasn't about to let anything stop me from competing; it meant too much to me. I had lain in bed too many nights thinking of this moment.

At the weight meet, everyone had to weigh in a few hours beforehand to determine which weight class they would be put into. It had been four months since I really started watching what I ate and lifting weights intensely, and I had dropped a lot of weight. I went from 250 pounds to around 200 and had just missed the 198-pound weight class. Now I was stuck in the 220 weight class.

The school's gym had about eight different stations where competitors would be lifting simultaneously. The lifter's opening weight would determine which station they would get. One of the registration tables had information about the school's powerlifting records from previous years. The bench press record for my weight class was 275 pounds.

Each lifter would have three lifts, choosing a weight to start with and writing it down on a sheet along with the wavier. You could not lower the weight even if you started with one that was too heavy. At each station, the lightest lifter would start and the heaviest lifter would lift last.

The meet began with squats and after all the lifters had lifted, they would move to bench press then power cleans. It was a while before I started. I was put in the station that had all the heaviest lifters.

While squats were going on, I was nervous and anxious. I had my headphones on, listening to the *Rocky 4* soundtrack or Metallica's *Black Album*. Certain songs from each album put me in the zone, plus I wore a specific shirt and pair of sweatpants that made me feel stronger and that I seemed to lift the heaviest while wearing. I always wore black sweatpants to cover up my AFOs so people wouldn't stare at my ankle braces; it bothered me mentally, particularly if others my own age saw them. Everything had to be just right or it messed with my head.

After squats were over, they moved the squat rack out of the gym and brought the benches in. Once the bench was set up, the lifters started warming up. There was 135 pounds on the bar; I waited my turn then rolled over there to warm up. When I wheeled over to the bench, everyone was staring at me, not knowing what to expect. You could tell they didn't expect me to lift a lot.

The way they stared at me, it seemed like they'd never seen a guy in a wheelchair before. As I transferred to the bench, I sat there for a second and pushed my wheelchair to the side. I then lay down and, as I grabbed the bar, moved my back around until I was centered on the bench. I was comfortable laying there. I adjusted my grip and lifted the weight off the rack. I lifted the 135 pounds easily for six reps then racked the weight, like everyone else had.

When the weight was 225 pounds, I warmed up with that for six reps with ease. Others would warm up even more, but I just waited for the competition.

The guys that opened with lighter weights started. There was a table by our station where two people sat, holding note cards with all the lifters' names and opening lifts. I was the second to last guy to be lifting at our station. The last guy was a friend of mine from school whose name was Willie. We had been competing against each other for the heaviest bench at Pomona. He benched more than me, but he also weighed about sixty more pounds.

Once they got close to our weight, we'd warm up once more with 275 pounds for one rep. The time was near; my opening weight was 315 pounds. This was my first lift at a powerlifting meet since my wreck. When I was next, I rolled up to the bench; everybody around the station and in the bleachers was watching. There were three 45-pound plates on each side of the bar. It was a massive amount of weight for a high school student to lift.

As I sat on the bench, there were three judges surrounding me each about five feet away, each holding a light switch hooked up to a wooden board. If the lifter moved his foot or head, lifted his butt off the bench or any of the things they were looking for, they would signal with a red light. If the lifter got two or three red lights, it would be considered a bad lift.

At this meet, all we had to do was touch our chest with the bar and lift the weight. At other meets, we'd have to hold the bar on our chest for a second then press the weight up. So this seemed easy—and I was in the zone.

Ramsey, Rocky, Lucus and some of my other friends had wrapped my arms with my Iron Wrap Zs. As they did, I began to yell really loudly: a snake's hiss sort of sound or a grunt to draw attention to myself. When I yelled like that, everyone knew that I was lifting and things would get quiet quickly then become loud from friends and people cheering me on.

Now, as I held on to my wheelchair, my hands and forearms were getting numb and turning white and purple with a tint of blue. The wraps cut off my blood circulation but I didn't care; the pain from how tightly they had wrapped me was phenomenal but I blocked it out. As they had pulled the straps, it felt like my flesh was ripping but it was worth it. In a way, I liked how it felt, as if it made my arms more powerful. More pain for more power was a fair trade, I thought.

I grabbed the bar with my cold, numb hands, lifted it up and held it there for a second then lowered it to my chest. I could feel my skin pulling apart as my elbows bent. As the bar touched my chest, I pushed with all my force, lifting it with explosive power.

The bar came off my chest so fast, locking my arms out with ease as if the weight I pushed were 135 pounds instead of 315. It was the best feeling in the world.

As soon as I racked the weight, they hurried to remove the wraps, but the discoloration in my hands and forearms stayed. Willie was after me and he screamed and yelled just like I did as he successfully completed his lift. I told them I wanted my next lift to be 335 pounds. Willie and I were the only two lifters left at our weight station who still had to lift.

I waited a minute or two and then I was back at it, screaming and yelling as they wrapped me again. I lifted the weight with ease then Willie did the same. I wanted my final lift to be 350 pounds. That would have been the most weight I ever lifted up to that point in my life, but I wasn't afraid. There were no other lifters, just Willie and me. We both had one lift left and both of us had won our weight classes (he was a heavy weight), so now we had to battle for the heaviest bench press medal.

I transferred back on the bench for my final lift and my friends wrapped me again. When I took the weight off the rack, there was a heavy pressure in my shoulder, but I just lowered the bar to my chest. Once I touched my chest, I pressed with all my might, giving it all I had. Without holding anything back, I pushed it with brute force. I had trained for many hours for this moment, this one chance.

The bar was going up, up, up and I did it! I locked out 350 pounds. As I held the weight at the top, I was excited and exhausted.

After I sat up and they took off the wraps, they told me there was an error. There was only 345 pounds on the bar, not 350. I couldn't believe that they put the wrong amount of weight on the bar and was angry when they asked me if I wanted another lift. So, after a few minutes, I would try 350 pounds again, but I was worn out. There are only so many times a person can try to max.

When I got back on the bench, my arms were all different colors from having been wrapped so many times. You could see lines of blood spots under the skin. It was wicked-looking but, despite that, they started to wrap me for the fourth time.

I was worn out from yelling, but I did it again. No matter what I felt physically, the adrenaline was overwhelming and I ended up lifting the 350 pounds. The Williamsburg bench press record for my weight class was 275 pounds and I just pushed up 350. I had broken their school record by 75 pounds!

Willie's final bench press lift was 375 pounds. I ended up getting a gold medal in my weight class and so did he. He also got the medal for the biggest bench press.

Pomona did quite well at that weight meet as a team, winning all sorts of medals. To this day, Willie's and my bench press records still stand at Williamsburg High School in Kansas, along with a few other lifters from Pomona. It was a great victory and did wonders for my confidence knowing there was a sport I could excel at even with the wheelchair.

■ ■ ■

After that meet, I was excited and hadn't felt so good in a long time. I never thought I could do that well. My family was thrilled for me. All that hard work had paid off, not only in achieving better balance, strength and circulation, but emotionally as well. I had accomplished something that many people only dream of doing their whole lives, and did it rather easily during my junior year. But that personal best only made me want to push myself harder in the weight room.

I ended up going to every weight meet my senior year, five or six in total. When I would go to the meets, it wasn't just about winning anymore. It was about breaking the school's record. However, there were only one or two other schools that actually kept records And some that did not place individual lifts, just a total of all three lifts. Even if I didn't get a medal, I would always win my weight division.

One of the largest weight meets we went to was Park Hill South, which, instead of going from lightest to heaviest, had all the lifters lift one time before attempting the second lift. It gave us a lot more time to rest between each lift and made the weight meet go faster.

Park Hill South's school record for my weight class was 310 pounds, and I was going to start with 315 on my opening lift. I had one spotter behind me and one on each side of the bar. At this weight meet, they did not allow us to use wraps but we could wear bench shirts. So I put on my new bench shirt before I went up to lift; the shirt was so tight that I needed two people to help me get it on, which was normal for that kind of apparel.

As soon as they called my name, I was ready. I transferred to the bench and yelled like I always did. Then I lay down and centered myself, but it just didn't feel right. I had only used the bench shirt a few times.

I lifted the bar and touched my chest then pushed it up hard. Instead of going straight up, the bar went up at an angle toward the rack. I pushed it halfway up and my elbows gave. It went straight down on my face, but as it was falling, I quickly turned my head to the right.

A full 315 pounds came crashing down right below my eye on my upper cheek. After a second or two, the spotters took the bar off my face; they were stunned. As I sat up, there was mostly silence, but I heard a few people say, "Oh, my God," "Did you see that?" and "What just happened?"

Some people came over to me to see if I was all right. I was fine but the bar had broken my glasses. You could tell it looked bad, though, because people thought it had killed me.

I know this sounds crazy, but it did not even hurt. They asked if I wanted to scratch my other two lifts, but I wanted to finish. I had my friends adjust my bench shirt, which felt too high in back, but when it was my turn to lift again, I could only bring the bar halfway up and the spotters had to take it. That really made me mad! Now I only had one more chance to lift 315 pounds, break the school record and get first place.

As I attempted my third lift, I pushed with everything I had but it wasn't good enough. I got it halfway up again and just couldn't lift any higher. After the spotters helped me rack the weight, I shot off the bench furiously and ripped off the shirt that was over my bench shirt. I was so pissed, I started to yell! I got in my wheelchair and had to wheel away to cool off, but I got over it after a while.

The next day I had a big black eye, which I thought was funny. Everyone at school and all the lifters at the Nautilus couldn't believe I had dropped 315 pounds on my face.

The last weight meet was State and I won first place in the 198-and-under weight class. Not only did I place first at bench, our school won many first, second and third places. Pomona had the highest point standing among all the schools and won the 2000 State 3A Kansas High School Weightlifting Championships. It was such an honor to be part of the team and have the opportunity to lift and motivate my other teammates.

I may have been wheelchair-bound but I never let that limit me. Sure, I couldn't do squats or power cleans, but I had my bench press and that's all that mattered. I just looked at what I could do and strove to be the best!

CHAPTER 20

Chicago

As the school year progressed, I was having fun hanging out with friends, but I hated the schoolwork. I was good at math but didn't like reading and writing. My main purpose n school was to have fun and enjoy it.

Even though I was in the wheelchair I would still pull pranks and get sent to the office. While I was in English class, I had one of my friends put my remote-controlled "cussing machine" in the tile ceiling in the front of the classroom while the teacher stepped out. The class wondered what we were doing—and when the teacher came back in, I waited a bit before pressing the button.

As soon as I pushed it, the phrase played loudly and the class started laughing. I got to press it a few times but then the teacher made us take it down. I had to confess it was mine or the whole class would have been in trouble, and I would never let someone else take the blame for something I did. So I got sent to the office. What I did not realize was that, because the library was the next room over from our classroom, the people in there had heard the machine, too.

So school was going pretty well and no one ever made fun of me because I was in a wheelchair, either at school or at weight meets. I was never in a clique; I talked to everybody. I remembered when I was a freshman and some of the seniors looked at me with an air of superiority; I swore I'd never be like that when I was in their place, so I even talked to some of the freshmen and made a few good friends with them.

■ ■ ■

When February came, I left for the Shriners' Hospital in Chicago again, only this time I would stay there for a week. Only my mother was going with me while they ran tests and had me perform more rehab.

There were two levels in the building and I was admitted to the top floor, where I could look down to the next floor from the railing on the side. On the bottom level they had a basketball court and a separate kids' area with blocks and toys. There was a foosball table, ping-pong, a piano, and a beautiful waterfall. There was also a staff of friendly nurses.

Each room was designed to hold four patients. My roommate was in a wheelchair and was paralyzed as well, but the other two beds were empty. My mother stayed with me the whole time, sleeping on a cot beside my bed.

As I looked around the place, I saw more and more patients in wheelchairs. Some were miserable and depressed, but others were outgoing.

The rehab room reminded me of Ransom, except their facility was a lot nicer and they had more equipment. More important, however, was my beautiful and caring therapist, Jennifer, with whom my mother and I got along quite well. She went through a range of motions with my legs and tested my leg strength—and she was impressed. I told her all the stuff I had been doing and she was amazed at how far I had advanced and wanted to see me walk. When she got me a pair of forearm crutches, I showed her and she was shocked at my progress.

Afterwards, we talked for a while about my AFOs and wheelchair. My calves and lower legs had shrunk a lot and now the AFOs were too big. She had me visit their casting department to make new AFOs, which felt like the same process I went through in Topeka.

With Jennifer, I did a lot of walking and she corrected my form a lot. They wanted to record my walking in their computer at the lab, so I ended up going to a separate room with Styrofoam balls stuck on different points of my body. The room was specially designed to record every move I made. I walked down and back, sideways and whichever way they wanted on a walking strip. Afterwards, they showed me a simulation of my walking; I was a stick figure on the computer. I did not know what they were going to use it for but if it helped them understand more, I would do anything they wanted.

When my braces were ready, they were smaller with little dime-size holes all around the back for ventilation and the foot supported the whole bottom of my feet, including my toes. This time they put a strap that could be tightened on the front of the foot where my ankle bent. When I tried on my braces, they fit well, but I had to wait to see if there was any redness or other problems. Jennifer wanted me to wear them and walk to try them out. She got her belt on and wrapped it around me, but when I began walking I was fine. I seemed to walk straighter and more upright in these AFOs.

■ ■ ■

Days were busy and things calmed down at night. There was always something going on, Monday through Friday. During the day it was mostly rehab with therapists but at night they had volunteers come in to help out with the patients. On the wall near the patients' rooms was a schedule of events taking place in the evenings. Some nights there was crafts, wheelchair basketball, movies, or other entertainment.

They served breakfast, lunch, and dinner at the same time every day down by the basketball court, unless the patient couldn't make it out of the room. If we were hungry between meals, the nurses would get us snacks. There was also a refrigerator constantly open for the patients to get what they wanted.

During late afternoons and nights, I had a lot of free time and would wander around talking to people. I saw one guy sitting outside his room all alone and could tell that something was severely wrong with his face. When I went over to talk to him, I started off by introducing myself and the more we talked, the more I brought up my personal life and why I was in the wheelchair, wanting to see if he would bring up what was wrong with him. It turned out he had eighteen or so tumors over his body and about ten of them were on his face. We talked for a bit more then he had to go. Afterwards, I headed back to my room and one of the nurses stopped me to say that she was shocked to see him talking to me. She told me that he didn't like to talk to many people.

When I went back to my room, I told my mom about the guy. I felt so sorry for him. Nothing is more of an eye-opener than actually seeing someone who is worse off than you. After what I had just experienced, I was so grateful that nothing else had happened in my wreck. I could have been much worse off with lost limbs, third-degree burns all over my body or brain damage. Then I thought of those people who actually had those things happen to them, and my heart went out to them. There are so many mean and rude people in this world who make fun of others that are different. People are quick to judge others before truly knowing them. It's hard when you have something wrong with you that makes you different from everybody, but that's when need to look on the positive side of life, or depression and anger will get the best of you Instead of asking if the glass is half empty or half full, the question you need to ask is: Are you grateful to even have a glass?

■ ■ ■

During my time in Chicago, I met a lot of different people who had all sorts of problems. A few (who I will mention) opened my eyes, made me grateful for what I had to work with, and made me want to do the best I could. After all, it could be a lot worse—and life is too precious and short not to appreciate the time we have.

My roommate was a passenger in the back seat when his friend rolled the vehicle and he became paralyzed from the neck down. He was on a special waterbed that rotated the whole time I was there. A month after I left, I found out that he died.

There was a girl there who was about three years old. She was in the back seat and her parents were in the front when they crashed. She became paralyzed from the waist down and her parents had died. Her grandmother was taking care of her. She was so cute in that tiny wheelchair but, being so young, she would have a harder time wanting to walk because the wheelchair was the only thing she had ever known.

There were so many different kids there: different nationalities, ages and injuries (not just spinal cord patients). When lunch and dinner were served, I got to see almost everyone and interact with them during games or activities. I was never shy about what happened to me, and most of the time would go up to different kids to begin conversations. Many of them were shy, but cheered up once I began talking to them.

Some of them had been in accidents recently and it was hard for them to talk to someone who hadn't experienced what they were going through. Even with those who try to understand, it's not the same if they haven't been through it themselves.

So the other patients and I bonded, and I was particularly excited to have a chance to play wheelchair basketball with them. When the staff started to bring out the wheelchairs, I realized that they were nothing like mine. I had an older model whose legs were removable, the back came up high on my back, and the tires were straight up and down. The wheelchairs that they brought out were nothing like I had ever seen before.

The seat cushion was not flat; it was angled downward toward the back. There was no armrest and the leg rest angled inward and was one solid piece. The tires were wider on the bottom than on top, and they had one small anti-wheelie bar on the back that was close to the ground. Those wheelchairs were so cool-looking.

There were approximately six to seven different wheelchairs that were all the same and Kris, the woman in charge, told me to pick one so I did. It even had a seatbelt! It was nice not having to deal with the armrest or the legs and it was compact, which was nice. As I began to push it, it moved smoothly and extremely fast and could turn on a dime. Kris told me that the smoothness was because of the tires, which were solid rubber and designed for hard, smooth surfaces. It could move faster because the wheels were cambered out a lot, meaning they were angled outward at the bottom, which also made it easier to push. Instead of having two front tires, there was one front tire in the center, which was why I could spin on a dime. This wheelchair rocked—and I was a speed machine with upper body strength!

There were a few other kids my age who wanted to play—some paraplegic, others not. The rules we followed were that we had to bounce or dribble the ball once every ten seconds and we played to fifteen points. Every shot made was one point, regardless of the three-point line. Kris demonstrated how to get the ball if it was on the floor, which was pretty awesome. We simply pushed the wheelchair right by the ball, leaned over and pushed the ball into the tire. The ball would then roll up the side of the tire onto our lap so we could grab it easily.

The hospital had a full-sized indoor basketball court with two nets that were adjustable in height. Kris adjusted them to about five and a half feet off the ground, just the right height for wheelchair dunking. There were four of us who played: two other guys, Kris and me (I ended up on her team).

I played around with the chair to get used to it and tried getting the ball off the floor. It seemed to come naturally to me. We started the game by giving the other team the ball and it was on. I became very serious and wanted to win. Since I had been in the chair for over a year, I could really move and maneuver. I charged the guy who had the ball really quickly, ramming the side of his wheelchair, stopping him from moving and knocking the ball out of his hands. Kris then stopped the game and told us not to do what I just did because that could break the wheelchairs, which cost thousands of dollars each.

We still got rough with the chairs, though; I just didn't am them like that first time. The wheelchairs' tires had an outer ring to grip besides the tire. It was coated with a rubber layer, and because we moved so fast and got so close to one another, our tires would grind and leave a scent of burnt rubber in the air.

I was always bad at shooting the ball but loved getting close to the basket and dunking; I was faster than the other guys so they could never stop me. Kris enjoyed shooting the ball and was good at it. I gave her the ball a lot because I liked teamwork and, besides, I could get it back pretty easily.

I loved playing wheelchair basketball. It was so intense and a great workout; my shoulders were on fire. We ended up playing two games and we won both. After the game, Kris and I began talking; we got along great. She told me that they were going to have wheelchair basketball again the next week if I wanted to play. I told her I would love to, but I was leaving that weekend.

I could tell she had a passion to work with kids with disabilities, just from the way she talked; her outgoing personality set her apart from the others. The Shriners were fortunate to have her!

It was an amazing experience to play wheelchair basketball, but then I got to thinking later that night: What else is there out there?

■ ■ ■

The day after the game, I met with someone from the hospital who was going to assist me with choosing and ordering a wheelchair. The man went over so many different options and what was best suited for me: if I wanted an armrest, anti-wheelie bars, handles for people to push me, and so on. I ended up choosing removable armrests, no anti-wheelie bars, no handles for people to push me, a solid foot rest, solid tires and a color that looked blue at one angle and green from a different angle. There were so many different options for the type of spokes, but I wanted the type with a grip coating on the tire. In the end, I was happy with my choice.

The week I was at the hospital went by so fast, and everyone enjoyed having my mother and me around. In just that short time of rehab, I got to know the entire therapy staff, who were all fun and outgoing. The therapists, nurses and medical staff helped me so much for the duration I was there and opened my eyes to how lucky and fortunate I was. I felt so blessed to have had the opportunity for them to treat me for that week. It was a humbling experience.

Sara was one of the workers who guided, helped and informed me about what was going on. Toward the end, she asked me if I would ever be interested in attending an SCI Camp, which was a spinal cord injury camp where four guys and four women who had spinal injuries got together for a week to participate in different activities such as rock climbing, scuba diving, and so much more. Right away I got excited and told her that I would love to be part of it. She said, "Great! I'll put you down as one of the four guys."

Soon after that, it was about time for me to leave. My mom and I said our goodbyes and thanked everyone. I learned so much and had a wonderful time. It was great being around others in the same condition I was in and seeing how they dealt with their situations and did things basic things like move around and open doors. Meeting them showed me how lucky I actually was. I had been blessed with the grace of God on August 17, 1998, and now I understood.

■ ■ ■

After I got back, I felt fantastic. I had busted my butt at rehab, home and at the gym, and it was all beginning to come together. It made me feel good that everyone was amazed at my progress and how far I had come. Before I had done it for myself, but now, after seeing other patients watching me walk through rehab, I realized that I gave others hope as well. My walking gave them inspiration and they saw that it could be done. Just their looks meant the world to me and it made me want to walk that much more. It wasn't only the patients who were inspired, either; my walking reinforced for the doctors and therapists why they do what they do in the first place.

So when I was back with Meg, I kept pushing myself hard at rehab in order to walk. I did what she asked and did extra at the house.

The time had almost come for me to leave high school; I only had a few months left before graduation. Every time I thought about graduation day, I also thought about the original choice I had of whether to take a year off or go to school. I had come a long way from the day of my wreck, but all that everyone really knew was that I went to rehab. They didn't know how much I had improved or that I could walk with forearm crutches. Most just remembered the article in the newspaper about a sixteen-year-old boy's paralyzing accident.

Then, one night, as I was lying in bed, I realized what I was supposed to do. It finally clicked, as if some spiritual force was guiding me: I had to walk across the stage at graduation. Thinking of that eased my mind and I began to cry. Walking across the stage to prove the doctors wrong, to show my family, friends, classmates, teammates, coaches, teachers and all of Pomona that it could be done.

They had all been there when I needed them the most, at a time that was the worst, the lowest, for me. This was a way I could say thank you for everything everyone had done for me. Most of all, it would be for my mother, father and myself. My parents had been beside me from day one and they had continued to always be there for me. As I thought about it, I cried, but I was smiling. Nothing was going to stop me from walking at graduation!

CHAPTER 21
Senior Prom

Before graduation, one of the hardest things was coming up: prom. Memories of junior year had came to mind; this year, I did not want to go by myself and relive the same feelings.

Throughout my junior and senior years, I was never in a relationship; I never wanted to try to get involved. I was very outgoing and motivated to push myself on many levels, but when it came to girls, I was bad, and being in the wheelchair made it that much worse.

I felt ugly and could never get past the thought that girls wouldn't want to be with me because I was in a wheelchair, when they could be with someone else who wasn't. So I never tried to get involved in a relationship with anyone, and instead I was miserable seeing my friends and others day in and day out at school spending time with people who they cared about and holding hands with their fingers interlocked. There were so many times I felt so alone and wished I had someone, but I didn't want to put any girl in the situation of asking them to go out with someone in a wheelchair.

But prom was coming and I needed a date. Most of the girls in our senior class were taken; they either had boyfriends or were already going with someone. At the time, I was good friends with one of my friend's sisters, who was a freshman. Her name was Amanda and she was a hot little thing. I also ended up being friends with her best friend, Imagine, and she was hot as well. Not only were they both good-looking, petite cheerleaders with amazing bodies, but they were also at the top of their class.

If I were going to go to prom, I wanted to go with either Amanda or Imagine. I was hoping that no one had asked them yet, and was curious if they would even want to go with me.

When I was in the library alone with Amanda, I brought up the fact that my friends were going to prom, and she mentioned that she wanted to go but couldn't because her mom wouldn't let her. That information hit hard, but I did not show that it affected me, even though I really wanted to go with her.

So I told her that was a shame and asked if Imagine was going to prom with anyone. She said no, so I asked if she thought Imagine would go with me. Amanda got excited and told me that she thought Imagine would want to go me if I invited her.

I felt good just knowing I had a chance to take this girl to prom. Now all I had to do was ask her.

This was my first time since being in the wheelchair that I approached a girl—and I had to do it for prom. When I told Amanda that I had originally wanted to take her, she just smiled and sort of blushed.

Later that day I had Imagine in my foreign language class, which was a mix of freshmen through seniors. I ended up going early to class to make sure I was there before she was. I was so nervous and my heart was beating fast.

A few minutes after she got there, I eased into conversation with her then asked if she was going to prom. She said no, then I asked her if she wanted to go with me. She immediately said yes with a smile on her face. When she said yes, it was the greatest feeling in the world and it was such a relief. I thought I was going to pass out. That was one of the hardest things I had ever done and yet it was so easy.

I wanted that night to be special. Even though Imagine was in a relationship with an underclassman, that didn't matter to me. I just wanted to go to prom with someone—even a friend—and I wanted to roll in style. So I chipped in with two other guys to rent a limo.

My mother went with me to pick out a tuxedo and helped me get dressed like in my junior year. As I got ready, she cried a little. This was her baby boy's senior prom and I had grown up. When she cried, my eyes watered, too, but I had to pull it together or else I would get all emotional and bust into tears.

We took pictures at the house then my father took me to the school, where I was meeting Imagine and getting into our limo. On the way, I was so nervous that my palms started sweating as I held her corsage.

My father and I got to the school early and he got my wheelchair out of the back of the car. The longer I sat there, the more my nervousness amplified. But, before I knew it, she arrived, looking gorgeous. She walked toward me in a stunning blue dress, which, like her hair and makeup, was flawless. It was as if she were an angel from heaven—and she was with me for that night! I was truly honored that she was my date.

My father and her family took some pictures of us together then the limo came and the other couples arrived. This was the first time we had ever been in a limo; the guys all sat on one side and the girls sat on the other, facing us.

We were excited during the ride, talking and having a good time, and soon we arrived at the fancy restaurant where we were going before prom. Since I was the only one in a wheelchair, everyone had to wait for me until the limo driver helped put my wheelchair together. It felt a bit odd but it didn't bother me too much.

When we went in, some of our friends were already there. The table was set up half with benches and half with chairs. I quickly guided Imagine to the bench and then transferred over to the bench as well. The host put my wheelchair to the side; that was my way of feeling normal.

I didn't want to sit near the edge of the table or sit across from Imagine in my wheelchair, so I sat beside her. I felt good. I know some of those other guys wished they had her for a date.

When we got back in the limo, each guy sat beside his date and we began to get loud, joking around and turning on the music. It was a lot of fun, and then I had an idea. Earlier that week at school, one of my friends sat in my wheelchair while I sat in a school's chair. Then I stood up and began pushing him around as I held onto the back of my wheelchair using the handlebars. As I pushed my friend around, the look we got from people was hysterical. The shock factor was great! We both got a big kick out of it, and since I was done with rehab and had trained for many hours to walk, it wasn't that hard to do.

So when we got close to the school, I asked Imagine if she wanted to sit in my wheelchair and have me push her in. She thought that was great and was all for it. I knew my family would be right out there as well as everyone else and we would shock them all with our entrance. It would be one-of-a-kind and no one could top it!

As the limo stopped, we felt like rock stars. We had been singing along to AC/DC in the limo and now there were people everywhere waiting for us. I stepped out and stood next to the limo, holding onto the open door. The song inside was blaring but I heard my mother, along with my friends, screaming my name.

Imagine and I looked at each other, waiting for my wheelchair to be put together. When the driver brought it to me, Imagine sat down in my wheelchair and I grabbed the back. My mother was shocked, yelling, "What are you doing?" Imagine and I just smiled as everyone stared at us in amazement!

What I did not think of at the time was that, earlier that week, my friend who I had been pushing did not weigh only 100 pounds. When I pushed him, I leaned into the wheelchair for support. Well, when I leaned into the wheelchair with Imagine in it, it popped up and went forward, with me holding onto the handlebars in back. As I fell down, she went backward so fast that both of her legs flew back and kicked me in the head.

Imagine was fine and so was I, but I was so embarrassed that I did not want to stick around for pictures. After we were in, though, I didn't think about it anymore because I started to talk to my friends.

Prom was set up beautifully and I felt like a king with my queen. Only, my throne had wheels.

Now the only thing I had to worry about was the slow songs. What was I going to do? Thoughts of last year came to mind again, but I couldn't let them get the best of me. Not this time, not my senior prom.

The DJ played fast songs in the beginning then a slow song. I asked Imagine to dance with me, although thoughts of misery were in my head. As I rolled to the dance floor with her beside me, all I wondered was, "How am I supposed to dance sitting in this wheelchair?" I couldn't dance face to face with her; my arms would be way out in front of me, so the only other way was if she stood by my side. That's what we did—and we could dance fairly closely with her next to me and me guiding my wheelchair with one hand and holding her with the other.

After that dance, the DJ played some more fast songs and Imagine and I danced among all the others. But when another slow song came on, this time I knew what I was going to do. We headed to the dance floor, but this time I stood up and grabbed her by the waist. However, standing up to dance with her didn't feel natural or comfortable. I was putting a lot of my weight on her, using her as my support, and I didn't like doing that.

I could tell she was worried as we danced so I leaned back, taking some of the pressure off her. Before I knew it, I began to fall. I let go of Imagine so I did not take her down with me, but my friend Lucus moved in quickly to catch me. I still fell, but he managed to soften how hard I hit the floor. I felt stupid and got back in my chair. Then I came up with another plan.

I took Imagine and we headed to the front of the stage. Once there, I got up and held onto the stage with one arm and grabbed her waist with my other one. I supported all my weight on the stage and got my balance. All the hours of rehab were worth it for this moment alone!

I was in a world of my own with my arm around my date's tiny waist. As I stood there, Lucus, Rocky and some of my friends would smile and make comments to me. It made me feel so good to be able to stand up; I felt normal and like one of the guys. It was another blessing from God that I could even do that. I would have given anything in the world to be able to dance like everyone else and they all took it for granted. But I adjusted to the situation and it worked out well.

Toward the end of the night, I got fatigued from standing and dancing. My lower back was throbbing and I had to sit down for some of the slow songs. During the fast songs, I could sit in my wheelchair and other girls would come up to me and dance. Life was good sometimes!

I asked the DJ to play some signature songs that the girls loved, including "Baby Got Back" by Sir Mix-A-Lot. It was his *Mack Daddy* album that I was listening to when the tire blew out on my Buick.

Prom was amazing and a night I'll remember forever. I was so grateful that Imagine went with me and I had one of the best times of my life with her. When she and I finally did get our pictures taken, I wanted to stand up. It was something I wanted to do for myself; I just didn't want to be in the wheelchair for my senior prom. However, that night meant a lot to me because I realized that girls could look past the fact that I was in a wheelchair. It was my own issues and problems that made me think that being in a wheelchair was holding me back. The wheelchair was a part of my life and there was nothing I could do about it but enjoy the time before it was gone.

CHAPTER 22

Graduation Practice

After prom, graduation was right around the corner. It was hard to believe that it was all almost over. Even after everything that had happened to me, the four years still seemed to go by so fast.

I had decided that, after high school, I wanted to take a year off to continue rehab on my own and become more dedicated at the Nautilus. I wasn't in any rush and after that year of training, I planned to start college. Even though some of my friends got scholarships and would continue to play football, I never got depressed that I wasn't going to college right away. In fact, I was more relieved than anything; I was tired of studying.

■ ■ ■

The time for graduation rehearsal came quickly. School was over for the seniors and we just had to practice in the gym, going over the order we would be walking in and what route we would be entering and leaving by. There were specific seats for each of us, and they had me set up my stereo (the one I used at the football games), which was going to play the graduation music.

We had to line up outside the gym in the halls according to our last names, so I had to wait a little since my last name is Scott. I had brought my forearm crutches with me to practice walking and had already told administrations that I had planned to walk at graduation.

I was nervous to try to walk in front of my classmates since most of them had never seen me walk before. When it was finally my turn to go, I started walking, focusing on doing it slowly to make sure I did not fall. As I walked, some schoolmates started to yell enthusiastically, even though it was just practice. I smiled at all the grinning and shocked faces. When I made it to the spot beside my fellow classmates, I just stood there happily, waiting for everyone else to arrive and for the principle to say the word to be seated.

Then it was time for us to practice going on stage to get our diplomas. When our row stood up, I realized how much I disliked that stage. The stairs that led up were the worst kind for me to climb, and there was no handrail. When it was my turn to go up, I was having problems with the first step, so Ramsey quickly came to my side. I gave him my right crutch and put my arm around his shoulders and used my left crutch up the stair. It worked perfectly.

As I got to the top of the stage, he gave me my crutch back and I walked to get my pretend diploma. Afterwards we went to the end of the stage and Ramsey came to my aid again. He pretended to flip the tassel on my cap then I handed him my crutch and put my arm around his shoulder as he helped me down the stairs. I was so thankful for his help and it relieved me so much to know that the steps were not going to be a factor during *actual* graduation the next day.

CHAPTER 23

The Final Day— Graduation!

B efore graduation, I had a lot of things going through my head; the thought of falling was at the top of the list.

It was also an emotional time for my mother, especially since we had been through a lot together. I always liked to joke around with her, though. When she was in another room, I would put on my cap and gown, hurry to the room she was in and stand in the doorway while her back was toward me. When I'd call her, she'd turn around and I'd have a big smile on my face. She would instantly get emotional then tears would come to my eyes as she gave me a hug.

■ ■ ■

When the time had actually come for graduation, my father took me to the school. As we headed to Pomona, seeing the cap and gown there by my side made me realize that it was almost over. I would never see most of my classmates and friends again. It would be like a summer break, only this time we wouldn't be returning to Pomona High.

As I looked out the window and remembered all the good times, my eyes watered, but I held back the tears and tried to pull it all together. I was at the school before I knew it, but I wasn't the only one there early. Other classmates were already there with their gowns on.

I had one final chance to talk to and joke around with my

friends and take a lot of pictures. This was the last time we'd ever be together like this so we had to make sure we captured the moment. When the bleachers and chairs started to fill up with friends and family, the graduating class was moved out to the hall. I transferred into a chair and had my forearm crutches beside me. My wheelchair was taken away so that it would already be out there when I walked.

The more people I saw, the more nervous I got. The band started playing and the first couple of rows lined up. It was time. As I sat in the chair, I kept thinking about falling. Soon they would call my name and I would have to walk in front of all of these people—and they all knew who I was. My wreck was one of the most talked-about events in the town for some time. This would be the first time they would see me walk since the accident—and they were not expecting it.

I did not want to mess up the moment by falling on my face. I had worked so hard and long for this and I wanted it to be perfect. I was getting cold from nerves and my lip started to tremble, but I did not have much time so I stood up and got in position. There was no turning back; I was lined up as the next person to walk down one side of the aisle. The classmate on the other side had to walk along the back to the center and turn before I started walking, which gave me a little more time. My heart was beating fast and all I could think about was not falling. I was waiting and waiting and as soon as my classmate made that turn, I was up!

As soon as I began walking, I was also praying not to fall. I knew that if I did fall, however, I could simply get back up—and that comforted me. After a few steps, everyone started clapping and yelling loudly for me, whistling and calling my name. I never expected that but it felt so good. I walked with my head down at an angle, watching my steps. As I got to the turn and began walking down the main aisle, the applause got even louder. When I looked at the crowd to the left and right of me, many people were crying and I saw my aunt bawling her eyes out.

Chills went down my spine as I walked toward the rest of my classmates, who were clapping and cheering me on as I approached. The feeling was so overwhelming that it is hard to put into words. All I could do was smile and focus on not falling. I finally walked to the spot where my wheelchair was and the claps and cheers died down. When everyone was in place, the principle said the word and we all sat down together.

As the ceremony continued, one of our classmates sang a song. When she was singing, I looked over at my schoolmates and it began to get to me: This was the last time we would be together as a class. Soon, tears were rolling down my cheeks. I did not care who saw me crying; my classmates meant a lot to me. The girl who sat to my right saw me crying and started to cry, too. She and I had been classmates at Pomona since kindergarten, and there were others there from the beginning as well.

After the singing and the speeches, we got to give flowers to our family. I rolled on over to them and they were in tears. As I gave them flowers, they each gave me a hug, holding me tight as we told each other, "I love you." I have never seen my mother and father cry so hard as on that day. Seeing them like that made me more emotional than I already was.

Soon I rolled away so we could move the ceremony forward. Organizers had put together a slideshow of our class and once that started and the music began to play, it got really bad for me. They played the graduation song by Vitamin C on my stereo, and I loved that song. It was about graduating and leaving your friends, which just amplified my emotions. I cried so hard that my eyes were burning from all the tears.

After the sideshow, the first row stood up and the principle started to read out names one by one. The crowd would clap or whistle for whomever was walking across the stage. When my row was next, I was ready. I placed the forearm crutches in front of me and off to the side. Ramsey sat a row behind me the whole time so he could help me as I walked up the stairs.

As the line got shorter to receive our diplomas, I became more nervous than before since I soon had to face the stairs leading up the stage. When I was next, I moved my crutches forward and took some steps in anticipation. The classmate before me had just shaken the principle's hand; that was my cue. With the crutches supporting my every move, I started to walk when they announced my name. Everyone started clapping, whistling, and yelling. Someone in the audience stood up and other people followed; soon everyone was standing for me.

As I moved slowly, one crutch and one step at a time, I could hear my heartbeat. When I got to the first step, Ramsey was waiting for me, dressed in a suit, and I handed him my right forearm crutch. I put my right arm around him and he put his left arm around me. I placed my left crutch on the first step then, with Ramsey's support, started climbing up the stairs slowly. It took me a while but I did it. Once I got to the top, the coach handed me my crutch and I walked to get my diploma. The crowd never stopped clapping and yelling, and it seemed to get even louder when I got up on the stage.

My tutor was the one giving me the diploma and she had tears in her eyes when I walked toward her. I tried to shake hands the best I could and she gave me the diploma with a firm hug and a big smile on her face. I handed my diploma to Ramsey, who helped me carry it as I walked to the end of the stage and waited for them to announce the next person. When I stopped and stood there at the edge of the stairs, I looked at the audience and Ramsey flipped the tassel on my cap. When he did that, the cheers I got were unbelievable! I felt so blessed that all those people supported me like they did. As I gave them a smile, Ramsey and I started walking down the stairs.

The crowd got a little quiet as I was descending, but then I got one final round of applause at the bottom. I had to shake a few hands then the cheers finally calmed down and I walked back to my spot.

After all of the diplomas were given out, the principle finally said, "Congratulations to the class of 2000." We stood up, threw our hats in the air and were then ready to leave the ceremony. My row was one of the first to exit. Instead of pushing myself out in the wheelchair or walking out with forearm crutches, I had it planned with Ramsey that he would sit in my wheelchair and I would push him out of the gym. I had another wheelchair in the row behind mine specifically for this exit.

Ramsey and I hurried to get situated. He sat in the second wheelchair and I grabbed the back supports. As I pushed him out of the gym, we got smiles and stares. Once we made it to the hall, I got back in my wheelchair and people came up to congratulate me, tell me how proud they were of me, how I had shocked them, and that they couldn't believe that I had walked. We were all supposed to go outside to line up but I got delayed from people constantly coming up to me.

Once I made it outside, I got hugs and kisses from my family, who again told me how much they loved me, and then Ramsey came over and I gave him a hug and thanked him.

Ramsey meant a lot to me. He had been there for me and was like another father, helping and guiding me in the weight room and with football since the time we met during the summer before my freshman year. He was one of the first ones at school to see me after my wreck and was there for me afterward as well. He is a great coach, teacher and friend.

Finally, it was time for me to go home and say goodbye to

Pomona High. I had some great times there and a lot of memories. My four years of school changed my life. I had been through more than the average teenager, but I kept going forward, looking at the positive side of life. Of course, I still wished that I could have played football my junior and senior years, but I felt that there was a purpose for me being in the wheelchair. I could have died, but I didn't—and that taught me that there is more to life than what you cannot do.

Heading home, it all seemed so surreal. Graduation was amazing; it was the greatest feeling I had ever experienced. Afterward, my family had a little graduation party waiting for me and I was grateful to have them all there.

Later that night, Lucus and I went to a bonfire party thrown by the seniors. Everyone was drinking except the two of us. We just sat around the bonfire talking, but once people started passing out and throwing up, we left. That was the last get-together for the class of 2000 from Pomona High.

CHAPTER 24
After Graduation

The day after graduation seemed like just another day. I knew some of my friends had received scholarships and were already planning for college, but I didn't receive any scholarships and wasn't going to have my schooling paid for, so there wasn't any point in my going immediately. Walking and working out honestly meant more to me than going back to school. I never really honestly cared for school itself; my family, friends, and working out arc what drove me.

My friend Rocky had received a football scholarship from Highland Community College to play tight end, so he wanted to get bigger and stronger. That's when he and I started working out together at the Ottawa Nautilus. Our friendship aside, Rocky liked my work ethic when it came to the gym because I really pushed myself and was serious about weights.

I would normally lead our workouts and knew which body parts we were going to target first and which exercises, sets and reps we were going to do that day. I visualized how each exercise would feel and tried to target each specific area, working the muscle from multiple angles. As we trained, the exercises, sets and reps would change, depending on how we felt. Listening to our bodies was what actually led our workouts.

Since school was out, I had more time and freedom to train whenever and however long I wanted. This was the perfect opportunity for me to really focus on my goals, so I did just that, training six days a week. From Monday through Friday, I went to the gym at around four and on Saturday, I went when I felt like it. Four in the afternoon was the perfect time for me; that was when people began to lift. The gym got busy around five then died down at six.

Being around people made me want to lift harder and heavier. That's why I went to the gym at the busiest time. I would lift until past six and sometimes close to seven. Lifting for that amount of time may seem too long, but it goes quickly, especially when you lift heavy. With bench pressing alone, it sometimes took thirty minutes or more for me to complete all my sets. I would always warm up with two light sets and stretch a little in between for about three to five minutes. Then how many sets and reps I was going to do determined how heavy I was going to lift.

Most of the time, I kept track of what I did in previous work-outs to give me an idea of how heavy I should train. When I picked the weight I was going to work out with, I did it differently than most people. I always determined how heavy I wanted to lift at the end of my workout and then I'd pick weights for the previous sets, working myself from the last lift to the first one. Using past workouts as a guideline also helped me choose a weight to use, as well as figuring out the percent chart of my max. Even then, I might have changed the weight I used depending on how I felt that day, because on some days you just feel stronger than on others.

Three to five sets of actually lifting did not take long; psyching myself up to lift that heavy and resting in between sets is what took so long. Every time I benched, it would have to feel just right and I couldn't have anything bothering me.

Bench pressing was the exercise that took me the longest. When I lay down on the bench, I had to line up the bar with the lines on the ceiling so that it was evenly centered on my head. Focusing would really take place in the second to last and the last sets of the lift—the heaviest lifts that really brought out the weird little habits in people, including myself.

As I lay on the bench lining everything up, I would grab the bar then wipe my hands on my shirt, sometimes multiple times. Then sometimes my face would itch and I would have to move around on the bench some more. I did those things without noticing; all I thought of was lifting the weights. If you watch anyone lifting heavy, they, too, will have these types of things they do multiple times right before they lift.

With all the other exercises, I had a bodybuilding concept with a powerlifting mindset. I went through magazines and books seeking knowledge about which muscles I should work on which days and how many sets and reps I should do. From that I set out the base of my workouts. At the time, I figured more was better, so this was my workout schedule:

Monday	Tuesday	Wednesday	Thursday	Friday	Saturday
Chest	Back	Shoulders	Back	Chest	Shoulders
Triceps	Biceps	Legs	Biceps	Triceps	Legs
Abs		Abs		Abs	

For each muscle group, I tried to target a certain number of sets. Below are the actual working sets, excluding any warm-up sets:

Chest	Back	Shoulder	Triceps	Biceps	Abs	Legs
16-20 sets	16-20 sets	14-16 sets	12-16 sets	12-16 sets	12-16 sets	16-20 sets

I tried to hit those numbers of sets each time I was working that muscle group. When working out, I went heavy all the time.

Looking back now, I realize that I trained foolishly, but I stuck with it. The more I learned, the more I switched my routine, getting smarter about how I trained. Back then, though, I did not think I was overtraining because I was getting stronger.

Working out for so many hours at the gym didn't bother me. Lifting as heavy as I did always seemed to take a long time, but I didn't care because I loved it! Bench pressing alone took a half-hour or more, but it never seemed to be that long.

The way I thought at the time was to train each body part twice a week and go heavy with every exercise and set—so that's what I did. I always started my chest workout with bench presses, doing three sets of three reps, five sets of five reps, or any type of low rep combo, making sure the weight went up with each set.

Workouts were hard and tough, but I wanted to be that guy who lifted more weight than anyone else—the strongest person in the gym. I knew the only way to get stronger was to lift heavy weight, and that is what drove me to train as I did.

CHAPTER 25

My Blazer

That summer, I purchased my second vehicle. My brother Mike told me and my parents about this black Blazer he'd found in a used car lot. He said it looked good and that we should check it out.

When we arrived at the used car lot, there was the black Blazer and a van. I was big into subwoofers at the time, so even though the Blazer was nice, I was leaning more toward the van because I was thinking of how many more subwoofers I could fit in the back.

But everyone talked me into getting the Blazer instead; it fit me better than that van. It was an '89 4x4 Chevy short-bed Blazer with a red stripe down the side—and buying it used up about all the money I had. I had worked full-time before my wreck, even though I went to school, but after then I had no money coming in—until I received a Social Security check from all the back months since my accident.

What was funny, however, was that even though I now had a Blazer, I couldn't drive it. I could move my legs and put my feet on the gas pedal but my accuracy was not that good. If I needed to move my feet quickly to step on the brake, I may not have been able to move my leg in time or my foot could've gotten stuck on something without my knowing, so I didn't want to take a chance.

I'd heard of hand controls in cars before, but I had no clue how they worked, what they looked like, where I could even get them, or who would install them. I called car dealerships and shops all around Kansas and no one had hand controls or could install them. On top of that, no one could refer me to anyone who had them or could install them. I was frustrated at the situation, but within the next couple of days, we get a phone call from a friend about someone who wanted to donate hand controls to me. I was so relieved and thankful.

I got the man's name and number and called to thank him. I also asked if he knew where we could go to get the hand controls installed. He told me that if we stopped by, he would install them for me. Excitement overcame me when I heard that.

He was a mechanic and his father had previously been in a wheelchair, so those hand controls were actually from his father, who had recently passed away. It was sad to hear that, but he wanted to donate them so that someone else could benefit from them. Thanking him again, I set a time for that weekend.

After getting off the phone, I was thrilled. My mother was beside me listening in the whole time, and she was happy for me as well. Soon afterward, we get a phone call from one of the guys I had previously talked to about hand controls and he found a place up in Nebraska that was able to install them. It was nice of him to call me back to help, but I was thankful that the man in Osage City had come into my life. He had saved me a huge hassle with my vehicle.

That weekend, my uncle, mother and I took my Blazer to Osage City, a little over thirty miles from Ottawa. The man I had spoken to was really nice and showed us around his shop. He wasn't just a mechanic; he restored antique cars as well. He had some awesome-looking vehicles, but I didn't know much about cars so I couldn't tell the years, makes and models.

We gave him the key to my Blazer and he explained what he would be doing under the steering wheel. He showed me the hand controls and where he would install them then gave me a couple of options about covering up the wires if I wanted to or just leaving them open. I just told him leaving them open was fine; it looked more high-tech. Anyway, whatever was easiest was fine with me.

He said he was going to get on it first that morning and it would take a couple of hours. We told him to take his time; we were grateful to him for just doing this in the first place.

When we returned to his shop after a few hours, he was almost done; there were just a few touch-ups left to do. The hand controls looked awesome! They were chrome with a black handle and were mounted on the base of my steering wheel, where a metal stick stuck out straight under my turn signal. At the base of the steering wheel, two metal shafts were connected to the stick. One was bolted to my brakes and the other to the gas pedal.

The hand controls worked by pressing the handle down toward the floor to give it gas and pushing the handle forward, like punching someone, in order to hit the brakes. It was just like a videogame! He had cut open a section under the steering wheel and I could see all the wires and where he had bolted them in. It looked that much more impressive and gave the Blazer a mean look. I loved it!

Then he wanted me to take it for a ride. I was worried, but got in the driver's seat as he sat in the passenger seat. My mother and uncle looked concerned as I closed the door.

He told me to start it up so I did, but this was my first time driving since my wreck. Over a year and a half had passed since I'd been behind the wheel and that kind of freaked me out. At the same time, I was excited to test out the hand controls.

He told me to push the controls forward and put it in reverse. As I did, I could feel the tension in the springs and the movement in the controls. When I put it in reverse, I could feel, through my hand, the Blazer shifting gears. As I slowly let up from the brake, the Blazer was backing up. I turned the steering wheel and let off the controls some.

Maneuvering the vehicle took coordination. After backing up some, I was in an alley and had to push forward on the controls again to put on the brakes. Shifting the gear into drive felt great but letting off the brake meant that I started moving forward. The controls were touchy and the Blazer began to take off right away. I also gave it too much gas.

Learning the feel of the controls was hard at first, but I got the hang of using them fairly fast. We drove a little and headed back to his shop, where my mother and uncle were standing in amazement. I thanked the man again for everything he'd done then asked my mother (jokingly) if she wanted me to drive home. Her reply was, "I don't think so."

The next day seemed to come slowly; I was too excited to go for a ride. My uncle and I went out for a test drive so that I could get used to the hand controls before I took my driver's test again. We went down streets that had little traffic so I could put on the brakes as I turned corners as well as practice stopping smoothly. For some reason, driving with the hand controls felt like second nature to me, like I had used them before.

It just took a while to get used to how hard to push down and forward on the controls so that the car sped up and stopped smoothly. It did feel a little weird at first to drive with my hands and not my feet, but it was just something I had to do.

Later that week I went in for my driving test and passed easily. They put "mechanical aid" at the bottom of my driver's license under "restrictions." It was the first time I'd ever seen or heard of that.

Being able to drive was one thing, but now I had another problem: How was I supposed to get my wheelchair into the Blazer? Sure, someone could help me load it, but what would I do when I was alone? Sitting in the car, I thought of a way to get my wheelchair in the backseat: taking off the tires and putting them in the backseat first since trying to get the main part of the wheelchair through the door was nothing but a pain. Even then, with my wheelchair in the back, how could more than one person ride in there with me? Frustration was getting the best of me…then it hit me!

I would just put the wheelchair in the back compartment of the Blazer! PERFECT! That thought was like a breath of fresh air. But could I really lift my wheelchair and put it in the back of my Blazer while standing? I rolled back there to check it out, unlatched the tire, popped the glass and let down the tailgate. Next I got out of my wheelchair and tried to reach down to grab the center of the tire, trying to pop it out while holding on to the Blazer. Taking one tire off and putting it in the back seemed like a lot of reaching down and up. Then another brilliant idea came to mind: just lift the whole wheelchair up.

Since I lifted all the time, the wheelchair couldn't be that bad to lift, even though the weight was unevenly distributed. The bar that ran across the back of the chair felt the most secure and seemed like the best part to lift, so I grabbed that part of the chair, which altogether weighed no more than twenty-five to thirty-five pounds. But I was concentrating so hard that I totally forgot how light the chair was and was getting ready to lift it with all my force. I pulled up on the chair so hard that it began to shoot straight up in the air! Its lightness caught me off-guard but I slowed down really quickly or I would have thrown the chair through the back glass of my Blazer.

It took me literally one second to get my wheelchair in the back. I just put the other tire on and moved it as far back toward the seat as I could. It fit perfectly when I closed the gate. After that, I held on to the top of the rack as I walked around to the front door. The whole thing worked out perfectly and I could not have asked for it to go more smoothly.

But, before long, I ran into a problem with having my wheelchair in the back. My stereo only had a tape deck, which didn't have enough bass. After a week, I couldn't take it any longer and reinstalled the CD player and subwoofers from my old car. With the subwoofers in the back, I didn't have room to just set my wheel-chair in there, so I had to take off its tires and put one on each side of the speaker box. Then I folded the back of the wheelchair down and put it on the box itself. It made my day when both fit!

I was so happy and felt so blessed to be able to drive again. It's one thing to be wheelchair-bound, but not having the freedom to go where you want when you want to is another thing altogether. It was so exciting to be able to do some of the things that I once did. It was as if driving had been a missing piece to the puzzle of my life, and now I was that much closer to making myself complete once again.

CHAPTER 26

Spinal Cord Injury (SCI) Camp

The last time I was at the Shriners', I had heard about the SCI camp where four guys and four girls in wheelchairs were picked to try scuba diving, sledge hockey, wheelchair basketball, rock climbing, and many more activities. It would last a week and all of the participants would stay at the Shriners' Hospital. Before hearing about it, I did not think that some of those activities were even possible being in a wheelchair. Now, I was ready to find out firsthand!

Once my mother and I arrived at the hospital, I went to my room, which I'd be sharing with the other guys. The girls' room was right beside ours, and I saw some of them wheel by, so I went to their room to talk to them and get to know them.

When everyone finally showed up, it was crazy. I had seen a few people in wheelchairs from the previous visits, but seven other people in wheelchairs in two rooms was an eye-opener! It was interesting for me to see how mobile and self-efficient everyone was.

That night, we all got together to talk and we told each other how we had become wheelchair-bound. Some of them had injuries higher in the spine, so that their grip and hands had impairments. Some were complete and others incomplete, and some had close to the same level of injury that I did. However, everyone seemed to be over what had happened to them and they weren't depressed about it.

Later that night, when the girls went back to their room, the guys talked about the bathroom situation so we could time things out. With the bowel program, we had to set a schedule to reduce the chance of having an accident. One guy did his program at night, I did mine in the morning, and the other two did not actually stick to a program, but just went whenever they felt they had to go.

I always got up early and did my program first thing in the morning so the other guys would have over an hour if they needed to get into the bathroom. Most of the time, when I got out of the bathroom, they would still be in bed. So I woke them up to make sure we'd be ready by the time we were supposed to leave.

Once we'd eaten breakfast and were ready, we headed to the main lobby and were loaded into one of the Shriners' shuttle buses outside the main entrance. It took a while to load all eight of us into the bus, which was pretty big and had a wheelchair lift that came out of the side. Once the lift was down on the ground, one person in a wheelchair would wheel onto the square ramp (which had edges that came up about two inches on all sides, so that the wheelchair's tires would not fall off the end) and was strapped into place. Then the final two-inch edge was lifted up to enclose the wheelchair.

The chair and passenger were then lifted up three feet or so and unstrapped to roll into the van toward their seat. They would then transfer over to the seat, using a transfer board, receiving assistance or just lifting themselves up, depending on their level of mobility. Transferring was easier for some than others, because we had to rely on our upper body strength. If a person didn't have upper body strength to help lift themselves to transfer, it only made the process longer and life more challenging for them.

Along with upper body strength comes balance. A person's level of injury determines how much they can lean forward, backward and to the sides before falling over. My injury was at T-12 L-1 and, in the beginning, I had the hardest time sitting up, even while holding on to the wheelchair, a bed or anything that I could grab, so I know how hard it can be. Watching everyone transfer,

I noticed how some struggled, which made me realize how much weightlifting benefitted me and could benefit them. My mobility and control were far greater than anyone else's and I owed it all to lifting weights. The constant day-in and day-out of being so active strengthened my upper body to the point where my lower back and ab muscles made me more mobile.

Once loaded on the bus, we headed to an aquatic shop—and when we got there, it took just as long to unload as it did to load! At the shop, we picked out snorkels and a mask then headed out back to a full-size swimming pool. They explained that we were going to get suited up and scuba dive in the pool with certified divers. They taught us how to equalize our ears, control our breathing (and to make sure we breathed at all times), and adjust our BCD (the vest), as well as other safety precautions.

I was so excited to get the chance to scuba dive, even if it was in a pool. I'd heard so many people talk about how they wanted to go scuba diving but never had the time—and it was just awesome for me to have the opportunity to actually do it. Others suited up and went in before me, but that was fine. It was harder for everybody else and some needed more time than others.

Two or three of us went in the water together and had one or two divers with us at all times. When it was my turn, I put on a wet suit and they showed me how to inflate the BCD with the regulator (mouthpiece). That way I would float when I got into the water with the tank on me.

After they finished explaining everything, I transferred to the floor and scooted to the edge of the pool with my feet hanging in the water. Then they put on the BCD and strapped me in, told me to inflate my BCD, and showed me how to release the air out of it with a cord, so that when I was in the water, I would slowly descend.

I was ready! I inflated the BCD again, put the mask on my face and put the regulator in my mouth. They instructed me to roll forward into the water headfirst, with one hand on my mask and another on my regulator so that the water didn't knock them out when I went in. As I put my hands in place, I took a breath and leaned toward the pool; as I hit the water, it felt great.

One of the divers told me to make sure to equalize my ears as I went down and pull the cord to let air out of my vest, but to do it slowly so I wouldn't go down too fast. As I pulled the cord, I started to go under, but as soon as my head was fully submerged, my mask sprung a leak; to clear the water I had to tilt my head backward and blow out my nose. Soon after—poof—the water was gone! I then felt pressure in my ears, so I grabbed my nose and blew. I heard two pops and my ears were fine.

I didn't let the air out of my BCD too quickly because I didn't know how much to let out and didn't want to go down too fast. So it took me a few minutes to get to the middle of the pool. Even though I wasn't in the ocean, it was the most beautiful thing! I was hovering there in the middle with no effort. It was like I was free.

But I didn't stay in the middle too long before I started to go to the bottom. As I put air in the BCD with the regulator, however, I began floating back up. Trying to figure out how much air I needed in my BCD was the hard part. No matter how much I tried, it never seemed to be the right amount, but I floated decently.

After playing with an underwater torpedo toy, playing catch and swimming around a while, I wanted to get out of the pool so the others could get in. When I came to the side of the pool, Steve helped to unstrap my BCD then I grabbed the edge of the pool like a kangaroo and lifted myself out. That was an awesome feeling, like I was floating in space.

The excitement and emotion I heard from all the other partici-pants was entertaining, and watching them maneuver their bodies with their disabilities was interesting and awesome to see. Seeing others overcome difficult challenges gives you a new perspective.

After we were all out of the pool, we got back into our wheelchairs and sat on cushions, which were wrapped in plastic bags. We thanked everyone and then got back on the bus. Damp and excited, we headed back to the hospital, settling in for a while to get some of our strength back. Just that short amount of exertion took a lot of energy out of some of the participants. Such activities were not part of our average daily routine, but I was up for anything and ready for whatever came next.

■ ■ ■

Later that day, Kris and Sara (our camp counselors) told us that we were going to play sledge hockey. I had no clue what that was, but it sounded awesome. They explained that we would sit on sleds playing hockey. I was excited; though I didn't know exactly how it would work, I was ready for it. We loaded up on the bus again and headed out.

One of the other guys there was becoming competitive with me, even though I was a lot bigger than him. While we were playing basketball, he'd try to move more quickly than me or start trash-talking. So as we were heading to the ice hockey place, he told me he'd light me up, and I just laughed and said, "We'll see."

We went to a full-size skating rink—I had never been ice skating before in my life—and headed to where they had the sleds and gear set up for us. The sleds were made out of aluminum or steel and had a curved front where the feet were strapped down. Toward the back of the sled was a bucket seat that also had a strap to keep us from falling out. We took turns transferring to our sleds then getting suited up in hockey gear: shoulder pads, helmets, gloves, etc. Then we each received two mini-hockey sticks, a little longer than a foot in length, one for each hand. These hockey sticks had picks at the bottom to grip the ice so we could push ourselves along.

Putting on the shoulder pads, helmet, and all the other protection brought back memories of when I used to play football. It felt so good putting on all that gear; it just made me want to hit someone!

I pushed myself out into the rink and stuck the picks in the ice; I could feel how firmly they gripped. As I pushed myself, I moved pretty fast without actually even trying to. So then I really started pushing myself, getting into it and moving at a fast pace. To turn, I leaned all the way on my side until my leg was actually on the ice and I held my upper body up with my forearm. Doing that, I could turn very easily, and it helped me slow down and stopped me from crashing into the wall or other players.

After a few pushes and turns, I was confident in my skills. I then pushed over to the other guys and checked them as a joke, knocking them over, but not too hard. One of them had a tough time getting back up once he was on his side; I felt bad at first, but then he got the hang of getting back up. It was fun just sliding up to people and pushing them over. I'd slide over toward the girls really fast then turn to my side and stop, giving them a soft push to knock them over and just sort of play with them.

But then the guy who was in competition with me charged full-force toward my side as I was sitting still. He had a look to kill in his eyes. When he got close, I just checked the hell out of him, knocking him over like a little boy. Once he got up, we were side by side and I pushed him and knocked him over again.

There was a hockey puck on the ice that we'd pass to each other, but not really seriously. After a while, however, an actual sledge hockey team came out and asked us if we wanted to play with them. We were all for it and separated into teams.

As we began, I started pushing full-force toward the guy with the puck. Right before I got to him, however, he passed it. Heading toward the new guy with the puck, I was planning to plough him over—and that's just what I did. Once I knocked him over, I took the puck and it was on.

After that, the other team didn't take it easy on me, which was fine because I hit them with everything I had. They came at me trying to knock me over, but they couldn't and sometimes I'd knock them over while they were trying to get me.

Those guys could move so much faster and smoother than the rest of us; it was obvious they had been doing this for some time. The way they worked together was awesome, and we thanked them for letting us play with them.

After we returned from each activity, it was time for us to hang out and talk—or joke and mess around. For example, most of us had muscle spasms in our legs from being in wheelchairs—some of us worse than others. My spasms were never that bad, but one guy had it really bad whenever water touched his leg. He showed us how, when he flicked water on his leg, it'd go into crazy convulsions. But he just laughed and threw more water on his leg.

Later that night, one of the guys thought it would be funny to flick water on the other guy's leg while he was sleeping, so we ended up getting a toothbrush and a cup of water and rolled over quietly to the side of his bed. As we uncovered his leg, we had to hold in the laughter so as not to wake him up. He was lying so peacefully on his back, not expecting anything, and we wet the tip of the toothbrush then launched a spray attack. Water went all over his leg, instantly causing those hardcore spasms.

That woke him up very quickly and he started cussing at us playfully; we died laughing. He was shaking so hard that he almost fell out of bed. So another guy flicked more water on him and he cussed at us some more. It was one of the funniest things I had ever seen–and he was totally cool with it.

■ ■ ■

The next morning, we headed out to the lake to kayak, which was something I'd never done before but always wanted to try. It was a beautiful day at the lake—perfect for being on the water.

Most of us got into single-seater, closed-top kayaks, which was difficult because we didn't have that range of movement to allow us to easily bend or lift our legs. But we did whatever it took to angle our legs and bodies just right so that we could get into the kayaks. Once we all had life vests and paddles, we were ready to roll.

Being on the water was amazing, like gliding through air. At first, it took some coordination to angle the paddle correctly, turn it properly to move, and alternate it from side to side with a lot of force in order to move more quickly. But once I got that down, all I wanted to do was haul ass up and down the river. However, I was told to slow down because they wanted us to stick together.

We headed up the lake together and eventually split up into two different groups: one that was slower, enjoying the scenery, and the other that went around the lake faster, while still enjoying Mother Nature! I was in the latter group—and I finally got to unleash the speed! All that weightlifting helped when I was in the kayak. Not only could I move faster, but I could paddle for a long time without getting exhausted.

Toward the end, we got back together as a group and watched the instructor demonstrate some skills. He explained that he was going to do a side roll to show us that, if we ever tipped upside down, we could push ourselves back over. He tipped himself over and went under water. Two seconds later, he was back up, having done a 360-degree roll like it was nothing. He said that all we had to do was use the paddle to push down on the water so that we'd turn back around. He demonstrated it again and once he popped back up, I could see how he did it.

Then he asked for volunteers, and instantly the competitive guy raised his hand. The instructor waited close by, just in case he became stuck. So the guy went for it and after a few seconds, he did it successfully. After he did it, I had to try. So I tipped myself over then pushed with the paddle to get myself to flip around. Flipping over was actually easy, but the build-up of thinking about doing it was the scary part, which is usual in life.

■ ■ ■

Later that evening, we headed out to play basketball at the facility where a local wheelchair basketball team practiced. The nets, however, were set on regular ten-foot posts, which hadn't been lowered for the wheelchair athletes. I wasn't crazy about that since we couldn't jump; in fact, if I lifted my arm up in the wheelchair, it would come only to a little over five feet. That would be like having fifteen-foot posts in regular basketball.

We transferred into the special wheelchairs and practiced shooting. Then some of the guys from the wheelchair basketball team showed up and we were going to play a couple of games with them, which would be fun. The rules were that we had to bounce the ball one time every two pushes or we had to pass. They were simple, but easy to forget sometimes in the heat of the moment.

Before the game even began, I knew it was going to be intense. After we picked teams, I wrapped a piece of cloth around my head like a ninja headband.

The game was heated and my plan was to rip the ball away from the others and pass it to someone who had better shooting skills than me. I sucked at shooting baskets, even before my accident!

Playing wheelchair basketball, or any activity that involves moving fast, burns the crap out of your shoulders. So even though the other players weren't into being as rough as I was, I was still getting quite a workout. The other team passed the ball a lot and had great teamwork skills—but I'm sure the guy I covered hated getting the ball because I was all over him! When I play a game, I mean business; I hate losing and will try my damndest at whatever I'm doing.

The game grew more intense and the scent of burnt rubber hovered in the air as people flew, flipped, and tipped over out of their wheelchairs. It wouldn't have surprised me if people lost fingers playing this sport.

After playing a few games, sweat was dripping off my face and my shirt was stuck to my back. During and after, I had to do pressure relief because my butt got so hot; lifting up, I could feel the heat coming from the cushion. Playing with the team—and just playing basketball in general—was a lot of fun. The SCI camp was so amazing. I'd done more in the last couple of days than in the twenty-two months since my accident back home in Kansas!

CHAPTER 27

More Sports at SCI Camp

Our next activity at camp was going to the gym. Of course, I was psyched!

Kris and Sara were going to show us around, check our body fat and other intriguing activities. I was so enthusiastic because I loved seeing new weightlifting facilities and checking out what different types of equipment, setups, and atmospheres gyms had.

On the bus, the competitive guy boasted he'd have lower body fat than me. I countered that just because he was smaller didn't mean he'd have less body fat. But we'd soon find out…

The gym was nice and big and the equipment was spaced out very well. Some gyms were so compact that it was hard to get to certain machines. It even had a hand cycle machine for cardio that we could use for upper body workouts. That was the first time I'd ever seen one of those.

Soon, Kris and Sara took us to an area where they could check our body fat; I had been waiting for this moment to shut the other guy's face! They got their skin calipers out and took our skin fold measurements, as well as testing our blood pressure and giving us a strength, endurance and grip test. Afterwards, we got a print-out. My strength and grip were superior and my endurance was good. More importantly, the body fat: Mine was twelve percent. The other guy's was sixteen.

I appreciated my results because I worked out so much. However, one girl did beat me on body fat percentage, with seven percent, which is low, especially for a girl.

After we were tested, we got a chance to try some of the machines. I went over to the chest, tricep and bicep machines for a few sets because there were more varieties than at my gym. Whenever we moved from one machine to the next, other people would stare at us. Some played it off like they weren't looking, but you couldn't blame them. It isn't every day you see that many people in wheelchairs at the same time—and at a gym. I would have looked, too.

The girls weren't too fond of this gym activity of ours, but I loved every minute of it! The second event, however, was rock climbing. Eight teenagers in wheelchairs were going rock climbing. How were we going to do this? Just the idea of it blew my mind.

Our destination was an indoor rock climbing area, which I had never been to before. The place was sweet; it had all these plastic rock-looking things in all different colors and sizes on the wall. People were using them to grip and place their feet. I asked why they were different colors and a worker told me that the colors indicated the level of difficulty. Once you started with a color, you were supposed to stick with it until you reached the top.

Looking closely, I could tell which ones were the hardest levels. The beginners were the size of your hands or bigger and close together, whereas the hardest level was about an inch in size and there weren't a whole lot to grab on to. You had to be Spiderman or something to reach those on top.

The walls did not just go straight up, either; some angled inward. People climbed without harnesses or cables, but the floor had a lot of cushion or foam. A few climbers were scaling the wall like it was nothing. One girl was doing the hardest level and she was just ripped. You could see the muscle definition in her shoulders and back.

After seeing that, I was like, "Yeah, right." I could use some of my leg strength to hold me and climb with my upper body, but the rest of our group couldn't climb the wall with their upper body strength alone.

It turned out that rock climbing wasn't exactly what we were going to do. It was more like a lot of pull-ups. A cable went straight up about fifty feet with a bar attached to it. We wore a harness that attached to the cable and once the bar was in place, it locked and couldn't move down. We were supposed to push the bar up until it locked then pull ourselves up. We'd repeat this until we got to the top then they would slowly release us to the bottom.

The girls went first. The one girl who had hand problems did the best she could; she wanted to climb up to the top so badly, but ended up going about thirteen feet. She impressed me, though. She may not have gotten to the top, but in my opinion, she went further than the rest of us. She pushed her body to the max, which is all you can ask.

One girl actually made it to the top, one went about ten feet and another couldn't even get off the ground. One of the guys almost made it all the way up and another barely made it to the top. The competitive guy and I were the only ones left. He went first and went up the cable pretty easily. Once he got down to the bottom, they told us that the record for someone in a wheelchair was doing it five times, so we got the chance to do it as many times as we wanted.

Of course, the guy went up again—and I realized that I had to get up there more times than he did and beat the record. He went up the cable more slowly each time and finished after four. I was glad he didn't tie the record because then I'd have had to listen to him go on about it.

I wasn't worried, but focused. I wanted to beat him and take the record. I could easily do chin-ups ten times but I never did them for endurance. As they strapped me in, I kept repeating, "It's only five times." They knew that if anyone could break the record, I could.

I was in position and grabbed the bar then easily pushed it up and pulled myself up. As soon as I lifted my weight, I knew it was going to be easy for me. I was at the top in no time. They got me back down and I went up again and again.

Going up the seventh time, my arms were burning badly. I eventually made it up a seventh time and was done. I was satisfied.

Even though our activity differed from rock climbing, I took it very seriously and it was a lot of fun. We had already done a whole lot of new things I had never dreamt of doing—but camp was only about halfway over!

■ ■ ■

Next, we were going to play tennis. To do so, we got in the same wheelchairs we used for basketball and went down to the tennis courts a few blocks away. There were three or four outdoor courts side by side; it was a very nice setup. A man in a wheelchair was waiting on us; it turned out that he was a major wheelchair tennis player who was going to show us some skills.

We each got a tennis racket and he showed us how to correctly hit the ball and maneuver in the wheelchair while holding the racket. The girl who had little strength in her hands had her racket taped to her hand.

As the tennis pro demonstrated, I could tell he had been playing for a long time because he moved so fast. We lined up side by side with a lot of space in between, then he hit balls to us and we would hit them back.

Eventually we played full-court as teams. We hit the balls back and forth but didn't play an actual game. It was hard enough for everyone to get the basics. I had a tendency to hit the ball too hard, causing it to go flying, and my aim was terrible. But after hitting the ball a few times, I got the hang of it. The best part for me, however, was when the ball hit my opponent!

Tennis was a great workout but we had to have good coordination and many other skills to be even halfway decent at the game. I enjoyed it, but I still preferred weightlifting.

Later that same day, we headed out for the next adventure of the week: horseback riding. This was going to be interesting and scary at the same time. I wondered how we were going to get on the horses and how the others were going to keep their balance once they were up there.

When we arrived at the ranch, I felt like a country boy; I should have worn a cowboy hat and boots. The scent of manure in the air sure helped! There were cattle and horses beyond the fence and tractors everywhere.

Horseback riding was never that exciting to me but I was looking forward to trying it again. Most of the girls were thrilled, though. We went into an open building and there were a few barrels set up, making it look like an oval dirt track. A ramp led up to the horses' backs; we'd use that to get on.

Two people at a time would go up the ramp, transfer on the deck and scoot to the edge. When the horse grew still, we'd get help putting one leg over the saddle and transferring onto the horse so we didn't fall. Once in place, we went around the oval track and they taught us different commands to make the horse move, as well as teaching us to shake or pull on the strap that went around its head. I went around the track a bunch of times; it was fun, but not exactly my cup of tea.

■ ■ ■

The final activity was more my speed: We got to try out the hand cycles. The Shriners' playground had a curvy track outside, and the competitive guy and I ended up getting on the cycles first.

We sat in our seats with our legs straight out in front of us; there was one tire in front, two in back and handles directly in front of us that turned to make us move. It was just like a bike except we pedaled with our hands. To turn, we simply touched the outside rim of the tire, slowing it down and making it turn however much we wanted, just like a wheelchair.

The other guy got settled before I did and started going around the track. Then I was off! I pedaled fast, trying to catch him—and eventually I did. After a few times around the track, I paused to get some water and the instructors noticed something wrong with the other guy's legs. The tires were rubbing skin off his inner knees. He had pink spots where the skin was missing. I quickly checked my legs to see if I had the same thing, but I didn't. Seeing him like that, however, was freaky. They wrapped his legs up where the tire was rubbing and figured out how to spread them so they wouldn't touch the tires.

Once I began going around the track again, I was pushing the pedals as hard and fast as I possibly could. My shoulders were burning badly but it was so fun to move at such a quick pace. After quite a few times around the track, they asked me if I wanted to try the other bike that you used with your legs. I was all for it.

As I sat in this new bike, I liked the way it felt (actually, I liked both of them). But now it felt as if I were preparing for a race. Once set up, I pedaled off and felt free. Pedaling took much less effort and energy since I was using my legs. I could go much longer in this bike than the other, which totally made my day.

To cool down afterwards, I decided to start a water fight. There was a drinking fountain right beside the track so I filled up empty Gatorade bottles with ice cold water and rolled over to one of the guys. He saw the big smile on my face and the bottles in my lap and instantly knew what was going to happen! He began to roll away but it was too late for that. I grabbed a bottle and squirted the freezing water at him. You could tell it was cold from the girly squeals that came out of him!

The war was on! He grabbed something to fill up with water as

I headed back to fill the bottle again. We ended up soaking each other and laughing the whole time. Our cushions got so wet that we had to sit on towels for sometime after that while they dried off. It was all worth it, though.

■ ■ ■

On our last day of camp, our families arrived and it was nice meeting everyone. Even though my mother had been nearby the whole time, she had given me my space and now it was nice to socialize with her. The whole week I felt bad because she stayed behind while I went to the activities. At times, I wished she were there. But throughout the week, I'd tell her what we were doing and she'd sound excited for me. My mother is a great woman who understands me. We have a strong bond and think alike. She means the world to me and I love her with all my heart.

That evening, there was a special room set up for a dinner banquette and they showed our families a video of all the things we'd done during camp. One of the girls also made a home video and they ended up showing that, too. Watching it made me realize how fast the week had gone by; I couldn't believe we had done all that in one week! Our families also got a big kick out of the stuff we did and said. As they watched, I could hear laughs and see their smiles. My mother's eyes watered as she watched the footage—and she told me how proud she was to have me as her son.

That was a great evening to reflect on all the things we'd done—and on top of that, Kris and Sara had awards for all of us. They spoke about each of us before calling us up and giving us individual awards that displayed our characteristics. As far as I was concerned, though, it was an honor just to be a part of this whole trip.

When we said our goodbyes the next day, no one was ready to go. I really grew close to one of the guys there, even though we had only known each other a week. I was so grateful and felt so blessed to have been given the chance to be part of the camp; it allowed me to see what opportunities were out there even though I was in a wheelchair. Knowing that anything was possible was a great feeling!

CHAPTER 28

Amanda

I had an awesome time at camp, but I was glad to be back home. After the trip, I couldn't help but think about Amanda, the girl I had wanted to take to prom. So I gave her a call one night but didn't tell her I was home because I wanted to surprise her. And I did just that!

I had a couple of gifts and drove out to her house the day after I returned. Her mom was outside and happy to see me. She told me Amanda was inside sleeping and offered to go wake her up, but I asked if I could wake her up instead. Her mother smiled and agreed; she helped me into the house and I headed to Amanda's room.

Once there, I sat on her bed and called her name, softly at first then louder and louder. She started getting pissy and didn't want to get up, thinking I was her father or brother. Once she realized it was me, she shot up and gave me a hug.

She was so happy to see me. I offered to let her get back to sleep, but she just smiled and said, "No, stay." We talked for a while then I gave her a gift. She melted when I gave it to her; it meant so much to her that I had thought of her when I was gone.

Then I told her I had something else for her on the floor beside her. She looked down but didn't see anything. As she sat back up and turned to face me, I moved in for a kiss. My heart was beating so hard since I didn't know how she was going to react, but it all turned out to be good. She didn't stop me and we kept kissing.

It was the best thing in the world—or so I thought. But the kiss turned out to take a toll on our friendship and we weren't the same around each other after that. I could sense and feel it. At the end of the week, she told me she didn't want to be anything more than friends. She missed our friendship and hated the fact that we had both changed around each other. I said it was fine, but I couldn't stay around long after that. Hearing those words crushed me.

I was devastated. As I drove away, the tears flowed down my face. The one chance I'd had with her was gone and it was obvious that her feelings for me weren't as strong as mine were for her.

I cried for weeks and weeks trying to deal with the pain. She would call and I would ask her why she thought things between us wouldn't work out. But I was just in denial and wanting something that wasn't going to happen.

After she got back together with her boyfriend, we eventually talked on the phone sometimes but it was different. I had gotten over my strong feelings for her but it was too late. Our bond would never be the same. She was an awesome friend and the choice to make more of our friendship turned out to be a mistake. Of all the lessons in my life, that one was very hard to learn.

CHAPTER 29

Lucus

It's interesting how everything comes together in life when you least expect it.

Lucus and I have been good friends for many years, going back as far as sixth grade when he first transferred to Pomona. Our first real interaction was during an argument over a girl, shortly after his arrival, at a Halloween party on his parents' farm. We quickly settled our differences and from that point on the bond of our friendship continued to grow and strengthen. As we got older, Lucus was forced to deal with many physical and emotional challenges due to being an albino.

Lucus's appearance consisted of pale skin coupled with an almost luminescent head of bright white hair. For him, tanning was not an option since even minor exposure to sunlight produced painful burns. As if he didn't already have enough challenges, Lucus's albinism also severely limited his vision. Even with his Coke-bottle glasses, he was borderline legally blind.

As one could imagine, our classmates constantly picked on him throughout school. I think we all understand just how cruel children can be with even the smallest amount of ammunition, and given Lucus's many highly visible differences, I'm sure it's not difficult to imagine the verbal onslaught he had to endure at times. Even outside of school, Lucus had difficulty dealing with people who could not understand or appreciate his uniqueness.

Early on, Lucus was very humble and subservient in the face of the badgering and name-calling, always hanging his head and trying his best to disappear. However, I had a different reaction. It really pissed me off to bear witness to such cruelty and I made it a point to let people know how I felt.

I recall that Lucus endured the worst of it during our freshman year of high school. The seniors liked to make comments during our foreign language class when the teacher was out of the room. I remember thinking, *Just who in the hell do these guys think they are?* A rage had been brewing deeply within me until one day I could no longer contain it. My palms sweaty, my heart racing, and my head hot with anger, I stood up one day and shouted, "YOU BETTER SHUT YOUR F---ING MOUTHS!" The words just erupted—words of caution to a group of seniors that far outnumbered me.

Under normal circumstances I think just about any freshman would have been afraid of issuing such a verbal challenge that begged to be contested, but I didn't care about the consequences. A look of astonishment passed over their faces as the classroom grew silent. As one of the seniors rose to his feet, I stepped forward, not only standing my ground but also pushing ahead and purposefully invading his personal space until I stood only a few inches away. We stood with our eyes locked while our unspoken facial cues established my resolve.

The tension was quickly broken as the teacher entered the room. At that moment I knew that despite my anger and disgust, I wasn't able to feel even one-tenth of the emotional pain that Lucus must have been feeling. Interestingly, it was only two years later that I, too, became unique and could truly understand how a stranger's stare could make a person feel so different.

Even with the chips stacked against him, Lucus somehow managed to beat all the odds with his condition. Perhaps one of his greatest accomplishments came during his senior year of high school. After much time and effort, he was able to get his driver's license. To you and me this may not seem like a very big deal but anyone within the albino community will tell you how rare that actually is. Lucus and I have both managed to accomplish things within our lives that everyone said couldn't be done. Growing up, we helped each other surpass all expectations and lead successful lives. For this reason we have a bond that can never be broken.

■ ■ ■

Months after high school ended, Lucus and I still hung out on and off. At the time he was busy with work and preparing to go straight into college, but the added pressure of having a daughter on the way really made him focused. He wanted the best for her and would do whatever it took to succeed.

On July 8, 2000, Kaycie was born. I stayed for hours waiting with their families. I didn't care how long it took; I just wanted to be there for Lucus. When I finally got to see his daughter, she was beautiful with long black hair. Lucus was so proud of his baby girl and had a glow about him. I was glad to be there by his side.

A few weeks passed and Lucus asked me to be the godfather of his child. I was shocked and honored, and just knowing he trusted me like that really meant the world to me. He knew that I would be there for him and Kaycie no matter what.

CHAPTER 30

Neosho

After a year off, I actually wanted to go back to school—and from the beginning, I knew exactly what my goal was: to open my own gym and train people. I loved training so much that, deep inside, I felt it was what I was supposed to do with my life. So I decided to pursue a degree in business and get certified on the side.

I wanted to attend college close by so that I could live at home and therefore focus on my studies and weight training. There were two choices in town: Ottawa University and Neosho Community College. Ottawa U. was one of the most expensive colleges in the state; Neosho was not. The prices were like day and night, so I chose to go to Neosho.

School was school to me; the whole purpose in the end was to get my bachelor's degree in four years—as little time as possible! So I figured I'd go to Neosho for two years, graduate with an associate's degree then transfer to a university to finish.

I went to Neosho for the first time in the summer of 2001 to get information about the fall semester, which classes I had to take, enrollment dates, and so on—but as I got closer to campus, I became really nervous. The first visit should have been no big deal, but my heart beat faster when I thought about going to college.

The truth was, I didn't know what to expect. How big was the school? How many students attended? These and a million other thoughts went through my head as I drove toward the campus, so I turned up my stereo to try to get my mind off school and to ease my nervousness. The closer I got, however, the worse I felt.

All I wished for was the ride to be over. Then the school came into view—and I couldn't believe it!

Neosho was so small—tinier than my high school, even. It was a one-building school surrounded by nothing but parking spaces—and there weren't that many vehicles in the lot. The good thing, though, was that the building was handicap accessible. That was the biggest benefit for me because the more I had to worry about accessibility, the more handicapped I felt.

Seeing the school was a big relief and I exhaled slowly. I wasn't completely at ease, however, since I still didn't know what to expect. I drove up in front of the main entrance, parked in a handicap spot and went right up the cement ramp, which was all so convenient and gave me a good first impression. But as I entered the building, I noticed that there were no other students around.

The main office was twenty feet directly in front of me as soon as I came in, so I rolled up and saw an older woman working behind a sliding glass window. She was very friendly and asked me what I needed, and I told her I wanted to take classes in the fall. She smiled, gave me a bunch of papers to fill out and bring back on enrollment day, and told me I needed to take a pre-test on their computer before I could take any classes. I didn't ask questions, but left feeling like a new man!

Knowing I was moving on with my life felt amazing. I got goosebumps just thinking about it! Of course, I wasn't thrilled about the computer test, but when I got home and told my mother that I had taken the first step, she was elated, which made me feel all warm inside and even more certain that I had made the right move.

Still, that didn't stop me from procrastinating. I had a whole month to return with the completed paperwork but, before I knew it, I was filling it out the day before I had to go back to school. That made me feel like a real student again!

I looked over the class listings and times to see which ones fascinated me more than others, but it didn't matter. I needed to talk with the advisors to make sure I selected the right ones. So the following day I arrived at school around eleven in the morning— and it was packed. It was the first day of enrollment and I had come at the worst time, but I didn't know any better.

Inside, many tables were set up with people milling around everywhere. I looked around and noticed that the students came from a variety of ethnic backgrounds—unlike my high school, which was mostly Caucasian. I was really looking forward to getting to know their cultures and learning about their countries, and I liked the idea that we'd be attending classes together. But first I had to navigate those tables!

There was a certain order in which you had to visit them; if you went to the wrong table first, they'd send you to the right one, where you'd line up all over again. I found this out the hard way, which made my wait that much longer. After going to a couple of different tables, I was eventually sent into a room full of teachers/advisors who were assisting students in choosing the right classes for their majors. I rolled up to a spot and waited my turn, flipping through the pages of the course catalogue as if I knew what I was doing.

When it was finally my turn, the teacher pulled his chair around to my side of the table and shook my hand. We talked about my wanting to get a business degree and open a gym, and he asked if I had a prerequisite sheet. I had to admit that I had no clue what he was talking about! Instead, I showed him everything the woman had given me when I first came to the school. After a second of looking through all the papers, he grinned and told me to wait; half a minute later, he came back with a sheet that had all the requirements I needed to meet to graduate. I laughed and said, "I wish I'd had this all along." He smiled and told me that a business degree falls under the "Associates of Science," which didn't make any sense to me whatsoever.

The prerequisite sheet interested me, though. To graduate, I needed to have sixty-four hours total with a certain amount of credits in each of five categories. That alone intrigued me since it almost felt like a role-playing video game.

Everything depended on my choices and what I wanted to accomplish first—which I really liked, since it was all up to me. I also listened to some of my advisor's suggestions and decided to register for classes in all different subjects rather than focusing on one area right away.

The class I chose first as my science requirement was Human Anatomy and Physiology Lab and Lecture. My advisor kind of stared at me and said it was one of the toughest classes offered, but I told him I wanted to take Anatomy because I had always been fascinated by the human body and taking the class would also help me know my body better, which would benefit my workouts.

The funny thing was that my advisor turned out to be the one teaching that class. He was a short man with a little belly in his early thirties, and I could tell from sitting there and talking to him that I really liked his personality. He helped me finish picking the rest of my courses then sent me to the computer library.

"See you in class," I said excitedly.

After forty-five minutes of waiting in a huge line at the library, I was finally enrolled. I bought the books I needed and went home.

Later that week, however, I had to go back to Neosho to take the pre-test. The administrator explained that it didn't matter how well we did; they just wanted to keep records of how we started and where we'd end up.

When the test began, I had to read those long essays and answer questions to see how much attention I paid to the story. Well, the first couple of stories went smoothly, but then the administrator's words kept popping into my head: "It doesn't matter how well you do." Therefore, I started selecting answers randomly without caring if I was right. I was done in several minutes and left.

■ ■ ■

I was nervous on my first day of college, not knowing anyone and unsure how hard the classes were going to be—but I was also excited to meet new people and learn new things. What wasn't exciting, however, was my schedule. Neosho was different than most schools; each class was two hours and forty-five minutes long. That's a long time to have to pay attention—but the good part was that every class met only once a week.

For my first day, I bought a new bag with all new supplies—I wanted to be on top of my game. I also wanted to get to class thirty minutes before it began so that I'd be the first one there. It would bother me if I showed up and the classroom was already full of students because then everyone would turn to look when a new person came in. I knew that everyone was already going to stare at me for being in the wheelchair, so by arriving early, I'd already be settled and *I* would be the one to stare at *them* while they focused on finding a seat.

As I got ready to leave for school, my mother beamed with joy, which made me even happier. Most of all, I just wanted to make her proud. I loaded up my Blazer with school supplies, my mother took some pictures, and off I went.

Before I knew it, I was at the school, but I calmed down when I realized that almost no one would be there that early. I parked, maneuvered around the side of my Blazer and held on to the bike rack on top as I walked to the back to get my wheelchair out. No one was in the parking lot watching me, which left me to focus only on finding the right classroom. Once I got inside, I realized how funny that was. The room wasn't hard to find because the college only had two small hallways!

The classroom could hold about twenty students and the tables were set up in a big square; only the outsides touched. I sat at the table closest to the door just in case I had diarrhea or some other stomach problem. If something came up, I wanted to make sure I had a quick escape.

I moved the chair out of the spot where I wanted to sit and waited patiently. I was the only one there, but the more I thought about everyone coming, the more anxious I got—especially wondering if any hot girls would be in the class. Before I knew it, more and more people came in and the room started to fill up. Some tables had two or three student sitting at them, but I still sat by myself. All I could think about was how uncomfortable some of those people must have felt when they saw me in a wheelchair. I was different than them and I knew that was the main reason no one sat by me.

Eventually, someone did sit next to me and I smiled and said 'hi.' You couldn't actually say anything without everybody else hearing because of how small the room was, so it was as if my greeting was meant for everyone. There was a good mix of people: younger girls, older women, Japanese students, as well as a few other guys. There were around fifteen students altogether, but the small size of the room made it seem as though our class was huge.

The English Comp teacher came in and greeted us with a big smile and a few little jokes to loosen up the tension in the room. Shortly after, he took attendance and said to let him know if we went by a nickname. In the back of my mind, I prepared my story. I knew he'd want an explanation about my name; all teachers always did.

When he called "Clarence," I replied, "Here, but I go by the name Nick." He asked, "How do you get 'Nick' out of 'Clarence'?"

I laughed and explained, "My legal name is Clarence Raymond Scott and my older brother's name is Raymond Clarence Scott. See, my grandfather's name is Clarence and my father's is Raymond. Our dad wanted to name us after himself and his father. But when I was younger, my brother and sister couldn't say 'Clarence' and pronounced it as 'Nin.' From Nin, they started calling me Ninny.

My mother then turned Ninny into Nick, and from then on I've been Nick, but on all the legal documents I go by my real name, Clarence." I smiled and added, "It's as if I have a secret identity or something."

My explanation broke the ice. Everyone was smiling and looking at me—because of the story about my name, not because I was in a wheelchair.

Afterward, the professor told us what the class would be about then let us out early. All the classes that first week were pretty much the same—and I had to explain the story about my name over and over again. I didn't mind, though, because each time it got a laugh.

CHAPTER 31
School Days

My worst class was college algebra. I used to love math but the teachers make all the difference. The professor at Neosho was like a drill sergeant. She didn't take any crap and didn't care how many people she flunked. I could tell all that from the first day, when she kept us the entire time, talking fast and expecting everyone to keep up.

It had been a while since I'd taken high school algebra. I'd always been good at math but somehow she made me feel really stupid. I could tell many of the other students were having the same difficulties I was. When she called on individuals to answer questions, one guy said he had no clue what she was talking about. She got pissed and told us that we should know the basics; if we didn't, we were wasting her time and should think about taking beginning or intermediate algebra instead. Until then, I'd thought I knew my stuff.

When that first class was over, she gave us a huge assignment; that night, I tried to do the homework but it all just seemed to be too much for me. I wanted to drop that math class and take another one. The teacher had made me feel so stupid that that's exactly what I ended up doing.

I enrolled in beginning algebra, where my classmates were seven or eight women in their thirties who hadn't taken a math class in over ten years. I went from feeling like one of the dumbest students in class to being the smartest one, which really boosted my self-esteem. My new plan was to finish beginning algebra, take intermediate algebra then enroll again in college algebra with the same teacher. I wanted to prove a point.

That first semester, I also had Human Anatomy and Physiology (which everyone called A&P). In that class, I found out what the school was mainly about: Neosho was primarily a college geared toward nurses—which was fine by me. In A&P, there were twenty students, all women except me and another guy—and he was studying to become a male nurse.

Despite my advisor's initial warnings, A&P didn't seem too bad—but that was before our lab. The lab room had high tables that didn't move and stools that slid in underneath. This was really awkward for me. I didn't actually have a place where I could sit, so I rolled up to the side of the table, stayed in my wheelchair and put my books on top. I already felt weird enough around all those women, but then I didn't even have a proper spot. I hated that with a passion, but made it seem like no big deal. As it came time for the class to start, everyone sat on the stools, which made them so much taller, as if they were looking down on me.

Lab was different than lecture. The lecture part was about how the body functioned and the lab was about knowing the names of body parts inside and out. For that, there was a skeleton that hung from a pole; the professor called it Marie. Our teacher was awesome and made the class fun; no matter how interesting class was, though, the material was still tough as hell—and being in lab and lecture for over five hours was too much for anyone.

The lecture part was harder than anything else because we really had to understand the body; lab was all about memory. Every week in the lab we had a quiz, starting with the bones of the skull—but that was a piece of cake compared to things like the muscles in the hand and the nervous system.

My classmates talked about how A&P was one of the hardest classes at the college, especially with our teacher, who was known for flunking quite a few students. The more they talked about it, the more it got to me and began to freak me out. As the semester went on, it turned out that everything they'd said was true. A couple of the students in the lab were failing the quizzes, but I was thinking of the overall picture. I wanted to take college seriously and get good grades. I didn't want a GPA like I had in high school, which was a 2.05 from fooling around during classes and everything I went through with my wreck. The truth was, I didn't take high school seriously, but college was a fresh start. I dedicated myself to my schoolwork and put forth a lot of effort.

After each A&P class, I stayed behind and spent hours studying the modules until it all made sense. I even went to the lab during the professor's office hours, teaching myself then asking him any questions I had. When the tests came around, I was always one of the first to finish and consistently got A's.

The teacher always invited us to stay after class, which few students did in the beginning. Soon, however, others started showing up and we all studied together, asking questions and quizzing each other. That worked out well for everyone and the teacher really liked the fact that we put in such effort.

A few weeks into the semester, our study group ended up meeting on Wednesday or Thursday mornings, or sometimes on both days. When this started, something changed in me. I still stayed after school, went over the material with the teacher and studied on my own, but on those mornings, instead of us all studying together, I was pretty much teaching the other students and explaining what the professor had already taught. When I did that, everything I studied made so much more sense; I really had to know my stuff if I was going to explain it to them. After a couple of times, the pressure of getting an A was nothing compared to making sure I explained everything correctly to my classmates—and I loved the challenge of it.

Most of the time, we went over anatomy during the study sessions in order to prepare for the quizzes; besides Marie, there were heart, arm, leg, torso, brain and a few other models in the lab. I helped them with physiology as well, however, which was so much more difficult and intellectually intense.

There was so much to know in such a short time. I really wanted to learn the material, not just to earn a good grade but to help the other students and to understand the body better myself. For once in my life, I felt like the smartest one in class.

All of the hard work paid off with my grades and with the anatomy games we played, in which two students would go head to head to see who could name the muscle, vein, or whatever body part the professor was pointing to. The class laughed whenever it was my turn because they felt sorry for whomever I went against. I'd answer almost instantly but after a couple of turns, I'd stop and give others the chance to play. After all, I liked competition, but I didn't have anything to prove.

For the first time, I was seriously taking pride in my school-work. After one semester, I was already a different person than the one who didn't care how well he did on the enrollment pre-test. The A&P teacher always gave us extra credit questions on every quiz because so many people had a tough time; by the end of the semester, I had accumulated so much extra credit that I could have stopped taking quizzes for almost a month and still have gotten an A in the class, but I kept on taking them anyway.

After many hours of studying and investing my time, I ended up getting A's in both lab and lecture, although quite a few people failed. That was the most satisfying experience I have ever had in school. From just that class alone, I learned so much—not just about the body but about myself as a whole. I felt more confident. If I could get an A in one of the hardest classes the school offered, there was no telling what I could achieve.

When the semester was over, the professor thanked me and said that I had helped him a lot. I thanked him in return for everything and told him I'd learned more in his class than at any other time in my life, and not just book material. He asked me if I wanted to be a tutor for the next semester, so I jumped at the chance. Learning just seemed to come easily for me, especially with subjects I loved, and after studying so hard for A&P, I believed that any other class would be easy for me to handle.

School strengthened me mentally, just as weight training strengthened me physically. Even my workouts changed for the better with the knowledge I acquired from my anatomy class. The phrase "knowledge is power" really came to life for me during that first semester and finally made perfect sense.

■ ■ ■

My first semester also ended with a grade of A in beginning algebra; the following semester, I took intermediate algebra and got another A (as well as becoming an algebra tutor for other students). So, in the summer of my first year, I decided to retake college algebra with that same teacher who had initially scared me into dropping her class. I had the choice of taking it with a different professor, but I didn't want to.

I did everything I possibly could to prepare myself for her class, which had over twenty students. I knew what to expect from her when she first walked in, but I looked around the classroom and realized that the other students didn't know what was coming. As soon as she entered, the class got quiet. She had a cold, unhappy look on her face that could intimidate the hell out of you with just one glance.

The second we finished going over the syllabus, she started straight in again, just like the last time. She went over the material at the same fast pace and began talking about things I didn't recognize, even with all my preparation. I just sat there and took notes since I wasn't about to ask her any questions, but someone else did. She then proceeded to blow up at the kid, saying she didn't have time to explain the basics and that he should have come prepared. I could see him sink into his seat after that, but the professor just carried on like it was nothing.

Even though I had taken both beginning and intermediate algebra, I didn't understand what she was talking about for half the class. Just like last time, she gave us a huge assignment and I went home thinking that this summer was going to be torture. But I wasn't going to drop the class again.

The next week, I was ready. I showed up early, as usual, but only seven other students came to class. I couldn't believe that she had frightened so many people off on the first day, but then I realized that I had been one of those people less than a year ago.

When the professor entered the room, I had the assignment on top of my desk, ready to be handed in. It turned out not to be too bad, actually; it took a while to do, but was pretty easy overall. As the teacher collected the homework, I made a comment about how she scared off most the class and she just smiled and laughed.

From that point on, she changed; she slowed down her teaching and was more laid back. Being a hardass the first day was her way of testing the students, which was actually pretty funny. She found out who really wanted to be there—and, this time, I did.

As the summer went on, I came to appreciate her style of teaching more and more. Each lesson was straightforward and she was more than happy to explain things in detail. Once she went over everything, she gave us our assignment and answered any questions; then we could stay and do the homework there or leave. She'd be in her office if we needed any help.

She was awesome and hers was the best teaching style I had ever experienced: Get to the point, learn what you need to do, and do it. Even though some of the homework was tough, I still enjoyed that class because it wasn't boring. Plus I had proven to myself that I was up for the challenge.

■ ■ ■

Of course, I didn't enjoy every class during my college career. While some subjects came easily to me, like speech class (where my basic rules were to always speak on a subject I found fascinating, try to make it interesting for the listeners, maintain eye contact, and make the most of my natural gift of talking to people), others were absolute misery.

For example, I never liked to read and write, but my worst fear in English class was when I had to read aloud. We had to do that all the time in high school, and I thought I wouldn't have to do it anymore once I got to college. Well, I was wrong.

The peer pressure I felt about pronouncing every word correctly—even ones I didn't know—and trying not to mess up in front of everyone never left me and, in fact, caused me to make a lot of mistakes. I could never even concentrate on what other students were reading because I'd be too busy practicing in my head the page or paragraph I'd be forced to read.

When my turn finally came, you could hear the nervousness in my voice, no matter how hard I tried to hide it. I would end up mumbling words I didn't know and rushing to get it over with. It seemed strange to me that I'd have no trouble giving speeches but couldn't get through a few paragraphs reading aloud. However, even English class taught me something important for life: Our own fears can limit us more than our lack of ability.

CHAPTER 32

Halfway There

After two years at Neosho, I was done. During that time, I had helped many students pass the classes they most feared and I had met all the requirements for my associate's degree.

To me, it wasn't really a big deal because I still had two more years to go to get my bachelor's, but to my family and friends, it was an achievement. Graduation was going to be held at the main campus in Chanute, Kansas, and I was planning to go there by myself because I didn't see the point of anyone else having to sit through the whole ceremony just to see me get my associate's degree.

In fact, I didn't really want to attend, either, but my friends from school wanted me to go. For them, it was a big deal—so how could I really say no about something like our graduation?

Chanute was quite far away and I didn't really like to drive long distances, so my uncle insisted on taking me. My mother really wanted to come, too, but she was sick and I felt she should stay home and get better. I told her that this was only my associate's degree and she'd be there when I got my bachelor's in two years. Knowing that eased her mind and she agreed to stay home, even though this graduation meant a lot to her (though I knew my bachelor's would mean that much more).

When my uncle and I left, the weather was fine, but it got worse the further we traveled. The clouds grew darker as we drove through spurts of rain, and there were tornado watches in effect. As we got closer to Chanute, we passed an elderly couple in their seventies who were pulled over with a flat tire. Our hearts gave out and we stopped to help them. (Sure, you have to be careful when you do something like that, but I figured that if they tried to pull something on us, we could have taken them!)

My uncle pulled up behind them then got my wheelchair out of the back of his truck and we went over to ask if they needed our help. They gave us a grateful look and politely answered, "Yes, please." Although it only took us a few minutes to fix the tire, we could see how thankful they were. They even offered to pay us but we wouldn't take their money. Instead, they gave us each a hug and said, "May God go with you." That made me feel better about this trip to graduation.

A few hours later, we arrived and I pulled on my cap and gown. The weather was still bad and the wind was picking up, but there were masses of people wearing black and red gowns. I followed them into the gym, where I heard one of my classmates calling my name. Six of them had gathered together into a small—but proud—group.

As the graduates were lining up, I was told to go to the front of the line, where there was another guy in a wheelchair. Sitting there waiting to go on stage, I had memories of my high school graduation and, when the music started, my hands began to get cold and sweaty. Luckily, I noticed that the stage was wheelchair accessible. If that other guy in the wheelchair hadn't shown up for rehearsals the day before, it probably wouldn't have been.

The college president said a few words but all any of us cared about was hearing our names and getting our diplomas. I wondered if anybody was going to cheer for me when my name was called. The worst thing was hearing dead silence.

I grew nervous right before my name was announced: "Clarence Raymond Scott, Associate of Science." At first, I didn't hear a sound but as I rolled up to the stage, the audience and my classmates cheered, whistled and hollered, recognizing that I was the "Nick" they knew. It was an awesome feeling and I turned to the audience with a big smile, feeling very lucky for that show of love. The applause grew even louder when I shook the president's hand, especially from those who were from Ottawa and from the classmates I had helped throughout college.

It was such an honor to have had that type of impact on so many people's lives. It gave others hope and showed them that if there's a will, there's a way. After the ceremony, so many people came up to tell me that I was an inspiration, which made me so happy that I had decided to attend my graduation. It was a glorious day after all, despite the awful weather.

Back in my uncle's car, I silently thanked the Lord for giving me the power to come as far as I had. Tears of joy ran down my face when I realized I had reached the halfway mark in my college life. The achievement that it really was did not fully sink in until I stared into the grayish sky on my way home.

CHAPTER 33

A Beginning and an End

It was May 4, 2002, shortly after graduation, and my tuxedo was laid out. My good friend Daniel was getting married and I was going to be one of the groomsmen. Everything seemed perfect on the morning of his wedding. I had woken up to licks on my face from Cocoa, my twenty-pound Shih Tzu who was a puffy white ball of fur. I'd had him for a little over a year and he meant the world to me. He had to be by my side wherever I went in the house and always hopped in bed with me when I went to sleep at night.

I was really looking forward to the wedding until, a few hours later, my mother came to my room and said she needed to talk to me. I could tell something was wrong from the look on her face. We went out to the back porch, where she started to say, "I don't know how to tell you this…but Cocoa is dead."

I immediately broke down, not wanting to believe he was gone. With tears running down my face, I asked what had happened. She said that he'd just been run over on Main Street. Hearing the way he died only amplified my pain, but I needed to know—and I wanted to see where it had happened.

My mother took me out in front of our house and showed me the red stain on the street. When I saw that, my pain suddenly got worse, but I asked my mom to get his body back from the police officer who had taken him. I wanted to bury him close to home, where he could rest in peace.

Thirty minutes later, a police officer came and handed me a trash bag that held my baby. I thanked him for bringing Cocoa home, but the tears started again and just kept coming. I could see spots of red on the bottom of the bag and his smashed little head inside. It wasn't the first point in my life that I wished I could go back in time and change things, but I knew, no matter how badly I wanted it, that could never happen.

My family helped me dig a hole by our back tree and I took Cocoa's lifeless body out of the bag. His eyes seemed to look at me and his tiny tongue was hanging out of his mouth. I cried, asking the Lord why this had to happen—but I already knew how precious life was and that it could be taken at any time.

My mother had prepared a box with a little blanket for him to lie in for his eternal rest and, after placing him in it, bloodstains covered both of my hands. My heart felt as though it would break when I began to cover my baby with dirt. I wanted to be left alone with him for awhile and pray to the Lord to watch over him for me, but I knew I had to leave. Daniel's wedding was starting soon, and he was counting on me.

In a daze, I got cleaned up and dressed, trying my hardest to keep my thoughts off Cocoa so no one at the wedding would notice that I'd cried. It was a miserable day, but it wasn't about me. It was my friend's wedding day.

The ceremony was beautiful and with all the celebrating going on, I didn't have time to think about my loss. Right after the wedding, we headed for the reception, where I had a blast, along with everybody else.

I came home tired, but had to visit Cocoa one last time that night. I rolled out to the spot in the ground where he lay and said my goodbyes through fresh tears.

CHAPTER 34

Diveheart 2002

During my fall classes at Neosho, I got a call from Sara at the Shriners Hospital asking me if I wanted to go scuba diving the following summer in Key Largo, Florida, and become a certified diver. Of course, I said, "Yes!" but no word could explain how excited I truly was.

A few weeks later, I got a package from her stuffed with some legal documents I had to fill out and material from the Professional Association of Diving Instructors, including a dive video, a divers' manual, a surface interval credit table and a dive log. It had everything I needed to know about getting my PADI open water diver certification, but all I thought about was how I was going to be able to scuba dive with such little mobility in my legs. The idea of getting certified as a scuba diver was awesome, but I wasn't sure if it was even possible.

I studied the divers' manual every day so I'd be prepared and know the material, and, in no time, I finished all of the review questions in each chapter. This opportunity meant a lot to me. After all, Diveheart would be providing everything for me and the other five disabled patients from the Shriners Hospital, so I wanted to make the most of it—and the least I could do was learn my stuff.

Diveheart is a 501-C3 non-profit, volunteer-driven organization that relies on donations and fundraising activities to continue its work. It was founded in April 2001 to provide and support educational scuba diving and snorkeling programs for physically impaired children and adults in the hope that these experiences will provide both physical and psychological therapy. Personally speaking, I never would have even thought about going scuba diving without them, so I can attest that their programs do a lot to help broaden horizons.

■ ■ ■

When summer came, I had everything I needed in preparation for the trip, such as dive socks and leggings; everything else was going to be provided for us by Diveheart. Emotionally, I felt a mixture of excitement and nervousness. This would be the first time I'd ever be in a different state without any friends or family. Sure, that state was Florida, and I had always wanted to go there, but I couldn't help but wonder about the other people who were also going, particularly the two other guys and three girls with disabilities.

To make me feel more at ease, my mother accompanied me to Chicago, where we would all gather for the next part of the trip. When she and I boarded the shuttle bus to the meeting point at the airport, there were others standing outside—one young girl in particular caught my eye. She was missing her right arm from the elbow down, and I figured she might be one of the three girls heading to Key Largo with me. Once the bus took off, I sat patiently, waiting for the right time to start up a conversation with her.

She sat diagonally across from me so I just said, "Hey, are you going on the Diveheart trip?" She smiled and said, "Yes," and I could tell that she and her mom had been curious as to whether I was going, too. We all introduced ourselves and, after breaking the ice, Carolyn and I talked all the way to the airport; it was nice knowing one other person on the trip.

Once we got off the shuttle bus, we went inside but there was no one at the designated meeting area. Granted, we were thirty minutes early, but I began to get paranoid that we weren't in the right spot. Soon, though, I heard someone call my name. It was

Sara! Seeing her brought instant relief. She came over and gave us all a big hug.

Before long, others arrived and my wheelchair helped identify us as participants in the Diveheart program. There were a few people I knew from the Shriners, such as Kris, who I was delighted to see, but I didn't know the majority of them. Besides the six kids chosen to go, the other people who had gathered were all dive buddies.

Finally, two other girls and one guy arrived, all in wheelchairs. The girls were Amanda and Lindsey, whom I had never seen before, but the guy was Brandon from the SCI camp I attended back in 2000, and seeing him was awesome! Not too long after that, the third guy, AJ, showed up. He was a younger boy about fourteen or fifteen, and I couldn't tell what was wrong with him just by looking at him.

We all introduced ourselves and I met Jim, the president of Diveheart. He was a tall, tan, slender man in his late thirties, clean-shaven and very nice, and I could tell from the first time I shook his hand that he had a great personality. When we were around him, we couldn't help but smile. In fact, the entire atmosphere felt great; everybody was making conversation and we could feel the energy from all of our excitement.

Jim was on top of everything, making sure all the equipment and luggage was together, and, before we knew it, we were checking in and heading to our gate. My mother went with us as far as she could. Her baby boy was leaving her for the first time since that dreadful day, and she was overwhelmed with tears and sadness. I felt bad leaving her, but deep down she was happy for me and so proud. As our group continued on, I looked back and saw her standing there, alone, smiling and waving goodbye. She came to Chicago with me so I wouldn't be alone and here I was, leaving her. However, I knew she'd be flying back home in a few hours and that eased my mind.

We got to the gate and had little time before we began pre-boarding. They wanted AJ and Carolyn to board first then I was to follow. Airplanes are not wheelchair-accessible, so our chairs could only go so far inside. Kris helped some of the others get into their seats; she'd get in front of the wheelchair and grab the person behind the knees, and that person would hold her behind her neck. Kris would then manually lift them out of the wheelchair and put them in the airplane seat while others willingly lent a hand, providing extra support to ensure that no one fell. It took a little time, but we were off the ground before we knew it.

Our flight had a couple of stops, but we didn't have to switch planes; since all the kids sat by each other, we got to know one another pretty well during our time in the airplane. Once we arrived in Fort Lauderdale, however, we grew even more excited. Disembarking took awhile because we all had to get in our wheelchairs; we waited for everybody else to leave the plane before exiting ourselves then headed to baggage claim side-by-side as if we were one big wheelchair posse.

When the caravans arrived, it was time to load the bags and equipment and head to the hotel. While everyone was getting in, which was a bit of a struggle, Brandon and I were checking out the women—and, believe me, there was some nice scenery! I also couldn't get over how humid it was outside; I wasn't in Kansas anymore, that was for sure—and the palm trees and beautiful ocean I saw proved it. Back home, all we had was land and murky water.

Key Largo was a two-and-a-half-hour drive from the airport; it was raining hard, but that didn't dampen our excitement one bit. Once we finally pulled up to our hotel, I couldn't believe my eyes: There were chickens running around everywhere.

The instructors gave us all keys and a schedule for the week then we unloaded our bags and the girls and boys split up into our respective rooms, which had a connecting door. I thought that was going to be interesting.

The boys' room had only two beds but there were three of us, so we called the front desk and they brought us a fold-up bed, which took up what little space we had left. Our room was already outfitted with a handicap bathroom, all of which are built big so that wheelchairs can fit in. They're like the Cadillac of bathrooms! With three people, the extra bed, and the wide bathroom, there was barely enough room to fit a wheelchair, so Brandon and I had to come up with a quick method of getting by one another. One of us would go in between the beds while the other person rolled past, which worked perfectly.

I told my roommates that I would sleep in the fold-up bed and they could fight over the two big beds. They both said they'd take turns sleeping in the fold-up bed but I assured them I'd be fine. After we'd settled in, Kris and Sara came to see us to explain the rules: If we were to leave our rooms, we had to have someone with us at all times, even another kid, but if we wanted to go swimming, we had to have a dive buddy with us; also, no drugs or alcohol was permitted whatsoever. We were fine with their rules because, if it hadn't been for them, we wouldn't have been there in the first place.

After Kris and Sara left, my roommates and I decided to check out the pool area. The pool itself was a nice size and there were lawn chairs, a white fence and a tiki bar built like a little hut. Further down was a great beach with palm trees and outdoor tables, like our own private paradise. However, off to the side was a sign that read, "CAUTION: MANATEE AREA." I thought to myself, *What is a manatee?*

The rain had stopped and the mosquitoes starting coming out. It was horrible! There were tons of the little blood-sucking monsters everywhere. Even when we went back to our room, we were still getting bit by them. They somehow got to us even in the bathroom!

Soon after dinner, the other boys and I decided to go to bed.

I planned to get up the next day at 5:45 a.m. to do my morning routine and make sure that we were in the conference room well before our diving class started at eight-thirty. If we were late, that would only slow things down—which was the last thing we wanted.

■ ■ ■

The next morning, after feasting on the hotel's all-you-can-eat buffet, everyone filed into the conference room. Jim had placed the bags containing the equipment on the floor and handed out folders filled with the main points of the open water dive manual. There was a lot of information in that thick folder and even though I had studied, I still didn't recognize some of the demonstrations.

Jim was going to be our main instructor. He had been scuba diving for many years and had multiple certifications, including some of the highest achievable, which meant he could teach beginning students as well as other scuba instructors. Several dive instructors were there to help, and we were so blessed to have these wonderful people with us. They took time out of their lives specifically to be there, although the trip wasn't free for them like it was for us; they paid for everything on their own. They could have chosen to spend their time and money elsewhere, but they chose to spend it with us—and it takes an exceptional individual to take part in something like this!

After all the introductions, we started right in on the book-work. First, we turned in the knowledge review sections that we had already prepared at home then Jim started going over chapter one. Since we had all read the book and done the reviews, everything went smoothly and soon he began giving us equipment to demonstrate on. We made sure we could secure the tank to the BCD, separate the hose correctly and perform other vital tasks.

After hours had passed and we proved that we could use the

equipment, it was time to train in the pool. I was so excited about how awesome it was going to be, though some of the others seemed anxious, fearing they might fail. That's the beauty of it, though; being in a wheelchair is all about adapting to change and learning which adjustments you personally need to make to overcome hindrances. For me, it's a rush to meet any challenge and push myself to the limit.

I put on my blue Lycra wet suit and Lycra socks to protect my feet from getting any surface damage (since I had previously skinned the top of my feet getting out of the pool back home). Other than that, I was only concerned about my contact lenses; this was the first year I had worn them and was worried that the water would flush them out, so I chose to wear my glasses when I went in.

Once my roomies were ready, we headed down to the pool, where our equipment was already laid out, and each of us was assigned a couple of dive buddies. Fortunately, I was assigned to a sexy woman in her late twenties, whom we referred to as "the weather bunny." My other dive buddy was an awesome guy, and they were both there to assist me. But before we got in the pool, we had to make sure everything was secure and working properly. I had the tank standing in front of me and put the BCD on it, but sitting in the wheelchair while adjusting everything was challenging. I made the final adjustments, however, and my buddies looked over my work. Then I was ready to go.

To get in the water, we had to transfer to the floor and sit at the edge of the pool. I put on my mask while my buddies got my BCD. They helped hold the tank up while I put the BCD on and tightened it. After double-checking the air, hose placement, and other little things, I filled up the vest and put on the fins. Once everything was set, I held one hand on my mask and the other on the regulator in my mouth to prevent them from getting knocked out when I hit the water. Then I leaned forward and went for it!

Hitting the water felt good. Even though it was just a pool, it felt amazing to wear all that scuba gear.

When everyone else got in and we were all floating at the top, Jim gave us the command to go slowly down to the bottom of the pool. Some of the kids had a hard time releasing the pressure in their ears but everyone got to the bottom eventually. Then we formed a half-circle around Jim so we could all see him demonstrate a specific skill because after he performed it, we would have to mimic his actions.

The first of the three exercises we had to do was to flood the masks halfway then remove the water by holding the mask at the top, tilting our heads backwards and blowing out our noses in order to remove all the water from the mask. Jim demonstrated it first, but when it was my turn, I barely pulled the bottom of my mask and it instantly flooded with water. My eyes were burning and, without thinking, I began breathing through my nose. Water went up my nose and I started choking. It startled me badly but I knew I had to calm down since Jim had told us that if we threw up, the vomit could go through the mouthpiece. So I closed my eyes and began focusing on breathing through my mouth. After a few seconds, I was fine and easily removed the water out of the mask.

The second and third tasks were to do a full flood along with a mask removal. Those were easier than the first since I had prepared myself for the instant rush of water. However, the reality of what we were going to do sank in when I was about to flood my mask for one of the tasks. If I got in trouble in the ocean, I couldn't just swim to the top from thirty feet down; many things can harm divers if they hurry to the surface.

Although these exercises weren't too hard for me, I put myself in the place of Carolyn, the girl with one arm. Knowing how much more difficult it would be for her, I realized I had no excuse as to why I couldn't do any of the tasks they asked of me. With that in mind, I didn't care how hard I might struggle. Having limited mobility increased the difficulty, but finding approaches to make it work was all about keeping an open mind.

We stayed in the water for quite some time, getting as much pool training as possible. Some struggled more than others but we all tried so hard.

■ ■ ■

After training, we stayed up late, and that's when the pranks started. Brandon and I waited for AJ to fall asleep before rolling like handicap ninjas in the dead silence of the night. With little light, Brandon had the camcorder recording as I held a razor and began to dry-shave AJ's left eyebrow. He woke up immediately and said, "What the hell are you doing?" and we busted out laughing.

No one on the trip was safe; they never knew what was going to happen or when. The focus of our pranks was primarily the girls—and in order for us to pull off some good ones, we needed a key to their room. We tried taking one of their keys, but then I learned the ultimate technique: The keys to our rooms had a plastic bar code strip, so we went to the front desk and told them that the pool had deactivated the key and asked them to rescan it for the girls' room. Instant access!

Getting into their room allowed us to pull off one of the all-time best pranks. Normally, we didn't bring towels to the pool since we'd wait until we got back to our rooms to dry off. In the girls' room, there was a high shelf and the girls in the wheelchairs would have to reach up to pull down a towel. We dumped a big container of baby powder on one of the top towels so that it would cover whichever girl tried to get it down. (It worked beautifully, but the girls managed to get the last laugh by keeping that a secret until after the trip. They didn't want us to have the satisfaction of knowing how badly they got burned!)

■ ■ ■

It wasn't all fun and games, though. We continued studying in the conference room until we were done with all the chapters then we took the exam and everyone passed. It was such a relief to have finished. The material wasn't hard but it was mentally draining. However, the information we learned was essential for our survival in the ocean and a lot of it was exciting; being aware of our surroundings was key, just like it was for being in a wheelchair.

Some of the other kids felt that they were too slow in developing the necessary skills during pool training. I told them, "Just do the best you can because that's all you can do," and reminded them that scuba diving wasn't a competitive sport so they should just enjoy it and have fun, because that's what it was all about.

During the second day of pool training, I realized how tremendous scuba diving really was. I was down at the deep end of the pool with my diving buddy, hovering vertically halfway between the surface and the bottom. At that point in time, I was weightless and felt free. It was as if I had my legs back and could stand without a struggle for the first time since my wreck. Time seemed to stand still and I was overcome with chills. Standing there like that, I saw all the others and wondered if they even realized that they were standing, too.

CHAPTER 35
The Ocean

With all the bookwork done and the majority of the skills completed, we were going to scuba dive in the ocean for the first time. Everything was so overwhelming. We had only been in Florida for a few days and had already learned so much. But I was ready for anything and willing to do whatever the Diveheart instructors asked.

I was eager to set sail but the boat still had to be prepared for departure. The boat was named *The Lost Continent* and our captain was the famous Captain Slate, who is known for feeding barracudas with his mouth and has been on *Ripley's Believe It Or Not!*

Loading *The Lost Continent* was a challenge. There was a two-and-a-half-foot-wide metal ramp with six-inch side guards attached to the boat for us to bring our air tanks and gear on board. The dive buddies helped guide the wheelchairs onto the boat and helped me walk, or else I'd lift my butt and scoot down to the boat. It was my choice not to bring my wheelchair in order to make more room on board.

Even though I left my wheelchair, I brought along my seat cushion so I wouldn't develop any ulcer sores while sitting on the boat's hard bench. It had been forever since I'd been on a boat and the feeling I got from being on the water was like no other. We took off shortly after boarding then started to pick up the pace. The wind felt good on my face and body as we headed to the dive site. This was the first time I had ever seen the ocean this close and it was beautiful. Just sitting there staring at the endless body of water, I couldn't help but think how lucky I was.

When we arrived at the dive site, the water surrounding us was the prettiest color of light blue and the sun was heating us from above. Our tanks were lined up behind the benches on the boat and everyone starting to find the spot where our stuff was. The buddies had already put the BCDs on and we only needed to attach the rest to the tank and check to make sure everything was working and secure. Then we were ready to get in the water.

They wanted me to go in first. The dive buddies had determined an order for each person to enter the water, then we'd get out in reverse order. This meant not only was I the first in, but I'd also be the last out.

I moved to the back of the boat and sat on the very edge with my legs hanging in the water. Someone brought me my gear while others held on to my shoulder so that I didn't fall in. I locked and secured everything, checked my regulator and gauges and filled up my BCD. With my mask and fins on and the regulator in my mouth, they gave me the sign to go. This was it!

It felt like things were in slow motion as I leaned forward until I hit that water. It was an awesome feeling to be in the ocean. I looked at the dive instructors on board, gave them the "okay" signal and grabbed the rope to be near my dive buddy, who was already in the water. My buddy and I headed out to the end of the rope, which was attached to a buoy, and waited for the others to get in the water.

As we waited, I looked down in the water and couldn't believe how clear it was. It seemed like the bottom was only five feet away instead of thirty feet, and there were so many different fish that we'd be swimming among. I switched to my snorkel to save air while we were waiting and that's when I got a big mouthful of the ocean. It was the nastiest water I had ever tasted in my life—so much saltier than what we had back in Kansas. My buddy laughed at my reaction and just told me not to drink the water.

The rope attached to the buoy was also tied to another rope that went to the bottom of the ocean. When everyone was in, we used that rope to ensure that we didn't go down too fast. On my way down, the ocean was so beautiful and everything appeared so much closer than it actually was. My buddies kept eye contact with me as we went down to make sure everything was all right—and, honestly, it couldn't have been better.

At the bottom, there was a huge, fascinating reef and so much sea life in such a small area. But I had to admit that moving around was difficult. I was still getting used to how much air I needed in my BCD, and at times I caught myself floating above or below the others.

After checking out the area and seeing some amazing neon fish, we slowly headed back up. Even though I had fins on my feet, I mostly swam with my arms, which took a lot of energy and caused me to suck down the air in my tank. My buddies and I were last in line to go back up the rope and onto the boat, so we waited with our BCDs fully inflated as the lengthy process went on. Getting onboard wasn't easy without the use of our legs. We could only rely on our upper body strength, so some of the kids couldn't get themselves up and required the use of the boat's crane.

My buddies and I hung out, holding on to the rope and talking about the creatures we saw. I told them it was incredible to swim among the sea life; seeing them close up in their environment was a remarkable experience. As we talked, the nasty ocean water kept getting in my mouth and, every now and then, I swallowed small amounts. It really added up twenty to thirty minutes later, and I began to not feel so great when it was finally my turn to board. I held on to the back of the boat and released my BCD so there would be less weight for me to lift up. Other than that, getting on the boat was like getting out of a swimming pool; I waited for the water to calm then lifted myself right *onto The Lost Continent.*

On board, everyone was excited but worn out as we took a break. The salty water I had swallowed was getting my stomach upset but I played it off as nothing because I didn't want to have to stop scuba diving. Fortunately, as I ate some snacks, my stomach started to feel better and I was joking around with the others in no time. But I kept my buddy's advice not to drink the water in the back of my mind.

After half an hour, we began gearing up for the next dive, which was close to the first site. This time, the order didn't matter; whoever was ready went in and the captain directed us where to swim. When I got back into the water the second time, I was a lot more relaxed and aware of my surroundings. I saw a nurse shark and a stingray, and couldn't help admiring how they moved with such efficiency.

The captain how told us to swim toward a statue of Christ but, after being down in the water for a while, there was still no sign of the statue. Somehow, we had gotten off-course and were nowhere near the dive site. With little air left, we headed back toward the boat. I surfaced with my tank almost out of air, which is something you're not supposed to do, and it was then that my stomach really started acting up.

At the surface, my buddy made sure I was all right but when we got closer to the boat, I couldn't take it anymore. I began to vomit, heaving harder and harder each time. My buddies and the rest of the Diveheart crew tried their best to avoid the chunky, murky water, but it wasn't long before AJ started puking, too.

Sitting on the bench of the boat, I felt better; vomiting was exactly what I needed in order to relieve my stomach. As we headed back to the docks, the breeze and the view were amazing; I only wished my family could've been there with me to see and experience it all.

■ ■ ■

The plan for the next day was to swim with the dolphins then go down to Key West. We were thrilled; this was going to be the first time for us, as well as for our dive buddies.

The woman who worked there welcomed us and began to explain about the dolphins. She told us that dolphins use their sonar and can see right through a person, so if you have any metal on you or in you, the dolphins may get curious and stay around you longer. When she said that, all I could think was that the dolphins were in for a treat today! We had brought along our snorkels and goggles, but were given life vests. The area where we'd be swimming with the dolphins was huge. We went onto a special eight-by-ten-foot platform, which they lowered into the dark, greenish water. When the water came up to our chests, the platform stopped moving and we got off.

At first we split up, swimming wherever we wanted and hoping that a dolphin would swim nearby. They were playful creatures and every once in a while one would stop and look at us. I saw one dolphin follow AJ, staying directly behind his missing leg; the dolphin was there for quite some time, probably wondering what was wrong with him.

After a while, we all lined up against one wall and the woman explained that bigger objects and sounds made the dolphins curious. So we swam to the other side while making a lot of weird noises, which caused the dolphins to zoom by us. There were times when we could see all three dolphins side by side, which was incredible.

Before we left, the girls wanted to go into the dive shop, which was fine by me since I wanted to go down the ramp nearby. This particular ramp was awesome because it was attached to other ramps and I wanted the challenge of going down all of them without stopping. I picked up speed very quickly and when I got close to the bottom of the first ramp, I had to grab the pole and sling myself around the corner to continue down the next one. By the time I was near the bottom of the ramp, I was completely hauling ass!

■ ■ ■

The next part of the adventure was Key West—and I was pumped and ready to roll. We headed down there at night, driving across the famous seven-mile bridge; soon after, I fell asleep but woke up full of excitement once we'd arrived.

We split up almost immediately after getting there. Brandon and I went off with our two dive buddies, Steve and George, and the others broke off into smaller groups as well. However, each of us had a walkie-talkie and a specific time to meet back by the van so we could all watch the legendary Key West sunset together.

Our group went our separate way, checking out the different stores and roaming the streets of Key West together—but all Brandon and I really cared about was checking out women. Eventually, after shopping and seeing the sights, we ran into the girls, who had gotten fake tattoos. With little time to spare, we all headed back toward the van, but as we got to the bridge, we started taking too many pictures and ended up missing the sunset!

■ ■ ■

The following morning, we continued our pool training. I was the only one completely finished, but I still went down to the pool to support the others. Jim only worked with two or three participants at a time, so while they were in pool doing their training, everybody else went to the hotel's beach to use the underwater propulsion vehicles.

After changing into my Lycra suit and grabbing my gear, I met the others and headed to the beach, where we saw manatees in the four-foot-deep water. I couldn't believe it! Brandon, AJ, Carolyn and I would go down to the docks by our hotel the first thing in the morning to see if we could actually find a manatee—now, here they were, and we were going to get to swim with them. They were gray and brown, huge, and resembled walruses. When we touched them, they had a unique texture and we could tell that they were related to elephants.

We admired the manatees for a while then got our underwater propulsion vehicles, which looked awesome! They were white, three-by-three feet with an aerodynamic design for maximum efficiency. Two-thirds of the way up on the machine, there were two separate handles as well as a toggle button used to make it move. We placed our arms on top of the vehicle, gripped the handles and off we went.

They moved slowly but when you're hanging on, it felt as though you were gliding quickly through the water. We didn't go that far from the beach, since they told us that the further out you go, the more jellyfish there are. Looking in the water, we could see hundreds of jellyfish below, some that were so small, and we knew we had to be careful. This was the first time in my life that I had ever seen a jellyfish.

After that adventure, we had plans to dive near the Christ statue again near Captain Slate's shop. I still hadn't seen it, but I knew it must have been awesome, given the way everyone talked about it.

Once we were back at the dive site, we geared up and went down. This time, we went straight to the statue. It was breathtaking: Jesus looking up at the sky with his hands raised over his head. It was so beautiful that everyone gathered around it. The statue was in about thirty feet of water and had all sorts of sea life living on it. We took pictures to capture the moment then went on our way.

Although we had practiced a couple of skills on the previous dive, we had to mimic the instructor much faster this time with more difficult tasks since we'd had a lot more experience. The fin pivot was one of the tougher skills for me. We laid on our stomachs with very little air in our BCDs and, only by breathing, we lifted our upper bodies off the bottom of the ocean. When we breathed out, we went back down while our feet were in constant contact with the ocean floor the whole time. Keeping balance was the most challenging part for me. My body would twist and I would fall on my side, which was frustrating. But once I slowed down and calmed myself, I became much better at it.

Some of the tasks were hard the first few times I tried them, but in the end I finished them all. At about that time, I started getting the breathing down and was able to keep the right amount of air in my BCD. Hovering in the water was an awesome experience, as though I were flying in the world of the sea.

That dive took a lot of energy out of everybody, especially the younger kids. Swimming was tough—and no wonder! After we got to the boat, we found out that there was a current. Everybody decided to call it quits after that dive and head back for the day.

The next day, we got two more dives in—and, unlike the first day, I didn't puke once! This was our last day of diving and it was a blast. We didn't come back until early afternoon then chilled at the hotel until dinnertime, when we had plans to go to a nice restaurant. The kids and I had something special in mind for our dive buddies and the Diveheart team. We had bought them some gifts at the stores in Key West (including a funny t-shirt for Jim with an off-color saying on it) and were going to surprise them with speeches at dinner.

We got to the restaurant and I waited for the right moment during all the laughing and joking. When it hit me, I knew to go for it. I grabbed the edge of the table, stood up and said, "Can I have your attention?" Then I thanked them all for coming and went into my speech, which came from the bottom of my heart. I could tell it meant a lot to them by the watery eyes I saw, but I also cracked some jokes to put everyone at ease.

After I finished, the other kids took over. I could tell they were nervous but they all did great. We gave our dive buddies their gifts and Jim turned red with laughter when he saw his shirt; then it was their turn to share their experiences with us. They said they also had such a great time and that helping us and being around us really opened their eyes. They'd never realized before what we had to go through and deal with every day. It was touching for me to find out that they had bonded with us as well as we had with them.

After the dive instructors had spoken, I thanked Kris and Sara. Without them, none of this would have taken place. They are extraordinary, phenomenal people and I have never seen such kindness and generosity as I have gotten from them.

■ ■ ■

That night, Jim called me to his room and told me how great it was working with me. He said he'd never seen anyone work as hard as I had, then revealed that I had finished all the requirements and was now a certified scuba diver! It was such an unbelievable feeling to know that I had done it, but Jim told me not to say anything to the others because some of them didn't get certified. I felt bad, but at least we all had the experience and the adventure. He then asked me to send Brandon to his room.

This trip with Diveheart was an exciting time in my life that brought me one step closer to becoming the man I was meant to be. It was such a blessing to be one of the six people who took part in this event and I felt really fortunate. God had given me the strength to overcome the tasks I was presented with, and now destiny was before me once again.

In the end, I had done what so many other people simply talk about. Becoming a certified scuba diver taught me that if I just believed in myself and strived to be the best, anything was possible.

CHAPTER 36
Amanda Vs. Riley

Almost a year after the first Diveheart trip, I got another call from Sara asking me if I'd like to go again the upcoming summer—only this time as a mentor! Stunned with honor, I said I'd be there for sure. I was floored to get the chance to go scuba diving again and especially to be a mentor to other kids.

After our 2002 trip together, Amanda and I had kept in touch, calling each other a couple times a week. She was having surgery a few days before I'd be leaving on the next trip, so I sent her flowers and said I'd come see her after her surgery. She was so excited—and so was I. After all, it had been a year since we'd seen each other last.

My mother and I arrived at the Shriners Hospital, but this time I was a visitor, not a patient. As we headed to Amanda's room, all the nurses smiled and greeted me as I rolled down the hall. I knocked on Amanda's door and was shocked when I went in: Riley was Amanda's roommate.

I met Riley the last time I'd come to Shriners for a checkup. All the nurses told me I should introduce myself to her so I did. She was a pretty girl, almost my age, with long hair and a slim body. Her injury level was close to my own but she had only been in the chair for a few months. She was friendly when I first met her but deep down I could tell she was depressed.

As we talked and I explained what happened to me, we bonded. Riley listened to me since I had been in the chair much longer than she had and had already experienced what she was about to go through. She was in the transferring stage, learning how to open doors in her wheelchair, and I felt bad for her because I knew how hard that was to do at first. It really bothered me when she struggled and my heart went out to her.

Even back then, I really liked Riley and found myself going back to her room often. Her mother became friends with my mother and it was sad when we left because we all really enjoyed each other's company. Afterwards, Riley and I spoke a couple times but we were both busy with school and just sort of stopped calling each other. Besides, I knew she had a boyfriend, anyway.

Now, here I was with Amanda and Riley in the same room! As I entered, Amanda was lying in bed but Riley was in her wheelchair and came right over to give me a hug. Right away, I could feel jealousy from Amanda. Riley had had no clue that I was the 'Nick' coming to see her roommate.

After my arrival, tension filled the air between the two girls. Amanda didn't want me to have anything to do with Riley, but I wasn't having that. I still talked to both girls, just at different times. I would spend time with Amanda in her room because she couldn't leave and time with Riley out of the room when the nurses had to attend to Amanda.

I enjoyed seeing them both but when Amanda started to act controlling like that, it was hard to want to be around her. I'm not a negative guy; I like life to be simple—and this situation was anything but. Even the nurses got in on it, telling Riley how pretty the flowers were that I brought for Amanda. The whole thing was kind of hilarious to me and I just tried to make it work for the few days I had there.

When it was time to leave, I was equally happy and sad. I had spent the majority of my visit with Amanda because she was the main reason I went there in the first place, but I wished I could have spent more time with Riley. After I said my goodbyes to both girls, Riley and I talked outside for a while longer then she gave me one last hug and I was gone. I'm sure the atmosphere in their room was interesting after I left!

CHAPTER 37

Diveheart 2003

A fter leaving the Shriners, my mother and I headed to a hotel close to the airport, where I'd be flying to Key Largo the next morning. It was hard for me to sleep that night since I was so excited thinking about all the new kids and dive buddies I was going to meet. I was especially thrilled to be able to concentrate on the dives and not to have to deal with all the bookwork and skill training that went along with getting certified.

My mom and I got to the airport early but only waited a couple of minutes before we were spotted by Kris and Sara, who gave us hugs and a warm greeting like always. It so nice seeing them again—and then came Jim. He looked very different and, at first, I couldn't recognize what it was. Then it hit me: He shaved his head bald!

That was awesome because I had shaved my head, too. A few months earlier, I had gotten a bad haircut that made me look like a goober, so I shaved my whole head with a razor as soon as I'd gotten home. In the following weeks, more and more people kept coming up to tell me how much I looked like Vin Diesel. Girls love Vin Diesel, so I had decided to keep it bald ever since.

Right away, Jim and I cracked up upon seeing each other bald. The moment was priceless and it felt like old times again, not as if an entire year had passed. Other dive buddies soon arrived—half of whom had come back from last year—but the kids were all new. A few of them were wheelchair-bound but others had different types of disabilities. We flew down to Key Largo and I stayed in the exact same hotel room as last year—though I was so much more at ease, having been through it all once before.

■ ■ ■

The next day, I didn't feel right not having to do all that paperwork while the other kids were doing it, so I sat in the conference room with my new dive buddy, going over all the information; I just didn't have to take any of the quizzes. The same went for the pool training; I just went to the deep end and worked on my hovering skills while the beginning divers went through their tasks. Jim's girlfriend was also there, training to be an instructor, so she worked with me on refreshing my skills.

I was basically a liaison on the trip; when the kids had problems, I tried to comfort them or help them as much as I could with anything that came up. But I would also inform Kris and Sara about what was going on so that they could assist in each situation with the best approach.

It was awesome just hanging out and getting to know everyone better—but other than during training, no one was safe from my pranks. The second night is when things really got started. I don't remember exactly how it happened, but I was trying to get Todd, one of the dive buddies, to shave his head. He wouldn't do it unless someone else agreed to go bald, too, so I hunted everyone down to ask if they'd shave their heads.

I just about gave up hope until April, one of the girls in a wheelchair, said she would do it. I was shocked! She had long, black hair that came down past her shoulders. After April agreed, Josh, another one of the kids on the trip, said he'd do it, too. This was better than I'd imagined! But before I could shave either one of them, Sara had to call their parents and ask for permission so that no one got in trouble.

After we got permission, Todd was surprised to learn that I'd actually gotten them to agree to shave their hair. Everybody was laughing at the situation, then April and I headed into the bathroom first while a crowd watched with cameras and camcorders ready. Before shaving her head completely bald, I asked her if she wanted me to give her a Mohawk, which I'd shave off the next night, and she excitedly agreed.

So I shortened all her hair on the sides and left an inch-and-a-half Mohawk from her forehead all the way to the back of her head. Then I used an electric shaver to make her head as smooth as a baby's butt on the sides and combed the Mohawk back like Steven Segal. After I was done, I just about died laughing, but I had to be serious when I was shaving her so that my hand would remain steady. After all, I wanted to make it look good. April got a big kick out of it, too, as did everyone watching. She was up for anything, which was so awesome.

Todd was next. He was outside by the pool, where some of the others were shaving a small heart in the back of his head. They had done such a good job that when it came my time to shave him completely bald, I left a little ring of hair ring around the heart. It looked so funny, like he had a hairy butt on the back of his head. Everybody was laughing so loud and I was practically crying from laughing so hard. We tried to talk him into leaving it like that for the rest of the trip but he wasn't going for that, so I finished the job, making his head super smooth.

Last was Josh, a skinny boy with red hair. We went back inside because the mosquitoes were eating us alive, and most of the gang followed us into the bathroom. I had to do something different with his hair, so I ended up giving him a reverse Mohawk. I shaved an inch-and-a-half strip down the center of his head then shaved the sides, but left two stripes of hair on the top of his head, which looked really stupid. On top of that, I talked him into shaving his eyebrows, and he ended up leaving it that way for the whole trip.

The next morning, we spiked April's hair up with some sticky gel and that Mohawk was HUGE! As we entered for breakfast, everyone on the trip thought it was awesome, but some of the entries in their Diveheart journals expressed how they really felt:

"Sweet Lord—It's only Sunday nite and three heads were already shaved! Someone hide me!"—Scuba Steve

"I agree with Scuba Steve, this is crazy. I am going to have to watch the baldies all week. There is no telling what else is going to happen this week!"—Big Daddy Dusty

"Yeah, I happen to agree with the two boys—Good God! What did I get myself into! Luckily I haven't sold myself for entertainment—so far—it's the first full day. I sure should have gone to church today!"—Ashley

"As Nick, Jim and George attack him, Todd says, 'And the last thing I heard was all this buzzing...'"—Debbie

As the day went on, people kept looking at them and didn't know what to think, especially Josh, with that goofy-looking haircut. But as the night came to a close, I finished shaving April's head and the whiteness of her newly bald scalp matched Todd's.

■ ■ ■

As if the pranks weren't crazy enough, on this trip we were going to try something new: swimming with SHARKS! The whole idea kind of freaked me out as we got closer to entering the water. The captain's wife went in first with her steel-chain gloves that she had duct taped at the wrist. She had a bucket with holes in it and an orange lid with a hole at the top. Then we all got in the water and sat at the bottom of the ocean in a big circle around her.

There were six or seven nurse sharks, ranging from about four to eight feet long. I didn't know what to make of the whole situation except to wonder what I would do if one of them attacked me. It's not like I could have just swam away; I would have had to face the situation at hand, and I had it all planned out, too. I swore I would poke the shark's eyes out and punch the hell out of its head until it let me go.

But the sharks were gentle giants that just followed the bucket of food. The captain's wife made her rounds to all of us and when she came by, the sharks would surround us. Then she'd pick them up and hand them to us so we could hold them if we wanted. The one she handed me wasn't like Jaws; it was more like a huge cat-fish. On the boat, we had all talked about kissing a shark on the head, so as I held it, I took the regulator out of my mouth and did just that. That was a crazy experience but fun—and definitely once-in-a-lifetime!

■ ■ ■

The whole trip was nonstop excitement. My pranks had gotten a lot better and I pulled off one of the best of my life during this time. Instead of pulling pranks on the girls, I recruited them, as well as a few of the dive buddies, to help me. And this time, I already had a key to everyone's room.

Pranks happened every night, after we were finished diving. Here are some of the highlights:

- I had gone in one room and put KY Jelly every-where: doorknobs, telephone, light switches… You name it, we jelled it. It was a woman's room so we put tons of KY Jelly on the toilet seat since most of the time they don't look before sitting down, and that is exactly what happened.
- We froze three shaving cream containers for a couple of days then stuck them in the bottom shelf of the small desk that had the phone on it,

which was located between the beds. Suppos-
edly, when the shaving cream thawed, the cans
expanded, causing the cream to go everywhere,
but it didn't make as much of a mess as I had
hoped.

- One night, we unscrewed all the lightbulbs and
  hid them in the room somewhere—even the
  bathroom lights.
- We stripped all the blankets, comforters and
  pillows from one room and hid them in someone else's room.

However, I've saved the best for last. To my knowledge, this prank
has never been pulled before. As I've mentioned, there were lots
of chickens running around Key Largo. Well, Mary Beth, one of
the dive buddies, said it would be funny if we put a chicken in
someone's room. I loved the idea, but was it even possible—and
how could we catch a chicken?

Then it hit me: At the dive shops, they had fishing nets! I could
buy one and try to catch a chicken with the net. Brilliant…or so I
thought. So after we went for an open water dive, I bought a net in
one of the shops and hid it between my back and the back of my
wheelchair.

That night, April wasn't feeling well from the dive earlier in
the day; a lot of heat had escaped from her head since she didn't
have any hair. She wanted to stay at the hotel while the rest of us
went out to dinner and Sara was going to stay with her. This was
a perfect opportunity! I said to Sara, "I'd like it if I could stay here
with April. Being the mentor of the trip, I want to be here for her."
Sara was shocked; I had totally caught her off-guard. She thought
that was so sweet and said, "That's fine, as long as it's alright with
April." April instantly agreed.

Soon everybody left and I turned to April and said, "Get your ass out of bed, if you feel up to it. We're going chicken hunting!" She laughed, knowing I had been waiting for the chance, and said, "I'm going! I'm definitely not going to miss this!"

We had about an hour to do this, so I showed her the fishing net and we went outside. It was nighttime and not too many chickens were out; even when we did find some, they would run like hell into the bushes before we could get near them. There was no way—and I mean no way—to catch a chicken just by speed alone.

So April and I went by the pool and asked anyone there if they could help. Everyone just gave us weird looks when we explained what we were trying to do, so I grew fed up. We were going to do this alone.

I had to come up with a strategy if we were going to have the slightest chance of catching a chicken. So my new plan was to make them run toward the hotel, where they couldn't get away too easily. That worked a little better, but they still managed to run past us even when we got them to the wall. People at the hotel just about died laughing at us when they saw us hunting chickens—and I guess I would have been laughing, too.

We were getting frustrated and running out of time, so our next approach was to force a chicken into the corner. As we rolled in from different angles, we guided the chicken behind a bush into the corner, which was perfect. Here was my chance! We were both five feet away from the bush and I told April not to move, then I slowly got out of my wheelchair and down on the ground, where I began crawling toward the chicken like Rambo. I inched my way closer and closer to the bush until I was right up next to it, keeping an eye on the chicken at all times.

My next move was risky but I had no choice. I didn't just want to stick the net out because the chicken would have shot out the other side like a bullet, so instead I reached around the far side of the bush, shaking my hand to try to scare the crap out of the bird and make it run out my side. When it did that, I was ready with the net in my right hand and caught it! And that was a mistake.

As soon as I got it in the net, that damn chicken made the worst sound in the world, as if I were going to kill it. The noise was so loud that I was worried that people would wonder just what we were doing. So I got back in my chair and told April we had to go now. We both pushed as quickly as possible to the room, holding something over the chicken to calm it down and so the staff couldn't see what we had.

At the room, I pulled out a key from my collection, opened the door, pushed the chicken quickly inside and closed the door. As soon as it was in the room, instant relief and excitement overcame me.

It wasn't but five minutes before everybody came back to the hotel. Some of the kids who knew my plan had figured out what I was trying to do and were even more excited than I was. I told them which dive buddy's room the chicken was in and we followed him to his door.

Of course, he knew something was going on from the way we were acting and opened the door slowly. The chicken didn't come flying out; in fact, no one saw anything at first. Then he spotted the chicken on top of the TV, looking at us. Everybody just about died laughing. "How did you catch a chicken?" he asked, and I simply smiled.

With my improved techniques, Ashley and I could catch chickens really quickly now, so the madness was far from over. We stuck two of them in Sara's room while she was out one evening and one in Jim's girlfriend's room, even though everybody warned me that Dawn didn't take jokes too well. I opened the curtain some so we could all watch from the outside when Dawn went into her room.

It took a few minutes for her to notice the bird, then she just looked at it, not knowing what to think. She called Jim in and they wondered aloud how it had gotten in there. Then they heard us laughing outside and opened the glass door. "Who did this?" Jim asked, smiling. Everyone answered, "Nick." He laughed louder and asked, "How did you catch a chicken?" Again, I didn't answer, but Steve wrote in the journal: "I never thought in a million years that a kid in a wheelchair could catch a chicken in a fishing net."

■ ■ ■

The trip had been so special and I learned and experienced so much. The memories we made were one-of-a-kind, and I know the others will remember them forever as well.

In my speech at our final dinner together, I thanked Kris, Sara and Jim for giving physically challenged individuals the chance of a lifetime. Trips like those were always so much fun and showed us that life is so precious and short and that we have to enjoy the time we have. There are some things we don't have control of, but we all have a choice in seeing our cup as half-empty or half-full.

CHAPTER 38

Las Vegas

After coming back from the Diveheart trip, I didn't have much time at home before leaving again. Lucus had gotten his bachelor's degree at DeVry and for his graduation present, his mom and stepdad were sending him to Las Vegas with a friend of his choice—and that friend was me! So the plan was that after I went scuba diving for a week, I'd come home for a week then fly to Las Vegas for four days. Life is good sometimes and I was planning to enjoy it!

Lucus and I were happy that his stepdad, Mike, who was both a father-figure and one of the guys, was going with us. That also made our families glad because there was no telling what the two of us would be getting into. This was the perfect time for celebration, after all; we had both recently turned twenty-one and graduated, and we were going to party hard!

In fact, the party started at the airport, where Lucus and I headed to the bar and each had three consecutive shots of Bacardi 151, followed by two huge glasses of beer, for which Mike joined us. Needless to say, Lucus and I were feeling pretty good when we got on the plane and weren't exactly the quietest passengers. When the flight attended asked if this was our first time going to Vegas, Lucus replied with our signature yell: "WOO-HOOOO! WE'RE GOING TO VEGAS!" What made it even funnier is that Mike said, "Lucus, *everyone* on the plane is going to Vegas." When he said that, we burst out laughing even more.

The flight attendant came around often and I would make my

pec muscles dance when she least expected it. Then she was talking to us about girls and I made a joke about Lucus not having any
game. As soon as I said that, she moved her hips around and said,
"And you do?" All three of us cracked up. Her timing was perfect,
and it was a blast just flying there.

The hotel we were staying in was New York, New York. It
was so awesome—it even had a roller coaster and there were slot
machines and beautiful women everywhere. Right away, I said to
Lucus, "I like Vegas!"

While we waited in line to check in, we were checking out all
the sights. But then we were called over to the front of the line at
another counter; apparently, since I was in a wheelchair, I didn't
have to wait in line. How sweet is that? It was definitely a good
start to the trip. We got into our rooms in no time then headed
down to do some gambling.

We made the rounds playing different games, but Lucus and
I loved roulette the most. Each day, we found ourselves at the
roulette table in different casinos. Before Vegas, I had only played
a couple of times after turning twenty-one, but I knew the game
inside and out from playing video games when I was younger. We
both won but Lucus was really on a streak. The excitement was
intense, especially with everyone around the table. Lucus and I
were up a few hundred dollars and decided to play big, so we each
bet a hundred on either black/red or even/odd. I'd pick one and
he'd choose the other so that one of us was bound to win unless 0
or 00 came out. Lucus hit on red and was then up $200.

Before he took his money, I said, "Let it ride…" He just looked
at me and I said, "Think about it. You have nothing to lose and if
you win, you'll be up $400." I can be very persuasive on occasion
and this was one of those times. Lucus said, "What the hell? Let
it ride!" Next thing we knew, it landed on red again. Lucus was
feeling good, we were getting loud and everybody around us was

wondering what was going on. So I told him again, "Let it ride!" He hesitated and I went on: "That'll be $800. Think about it!" After a few seconds of debating, he decided he had nothing to lose since he was just playing with some of his winnings and would still be up either way. So again he let it ride—and this time it landed on black. Lucus screamed, "NOOO!" as if someone had just stabbed him, but we didn't let any losses get in the way of our fun.

After gambling for a while, we headed to the hotel bar and got a few more shots of Bacardi 151. They weren't cheap, but we didn't care—this was a celebration! After that, we got a few beers and went to the dance club, Coyote Ugly. Mike wasn't a big fan of dance clubs so he didn't come—which meant that Lucus and I were on our own!

The club was packed and it was hard trying to get through everybody, especially with me in a wheelchair. We eventually got to the bar and I grabbed the edge and stood up. A little while later, a bouncer half my size came up to me and said I couldn't hold on to the bar. I explained my circumstances and he apologized and said it was cool.

But then other guys starting coming up beside me to order beers, and they'd lean on the bar, too. I was about three times their size, and I'd flare out my chest, deepen my voice, put on a serious look and tell them they couldn't lean on the bar. They'd instantly apologize and back away. I'd say, "It's okay. Just don't do it again." Lucus and I almost burst out laughing, but the bouncer saw me take care of them and gave me the thumbs-up. Being bald, big and looking like Vin Diesel has its advantages sometimes—not just because I could intimidate the hell out of most guys, but the women loved it! Let's just say girls were hanging all over me and Lucus when we left the club.

■ ■ ■

The next day, we were feeling great. We gambled, drank, went out on the Strip, gambled more, drank more, ate and took a nap. Once the sun set, we hit the bar again and had more shots of Bacardi 151 as well as a couple of beers. I called up some of the women who had given me their numbers the previous night and set up a time for Lucus and me to meet up with them and their girlfriends. But before that we had some time to kill so we decided to finish our beers then ride the roller coaster at our hotel.

The wait was pretty long and my wheelchair couldn't fit between the railing that snaked around the line. It was kind of annoying but Lucus and I were both liquored up and just kept laughing as we heard the announcement, "Alcohol and speed don't mix," repeated over and over. Since I couldn't get past the bars, I stood up and Lucus picked up my wheelchair and started to lift it over the rail. As I started walking forward, he accidentally hit me in the back of the head with my own wheelchair and I fell forward, hitting my forehead on the bar. I knelt on the floor, laughing hysterically, and Lucus did the same. The Bacardi 151 had really set in at that point!

We drew so much attention to ourselves by laughing so hard that one of the workers came over as I was getting back in my wheelchair. We thought we were going to get in trouble but instead he told us that we could go to the front of the line. It was awesome, just like when we had checked into the hotel!

So we went around the railing to the front of the line and got on first. I hadn't ridden a roller coaster since middle school—but this was the first time I'd been on one after drinking. That first drop really messed with my head, but after we went around once, they asked if we wanted to ride it again and I said, "Yeah!" After the second time, though, Lucus was about to throw up and we left so that the people behind us wouldn't have chunks blown all over them.

After that, we headed to Studio 54, where there was a huge

line out front, like an hour and a half wait. The first thing I said to myself was, *I wonder if we could just go straight in.* Lucus had the same thought, so I decided to try. All we needed was one second to come up with a plan.

Less than a minute later, Lucus came back with three women; he'd told them we could get them straight into the club. So we all headed to the front of the line and I said to the bouncer, "They told me to go here and you could get me in," even though I hadn't talked to anyone. I just figured that's what we'd been doing the whole time in Vegas and I was sticking with it. The guy asked, "Who's with you?" and I pointed to Lucus and the ladies. He must've been impressed because, before we knew it, he had stamped all our hands with "VIP."

It felt so good getting straight in that we went to the bar and I bought everybody drinks. That was a mistake because right after I did that, the three girls took off. But Lucus and I partied there for some time before meeting up with the women we'd called at Coyote Ugly. That night was a long one…but it turned out well for both of us!

■ ■ ■

That next day, we did our usual thing. As Mike, Lucus and I went out on the Strip, I'd talk to the beautiful women, just to get a grin from them. I'd started chatting to one girl walking beside me and, after a minute or so, she said, "I thought everybody in wheelchairs was mentally retarded." I couldn't believe she thought that; it really caught me off-guard.

I tried not to let her comment get me down, however. I remained positive and was looking forward to the show we'd gotten tickets for. Lucus and I were especially excited because this would be the first show we'd ever seen in Las Vegas. But as soon as we got there, we realized we couldn't get any closer than the back row because the place wasn't wheelchair-accessible. I didn't let that get to me, either, because it had happened several times in the past, but Mike was pissed. He said, "Just because he's in a wheelchair doesn't mean you have to treat him like a second-class citizen." After that, they put us as close to the stage as they possibly could, and Lucus and I thought that what Mike had said was awesome!

After four days and three nights in Vegas, it was time to go back to Kansas—but some of the memories of that trip still put a smile on our faces today.

CHAPTER 39

Powerlifting

Everywhere I went during my travels, my strength and size amazed people, especially since I was in a wheelchair; it was as if they had never seen anyone in a wheelchair as big as I was, nor had they believed that it was possible. That alone motivated me to get even bigger and stronger. So once I returned from my trips, I was back at the gym with my friend Rocky.

But as soon as summer was over, Rocky was getting ready to leave for Highland, so we busted our asses to make substantial gains in the meantime. Rocky went from a weight of 210 to 232 and his bench went up to 315, which was the most he'd ever benched.

Rocky was a close friend and an awesome workout partner. He was dependable and the level of intensity we brought to our workouts was exceptional. We knew that we could count on each other to bring out the best in one another, but now we had to go our separate ways.

After Rocky was gone, I still worked out. Life moves on, regardless of what happens, and you just have to roll with it. People saw me at the gym day in and day out, and some would come up to tell me that I looked bigger and ask what my bench max was. That boosted my self-esteem and made me want to work out that much harder. In a way, I wanted to bring people hope with my strength. I wanted them to see that if you set your mind to it, you can do anything.

After months of training, something clicked in my head and I decided to continue doing powerlifting competitions. I knew they were out there, but I didn't know where or when they were being held, so I did some research on the Internet and found the Natural Athlete Strength Association (NASA), which held competitions all over the country.

Luckily for me, there was one coming up in May 2001 in Wichita, Kansas, which was perfect because it gave me months to train beforehand. Besides, it was already winter and I hated the cold and snow, so I didn't mind spending hours inside the gym.

I was excited to read that the upcoming NASA competition not only had powerlifting but power sports. Powerlifting consisted of squats, bench pressing and deadlifts, and we were allowed to use bench shirts, squat suits and wraps (for squats, not bench pressing). Power sports consisted of curls (which was unusual), bench pressing and deadlifts, but we weren't allowed to use any supportive gear. That was fine because when I did bench presses, the bench shirt never actually helped me out that much; it was always the wraps that I benefited from.

My mother was excited when I told her my plan to join the competition. She had always been one hundred percent support-ive of whatever I wanted to do, which meant I didn't have to worry about her reaction and could instead focus on what lay ahead.

Besides getting bigger and stronger, lifting as heavy a weight as possible at this meet was my new goal. I researched how to increase my bench presses and found tips and tricks on improving my max. One suggestion was to have a wider grip, which involved more chest muscles than triceps (especially depending on the angle of your triceps). Benching with your elbows at a ninety-degree angle involves more chest strength, whereas benching with your elbows ducked in at a forty-five-degree angle brings the triceps into action more. Since your chest has more muscle than your triceps, it makes more sense that you can push more weight if you have a wider grip.

At the gym, I also saw many guys benching seven hundred or more pounds by grabbing the bar really wide, with their index fingers on the outer ring of the bar and their elbows kept in. The wider grip was also to decrease the distance that the bar had to travel from the chest to lockout.

All of this new information made me anxious for my next chest workout, when I planned to try these new techniques. As I lay down on that bench, I adjusted my body according to the recommendations I had read: I placed my feet differently, kept my shoulders back, widened and tightened my grip, and breathed differently. I had 135 pounds on the bar and that weight just about flew off my chest! It was so easy that I increased the weight to 225 pounds and pushed that a few times without much effort.

It was going great until the weight got even heavier. When I got to around 300 pounds, it became extremely hard—even harder than it had been with my normal grip. So I went back to how I normally held the bar and pushed it up like nothing. It didn't make sense but I was determined to figure out why that had happened.

After going over all the material I had and realizing that I hadn't done anything wrong, it hit me: My body simply hadn't adjusted to the new grip. With a wider grip, I was using a lot more chest muscles than triceps and I wasn't used to that. I needed to give my body more time to adjust.

Months of training passed and I could feel the change in my body. I was pushing heavier weights with ease and lifting heavier than ever before. I even felt different emotionally and oozed confidence. My chest adapted very nicely to the new stress I had put on it by benching with a wider grip. My bench press had increased and my chest had gotten bigger. Benching 300 pounds was a lot easier than it had previously been and I could rep 315 pounds two or three times without much difficulty. Even going up to 335 pounds raw was no problem. It had worked out perfectly and I'd go into my first weight meet since high school stronger than ever before.

When the competition was only a week away, I still had a lot of work to do. I was lifting light Monday through Thursday but still needed to lose weight to get in the lightest weight class possible. Most of the time, a heavier weight class means the guys can lift heavier, which makes it harder to win. So my plan was to drop as much weight as I could without becoming weaker or decreasing my max. It wasn't going to be easy—but that sure wasn't going to stop me from trying. After all, I never let it stop me before.

CHAPTER 40
The Transformation

D O NOT do what I am about to tell you regarding how I lost weight for the competition. It is dangerous.

Over the years that I've been competing, I've learned my body's limits, and the weight that I lost for this initial meet is what I call 'illusionary weight,' which means that it will return because it was mostly water weight.

However, many people wondered how I could possibly have done what I did in preparation for the NASA competition, so here it is. I call what I did a transformation. It is a combination of dehydration, starvation and suffocation. I started it just two days before the meet because it was so mentally tough to go through.

On the Wednesday morning before the competition, I weighed 197 pounds. That's when the transformation began. For the starvation part, I took multivitamins, ate barely anything and took protein drinks with little water. This continued from Wednesday to Friday morning, when they officially recorded my weight. If my stomach growled during that time, the trick I used was to sip on orange juice because it increases blood sugar levels and helps stop hunger some. Even though I consumed few calories, I still kept my nutrition as high as I could with as little food as possible.

The other processes were dehydration and suffocation to pull the water weight out of my body, since one gallon of water is equivalent to eight pounds. There were no saunas in the area near my home, so I had to come up with my own. I turned a portable heater to full blast in the bathroom then sat naked in the shower on my bench chair with the water running as hot as I could take it. Half of the water would spray on me and the rest would spray off to the side. Between the heater and the steam, the bathroom would become so hot that I'd suffer during this part of the transformation. I could only do it for about an hour since doing it too long can be dangerous, especially because I'd been drinking very little water in order to keep off excess water weight.

Nights were torture. I'd be starving as I lay in bed, and a few snacks weren't enough. Then I'd wake up the next day to repeat it all over again. Thursday was so much worse than the day before, but that morning I weighed 185 pounds. I had dropped twelve pounds but I kept going. Just one more day and I would be done.

That night, I almost couldn't take sitting in that hot shower. With little food and water, I felt absolutely miserable. My mother hated to watch me go through it and was against this procedure, but she also knew I would do whatever it took for the competition.

When Friday morning came around, I was so happy. Even though I was anxious to eat, I didn't have breakfast because I was going to weigh in at my rehab center. I was curious about my weight but didn't want to measure it at my house; I wanted to wait until I got to rehab. If it turned out that I didn't lose much more or that I'd somehow regained a few pounds, I wouldn't be mad because I knew I had done everything in my power to lose the weight and couldn't do any more.

When I got to rehab, everyone was excited to see me and they all noticed how much weight I had lost and muscle I had gained. It was a great feeling to show them how hard I'd been working. Meg was impressed, which meant more to me than anyone else's reaction because I'd worked with her for so long. I asked if she'd weigh me for the meet the next day and she was more than happy to do it.

As she got out the scale, I stripped down to my shorts. There were other people rehabbing nearby, so I couldn't get down to my underwear—but I was 'commando' in the shorts anyway. The lighter, the better!

It was hard standing on the scale without the support of my AFOs, so we went to the parallel bars, where I tried to balance myself. After I was standing pretty still, I let go of the bars so Meg could get a true reading of my weight. We did that a couple of times to make sure it was correct.

I weighed in at 175 pounds. I couldn't believe it! The hard work and suffering had paid off. Meg wrote my weight on an official hospital paper and dated and signed it. I told her how much I appreciated her help then headed back home, still in shock but excited to show my mother. Afterward, I ate a huge breakfast and drank a lot of skim milk to load back up, then took it easy for the rest of the day.

I hated the whole transformation procedure, but I was lighter than I had ever been as a result—and I was ready for the competition.

CHAPTER 41

The Day of the Competition

Before the weight meet the next day in Wichita, Kansas, Lucus spent the night at my house then drove down with me to the competition, about two hours away, and my uncle gave my mother a ride. My uncle's truck didn't have cruise control, so when I would have it on while driving, I'd pass them up easily and my mother would give me the evil eye as if I were speeding, so I had to hold down the hand control the whole time. When we got there, my left tricep was burning—and it would eventually cramp up on me.

I did not know what to expect at this competition. All I had ever known were high school powerlifting meets. It was a pretty big place with only one station, and the first thing I thought was that it was going to take forever.

I had sent my entry form and money weeks before the actual competition, and what I looked forward to at a powerlifting meet like this was that I could enter multiple divisions. Each division depended on your age, whether you'd ever won first at a national meet and how long you'd been anabolic steroid-free. I met all the qualifications of all of the divisions, so I entered them all: pure, pure novice, natural (open), teenage and junior for both curl and the bench press. Since the bench shirt never helped me that much and you're not allowed to use wraps on your elbows, I also decided to enter power sports, which is raw (unequipped) lifting for which all you're allowed to wear is a wrestling singlet.

After a few minutes of being there, I started talking to Lucus about whether or not he would enter the competition. I had caught him off-guard and at first he wasn't sure, but after some discussion he was in! We weren't certain if he could enter, though, because some meets would not allow you to lift if the entry form was submitted past the deadline date. Fortunately, this wasn't one of those meets and Lucus was allowed to join.

So we both headed to the weigh-in table, where we had to fill out membership and liability forms. Lucus entered a couple different bench press divisions, but no curls. He was not prepared for or comfortable doing them.

When they went to weigh me, I could tell that they didn't really know what to do and hadn't dealt with many people in wheelchairs. They were relieved when I gave them the paper with my weight on it: 175 pounds, official. After Lucus weighed in, I changed into the singlet I had bought off the Internet, and Lucus lucked out because they sold singlets there. We were both wearing black singlets and couldn't help but make fun of each other.

There were only a few familiar faces in the audience and no area that we could really call ours. Two other students who were still in Pomona High School showed up, and it was nice that they were there, but it wasn't the same as being in a school meet. It was every man and woman for themselves.

When they announced that all the lifters were to meet in back in the warm-up area, we knew the weight meet was going to start. Once everyone got back there, they went over all the rules and would soon post the order in which we would lift. It was simple: The list started with the lightest and ended with the heaviest. The amount of flights depended on the number of lifters. Everybody in flight one was going to lift once, going from the lightest to heaviest lifter. After that, everyone would lift a second time, and then repeat it for a third, which is why they couldn't put everyone in one flight. If there were a hundred lifters, everyone would be cold before it was time for their second lift. It was the same setup as in Park Hill South High School, when I had dropped the weight on my face.

The order was curl, squat, bench press then dead lift, which I liked because I got to lift right away. I started to warm up and Lucus stayed with me. As I was warming up, they posted the flights on the wall. Seeing the list was nerve-wracking because it became *real*—you knew exactly when you were going to lift.

There was just one flight on the list; thirty or forty people would be curling and I was in the last ten. My opening curl would be around 125 pounds, and I wanted forty-five-pound plates on each side (the weight we had to choose from was in kilograms, not pounds, so it always came out to an odd number when you converted it to pounds). I just wanted to start with something I knew I could get easily.

Since we would get three lifts, I planned roughly what I was going to lift next, though I never had a set number to lift at these powerlifting meets because I never knew how light or heavy the first lift was going to feel. It all depended on how bad the weight loss affected me, the energy from the crowd and especially the first lift.

Surprisingly, it was going faster than I had expected and I was soon up. I knew by what weight they had on the bar how many people were in front of me, and they called my name as I sat on the side in my wheelchair.

As I rolled up to the EZ curl bar, I was psyching myself up as I placed my hands in the close grip position. After rotating and adjusting the bar to fit the groves of my hands, I pulled it off the rack and rested it on my quads. I kicked my legs out and stood up straight, trying to make it as much of a full range of motion as I could. Everyone knew how much harder it was to lift that way because the bar was at a dead weight position and I couldn't use any momentum. After I put the bar on my legs, I looked at it, adjusted it once more then looked at the head judge.

Once I looked at him, he gave me the curl command and I curled with all my might. I curled that bar like it was nothing!

After lifting it, I got applause and cheers from the audience, and the judge gave me the command to let it down. I sat the bar back on my legs and two guys racked it. After that, I knew I wanted to increase the weight for my second lift to around 135 pounds.

As I headed to the announcer's table to tell them my next weight, I had to see which exact weight I was going to lift. They had kilogram charts on the table and the weight I chose was 62.5 kilograms, which was 137.5 pounds.

I went back to the warm-up area and people there told me it was a good lift—and that I made it look easy. I thanked them and got ready for my next lift, watching the others curl the heavier weight.

Before I knew it, they called my name again and loaded the bar. At that moment, it was me versus 137.5 pounds. As I went through the same adjustments as last time, all I could think about was not failing. I sat there with the weight in my hands and all I heard was my mother, uncle, Lucus and the crowed cheering me on. Right before I was about to battle this weight, I heard the judge call, "Curl!"

Again I curled that weight as hard as I could, lifting it with something approaching ease. Victory was mine! As I headed to the table again, I knew what my next weight was going to be: 143 pounds, a personal best. But I could tell I was getting close to my limit.

As I rolled up for my third lift, I mentally prepared for my final attempt. But as I held the weight in my hands, I knew right then that it was too much. Once you have lifted weights for a while, there's a certain instinct you get when you have the actual weight in your hands. From that feeling, you can usually tell what the outcome of the lift will be.

Even so, I curled with everything I had when I got the command. But the third lift ended up being too heavy; I got the bar up about halfway and that was it. I was mad at myself, even though people told me afterwards how awesome I did. I would just smile and tell them they did great as well, even though I was not satisfied with myself.

■ ■ ■

It was hours before the bench presses started—the only other lifts I could physically participate in and the only ones Lucus wanted to do. I had to wait for everyone to finish squats and the half-hour intermission to end before I had another chance to prove myself.

Once it started up again, they posted the flights for bench press. This time there was more than one; Lucus was in the first flight and I was in the second. As he was warming up, I stayed back with him, helping to plan what his second and third lifts would be.

There were three judges and they were very strict. They all sat in chairs, one on each side of the lifter and one behind. They were about five feet away from the lifer with white light switch boxes in their hands that were hooked up to a big, wooden, rectangular board on the side that had six lightbulbs on it. There was two rows of lights, three bulbs in each row. The top row consisted of all red bulbs and there were all white ones on the bottom.

Each judge had a specific thing to look for when a lifter benched. If the lifter did it right, they would get a white light from the judge. Wrong was a red light. If the lifter raised his right foot, he got a red light from the judge on his right. If the lifter lifted his head off the bench, he got a red light from the back judge. All white lights or one red, two white meant the lift was good, but if you got two or more red lights, the lift was bad.

On top of all your other body movements, you had to pause the bar on your chest. A lot of people think it is a one-second pause (which is true for high school), but actually it is a non-movement pause, meaning you have to hold the bar on your chest until it doesn't move, which shows that you are in control of the lift. I saw a guy hold the bar on his chest for five seconds. The judges did not give him the "press" command because he kept moving the bar while it was on his chest. Lowering the bar slowly shows more control and you have to hold it on your chest for less time. If you push the bar off your chest and it moves back down toward your chest, the lift is considered a falling movement and is automatically scored as bad.

Before Lucus lifted, he would pace back and forth or stand with his arms crossed and a weird look on his face, his nostrils flaring in and out from his heavy breathing as he tried to psych himself up. It looked strange, but then I wondered what people thought of me when I got ready to lift. It didn't matter, though. When you're about to lift, you don't care what others think. All you care about is doing whatever it takes to lift the weight.

Lucus would watch me and I would watch him and we'd inform each other how much we thought the other one should go up in weight after each lift. It was nice having my best friend by my side; it's a different feeling of comfort when a friend is there supporting you compared to how family supports you from the audience. But both give you that edge when it comes time to lift.

Lucus ended up with red lights during his first lift because he picked his head up off the bench. He would later get both of his other lifts, beating everyone in all his divisions.

After he was done, I had some time before it was my turn. The first flight ended and the second flight began warming up, but even when the second flight started, I still had time. My 292-pound opening was heavier than the majority in my flight.

As I warmed up with 135 pounds, it felt easy so I did 225. But when I put on 275 pounds to push one time, it did not feel right. The weight felt heavy, and as I sat up from the bench, the whole weight loss "transformation" thing crossed my mind. I did not know that it had affected me that much.

That was it for warming up. I needed to save as much energy as

I possibly could. But now I was worried about whether I was even going to get my opening lift. This was not good.

As the time for me to lift was getting closer, I was dreading it and trying to psych myself up at the same time. When they called my name, it was show time. As I lay down on the bench, things just seemed to bug me. I didn't know if it was just because the warm up had messed with my head, but the bench felt hard, my feet placement bothered me, my grip felt weird, and my head and face got itchy.

I lifted the weight off the rack and it felt really heavy. I was worried more about moving my head and feet and about the pause than anything. I lowered the bar pretty fast and held it on my chest, waiting for the press command. After a second or two I heard, "Press!" Once I heard that, I pushed the bar as hard as I could and it went up all right, but not speedily. I locked out and waited at the top for the rack command then racked it.

It was a good lift and I was happy for that. If you don't get your lift, you're not allowed to lower your weight. If you did not get the first lift, it wouldn't be wise to move up the weight unless you knew you could get it, and you would have to waste another lift trying the same weight.

After getting off the bench, I headed over to the announcers to tell them my next lift. The original plan was to try for around 335 or 340, but that wasn't going to happen. Mentally and physically, the weight was messing with me so I increased to 304 pounds. That diet had hurt me something severe. Don't get me wrong—I was doing well against my opponents, but I wasn't satisfied with my overall performance.

Lucus and I watched the few guys that were after me and they jumped the weight up to the 350- to 400-pound range. Thankfully, they were older than me because they would have beaten me bad if we were in the same age bracket. The guys I was going against lifted around 225 to 280 pounds.

I eventually lifted my second time, and something was just different. I couldn't get in that same psyched up phase that I normally do. It was like I was going to lift it to lift it. My face was still itching and I had to wipe my hands on my shirt before I started the lift. As I lifted that bar up, it was extremely heavy.

When I lowered it, I hoped I did not have to hold the bar on my chest for very long. When the bar did touch my chest, I pushed it up before too long and locked it out at the top. I was glad I got that lift because it meant that I officially pushed up over 300 pounds at a non-high school powerlifting meet, which was a pretty big accomplishment.

On my third lift, I wanted to attempt 314 pounds—but after knowing what 304 pounds felt like, 314 was going to be a challenge (and 335 or 340 were not even an option; I would have just made a fool of myself if I had tried them).

Sitting off to the side, I was in my own little world. I had some time before my third attempt and the closer it got, the more I tried to get myself angry, digging deep to find my inner strength. Before I knew it, they called my name and I transferred onto the bench. I sat there for a few seconds, trying to piss myself off more and more. I began to shake and yell out in short bursts before finally laying down. As I grabbed the bar, I focused my sight on the middle.

After a few itches, I took the bar off the rack and slowly lowered it to my chest. I took a deep breath in and held it. The bar came to a stop on my chest and it felt like forever until the judge said, "Press." Once I heard the command, I pushed with everything I had, only to push it halfway up before it stopped. The bar wouldn't move anymore, even after a couple of seconds. Then I heard, "Rack it." The spotters helped me lift and rack it. I failed. I sat up, mad, and just cussed softly out loud.

There were so many more flights left on the bench press and they still had to do deadlifts. So over the hours we had left, we talked about how well we did. With only a few months of actual training for power curls, I thought I did well enough, but I did not realize how good I actually was. I had beaten everyone in my weight class and had broken previous records—not just one record, but FIVE RECORDS in curls and THREE RECORDS in bench press!

I broke the curl record for the pure, pure novice, natural (open), teenage and junior divisions and the bench press record for the natural (open), teenage and junior divisions: eight records in total. That made me feel good, even though my lifts weren't that strong. Lucus won first place in all his divisions as well, but did not break any records.

For the awards ceremony, one of the main announcers called people's names and they would go up there and get theirs. They handed me an engraved plate that read:

NASA

STATE CHAMPIONSHIPS

POWERLIFTING, BENCHPRESS AND

POWERSPORTS

1ST PLACE

We also got to choose any trophy or plaque on the table and, of course, the people they called first (those who did the full meet and had a higher coefficient ratio) would always take the trophies. I wanted one so badly and hoped they would call my name quickly. But it didn't happen for me or Lucus. We just got plaques. That was disappointing but understandable since we only did individual lifts.

That night I received ten first-place plaques and eight certifications of my records (Lucus received two first-place plaques). We were thrilled with our victories. My mother was so proud of me that she did not need to say a word because I could see it in her eyes.

We loaded the plaques in the backseat of my Blazer, careful not to stack too many on top of each other so that they wouldn't get scratched. We also stuck any extra clothes we had between them to make sure no damage was done. I wasn't looking forward to the two-hour drive back, but I couldn't wait to look on the Internet for more upcoming competitions.

In August, they would have the World Cup Championship in Oklahoma City, Oklahoma. In order to be allowed to participate, you had to have won first place at a state, national or regional championship—and now Lucus and I both qualified. I called him immediately and asked if he wanted to join the World Powerlifting meet. He was in—and my mother and uncle would come along.

But, before that, I took all the awards I had won at NASA down to the gym and put them on the counter for everyone to see. I typed my name, body weight, how much I lifted, division and places on a sheet of paper to let people know just what I did.

As I was working out, people came up to shake my hand and were amazed that I had won all those awards. It was an overwhelming feeling—one I looked forward to achieving again.

CHAPTER 42

The World Cup Championship

After months of serious preparation and training, Lucus and I left the night before The World Cup Championship to stay in a hotel in Oklahoma City. The meet was being held at The Biltmore Hotel; it was a four-and-a-half-hour drive and we had to be there at 7 a.m, so we decided to book a room there. The morning of the competition, we checked out the area where the lifts were going to take place, and there were hundreds of trophies and plaques—some seven feet tall. I had never seen anything like that before, but I knew I wanted to leave with one.

The setup was the same as in the state competition, except with a lot more chairs for the audience. The event was going to take place over two days because there were so many competitors.

This meet had hundreds of entries. On Saturday, the lighter divisions lifted and on Sunday, the heavier divisions. By the end of the first day, they awarded the lighter divisions and, although I had benched and curled more weight than at the last meet, I was beaten in some of my divisions.

I received seven first places, two second places and one third place. Lucus trained and competed in curls as well, and received three first places. I ended up with two trophies and eight plaques and Lucus won one trophy and two plaques. We never expected to do that well and enjoyed every bit of it.

Then again, we almost always enjoyed ourselves, no matter what we were doing.

■ ■ ■

Lifting competitions were important to me, but they weren't the only things happening in life. For example, my friend Jack got married in the spring of 2002 but still kept lifting. I had met Jack in February 2002. He was forty-two years old, 5'6" with red hair and a very stocky build. From the first time we met, we got along very well. He would come down to the gym about the same time I did and we started working out together. Shortly after we met, he found out that I did powerlifting competitions, and I found out that he had competed back in 1989 and had been the German champion.

When we worked out, it was intense. I still lifted the same split, as heavy as possible. I didn't see any reason to change what I was doing since I kept getting stronger and bigger. Jack could push some weight and that made me want to lift even more. When he worked out with me, we benched really heavy and his bench press kept going up.

Then in July 2002, I was shocked as I entered the gym. Almost two years had passed and there stood Rocky. It was great to see him again and it felt as if it were yesterday. We talked about what we both were up to; he had completed his semester at Highland back in 2000 then pursued a profession as an electrician, earning his Block Journeyman Certification in January 2001. He lifted at his house, training on a home gym, but was now back at the gym. He had also been involved in arm-wrestling competitions and had won a few titles. That day, I introduced him to Jack and we all just connected, so the three of us started working out together. I tried to get Rocky and Jack to do powerlifting competitions, but they felt they wouldn't do well enough. Jack wanted to train a year or so before he started competing.

Lucus lived a distance away but continued to train at the YMCA in preparation for the competitions. I was going to school at Neosho at the time and Lucus was still taking classes at DeVry, although he had it tougher than I did since he also worked to provide for his daughter. Neither of us were exactly the party type; we were both more the responsible ones.

Lucus had his daughter three weekends of the month and drove down to Ottawa to get her. Most of the time, he would stop by after he dropped her off every Sunday to hang out for a while and sometimes I would drive up there on the weekends that he didn't have her or he would come down on the only weekend he had off. That was when we went to clubs, played pool, or just hung out.

Going to bars and clubs was always interesting; Lucus and I never drank because we weren't of age. I wasn't into drinking like most people, anyway; weightlifting was too important to me and alcohol made it that much longer for my body to heal. Besides, I didn't mind being the designated driver.

Most the time when we hung out, it was just the two of us. It was always fun no matter what we did; Lucus was the shy one but I didn't have any problems going up to women even though I was in a wheelchair. Women are attracted to personality and confidence, plus having a good build helps a bit.

Getting Lucus on the dance floor took a lot of talking but once we got out there, it was a lot of fun. We would go up to women and try to start up a conversation, and either they were interested and kept the discussion going or they would just answer and not say anything else. That was the cue to move on. Women would come up to us and there were many times when they gave me a "pity dance." It was all good, though, because once one started, others would start dancing with me, too. There were times when I had three women on me at once!

To really get people's attention, I would do multiple three-sixties while popping a wheelie. Then if I had enough room, Lucus and I would go into "The Spin," when Lucus would grab my right hand and start spinning me in circles. While in "The Spin," I would tighten my grip and keep my mid-section tight, guiding my wheel-chair by turning it with my waist.

After spinning so long, I would just let go in the direction I wanted, rolling at a fast speed, making movements with my arms, until I stopped the wheelchair instantly. After seeing that move, people were curious and would come up to us and tell us how awesome it was.

Actual bars with pool tables were where trouble always occurred; you never knew what could happen. When I played pool, I held on to the table and stood up to take some shots. Then, while still holding on, I would walk around the table and eventually sit back in my wheelchair. Well…there would be one drunk guy out of the blue every once in a while who would come up to me and tell me to get out of my wheelchair, that it wasn't funny to act like I had to be in one. Then Lucus would get close just in case the drunk wanted to start something, and I would explain why I was in the wheelchair and what had happened to put me there. I would rather not make a big deal out of it than get into a fight, but sometimes the explanation wasn't enough. So I would just ignore the guy and continue what I was doing.

When I'm confronted, it's as if the other people at the bar become united and are automatically on my side and have my back. Afterwards, they come up to me and wonder what was going on. It doesn't scare or bother me that drunk guys come up to me like that. They just don't understand the circumstances and are quick to judge.

There are many things that I have gone through, but the thing I hate with a passion is when people tap me on the head, which happens a lot in bars. The women don't bother me; they can touch, rub, or kiss my head—but for a guy, it's off limits.

Once, I was with my friends and all of a sudden felt three taps on the top of my head. Instantly, I stopped in place and turned around, and this guy had come directly up to tell me how much of an inspiration I was and how awesome I was. I was still pissed about the whole head-tapping thing and said to him, "For starters, you shouldn't tap people on the head to get their attention," then rolled away. That is one thing I don't care for. How would he like it if people came up and tapped him on the top or back of the head? Exactly.

■ ■ ■

Like I said, my friends and I tried to enjoy ourselves in almost every situation, from lifting in meets to mingling in bars. All I wanted was the same respect that I gave other people, and the same types of opportunities that everyone else had, without my wheelchair getting in the way of going to my limit.

CHAPTER 43

Best Chest

Lifting awards weren't the only kind I received. In fact, one other type of competition we were in was bad but so funny!

One Saturday, Lucus and I went to Coyotes in Lawrence. It was more of a country bar/dance club, but they did play some hip-hop. I'd been there before with Rocky and some other friends, but we normally went on a Thursday night, when they held the best butt contest for women. However, Saturday was the wet T-shirt contest for women and the best chest contest for men.

That's why we ended up going on a Saturday night in the first place—Lucus and I were planning to enter the best chest contest. We figured we both had a pretty good chance at winning. So we went to Wal-Mart and bought these small white t-shirts, making sure they were extra tight so the women could really see our "man cleavage" as we went around the club before the contest started. We wanted them to check us out and be that much more eager to cheer for us. I ended up wearing a medium and Lucus wore a small. That medium was so damn tight and my chest stuck out so bad. It was too funny, but we looked good.

We tried to determine the best time to actually show up at the club, because we didn't want to be the weird guys who came too early or late. We figured we would make our appearance around ten-thirty or quarter to eleven, giving us enough time to mingle and let the women check us out.

That night, we pulled up in my Blazer and the parking lot was packed. After seeing the lot so full, we started to jokingly cuss because soon we would be taking off our shirts in front of all these people and we were so nervous.

The one or two handicap parking spots were in use, so I ended up parking across the street. As we headed to the entrance, we talked about how nervous we were—but once we got in the club, we started to loosen up a bit. We were both under twenty-one, but we had to get something to drink and made sure it was in a cup so it looked like we were drinking beer.

The club was pretty big. As you walked in, pool tables were off to the left and there were two bars in the front and back. The dance floor was a huge, oval-shaped area and was directly in the center of the room. All the way around the outside of the dance floor was a ten-foot walkway that looked like a track. There was a high, wooden countertop with stools that surrounded the dance floor so people could drink and watch others dance.

As we went around, we mingled with the women, starting conversations, joking a bit and asking if they were going to cheer for us in the best chest contest. They would say, "YEAH" or "HELL, YEAH!" in reply. Then I would ask them if they were going to enter the wet T-shirt contest. Most said no, but I talked a few into it. I felt great as we kept making our rounds.

Eventually, we sat on the side, waiting for the contest to begin in about fifteen minutes, at midnight. We were both nervous but I had come up with the idea to rip off my shirt. But then I thought, *What if I try to rip my shirt off and it won't rip?* That freaked me out because then it would make me look weak and stupid. So I had the waitress get me a pair of scissors and I cut a slit in the neck seam to make sure the shirt would rip easily. After that, I began flexing my chest and arms, pumping the blood and trying to make my muscles as full as possible.

Before I knew it, the DJ announced that it was time for the best chest contest and called for all the guys who wanted to participate to come forth. There was a six-inch step that went down to the dance floor and I just rolled off the step while popping a wheelie. About halfway to the center, I ripped off my shirt. I ripped it like a hot knife through butter!

But I was nervous, and could tell Lucus was, too, as the crowd gathered around the dance floor. Once everybody was at the center, the DJ tried to get more people to compete and there ended up being around twelve of us. The DJ started to play some music and everybody started making their way around the dance floor, strutting their stuff. As I was making my rounds, some of the women were screaming for me and I would get close to the side, hold on to the edge, and stand up so they could feel my chest. After a few seconds, I would sit back down and kept a-movin'. My style wasn't all about just strutting—I would be flexing, popping wheelies, doing 360s, and all sorts of things. It was all about the crowd. Lucus was working it, too. Throughout the whole song, they shone a spotlight on us to single us out.

After the song finished, they got us all lined up and the guy with the microphone shined the spotlight while saying stuff like, "How did you like number one?" The women would cheer and then they would move to the next guy. When the light flashed on me, I started making my pecs dance then started flexing, and the crowd went crazy.

It got extremely loud and then the spotlight moved on to Lucus. After he asked the crowd how they liked him, it got quiet. I mean dead quiet. It was so silent that I actually heard a bottle hit the floor. Instantly, my heart dropped for him and I couldn't believe that not one single person cheered for him. As soon as the light went to the next person, I looked at him and he looked at me and I said with my eyes, "I am sorry." You could tell he wanted nothing more than to just get off that stage but he had to wait until the end of the contest.

After they went through all the guys, he picked three of us to stay for another round and I was one of them. Lucus walked fast off the dance floor.

In the second round, we did the same thing but worked it that much harder to the new song and afterwards lined up again. The cheers were loud but mine were louder and I ended up winning that night. My reward was that I got to spray down the girls with water for the wet T-shirt contest. They brought out a kiddy pool and a pressurized water sprayer and I had to keep pumping the metal can. Then the girls came out and I went to work. The winner of the wet T-shirt contest got $200.

After it was over, it hit me that I hadn't brought an extra shirt. A few girls started coming up to me but I saw Lucus waving me over and he said, "Let's go." After everything he just had just gone through, I wasn't going to stick around, even though all these women wanted to talk me.

Almost a year later, we went back and I participated in the contest once again. Lucus wasn't about to even consider doing it again; this time, I was in it solo. The turnout was awesome and I won it in the first round! The reward was the same for winning and it was all good. But, shortly after that night, Coyotes in Lawrence stopped holding the best chest contest for guys.

I guess I retired the champion.

CHAPTER 44

The Bench Press Club

Even though Lucus didn't live close by, we continued entering competitions throughout 2002, and we returned to the 2002 World Cup Championships.

Between the two years that we competed, I won thirty-six first places, two second places and one third place, and a total of eleven trophies and twenty-eight plaques. Lucus won four first places and three second places for a total of three trophies and four plaques. Our lifts did increase and I broke some of my old records by curling 154.3 pounds at the World Cup.

After those two years, however, Lucus and I stopped competing; at the time, we had other things going on. Deep inside, I wanted to convert to bodybuilding but I still wanted to have a big bench press. I just did not want to compete anymore.

■ ■ ■

It all came together about a month after the 2002 World Cup. The Ottawa Nautilus had a bench press club in the past but it died out before I ever lifted there. I did not know anything about them and there were no records of the club, but I heard that it had existed.

That's what I wanted to do next: bring back the bench press club! It would spark this phenomenon down at the gym and make people want to push themselves harder. It would keep challenging them to be better without even knowing it. Just the thought of that sent chills all over my body. It was a way I could push people without even having to talk to them.

So I decided to begin anew. I approached the owner of the gym as well as the general manager and told them what I wanted to do. They were more than happy to do whatever I wanted because they knew I had been involved with powerlifting since I started working out there. The owner was even going to have a bench press club shirt made for the Ottawa Nautilus and each person's first shirt would be free.

When I was younger, my brother had a bench press shirt that had a weight of 225 pounds on it and I thought that was the coolest thing in the world. The shirt was a way to show off what you accomplished without saying a single word. I always wanted one but my school stopped producing them. I knew how much bench shirts meant to me and I knew others would like them as well.

But the main reason I wanted to start the club back up was to motivate people to want to lift more weight than ever. Too many people were happy just with the concept of "staying in shape" and that drove me nuts. The bench press club was the perfect opportunity for me to help these people push themselves harder and strive for something higher.

So on Monday, October 14, 2002, Rocky, Jack and I maxed on bench press. I kept records of our max, weight and age, and that night I designed an Excel spreadsheet for the bench press club. I designed it to compare everything you can imagine: weight class, age class, overall, and heaviest, so that everyone could see who was in their weight class, age class, and where they ranked in the gym. With the overall, it wasn't fair that a 150-pound guy would have to bench against someone weighing 250 pounds, so to make things even, I ranked people on their power ratio.

To calculate that, the lifter divides the weight they lift by their body weight. So, if a 150-pound guy benches his bodyweight (150 pounds), his ratio is 1.00%, and the 250-pound guy would have to bench his bodyweight (250 pounds) to be equally strong. If the 250-pound guy benches 300 pounds, that gives him a 1.2% ratio

(300/250=1.2), and if the 150-pound guy benches 185 pounds, his ratio is 1.2333% (185/150=1.2333). This means the 150-pound guy is pound for pound stronger than the bigger guy who benches 300 pounds. But the 250-pound guy would rank much higher in the heaviest category.

Compared to powerlifting meets, my rules were simple. The bench press club was meant for everyone to do their absolute best. It is extremely hard to do your best at a meet because of all the pressure and rules. At meets, even if you locked out the weight, the lift may still be bad. Something as simple as moving your feet or lifting your head off the bench would red light the lift, meaning it didn't count.

For my club, I did not want to put that type of pressure on any lifter. That is how my rules came about. The only two rules that I was extremely strict on was touching the bar to your chest and not allowing the spotter to touch the bar as the lifter was lifting the weight.

The thing that pisses me off the most is when the spotter touches the bar when someone is maxing. I can understand helping the lifter once the weight is not moving for a couple of seconds or is coming down, but not when the bar is still moving or stops for a slight second. I have seen so many spotters put one or two fingers on the bar and when I ask them why they touched it, they immediately say they didn't or that they weren't lifting the weight and that the lifter was doing it all. This will only make me more upset. It's true that the spotter may not lift very much weight, but in the end the lifter will always doubt and wonder if he or she could have actually lifted it on their own. Even if the spotter puts his pinky on the bar, it still bothers me because if someone is trying to max, either they will lift the weight or they won't.

I'm not the only one who gets mad when a spotter touches the bar. There are many times when a lifter is going to max and they ask for a spot. They will tell the spotter that they are maxing but the spotter will still touch the bar, even if the lifter specifically tells them not to. There have been times when I told the spotter not to touch the bar unless I ask for help, even if it is coming back down on me. So what does the spotter do? He touches the bar. When that happened, I started to let the weight come back down. I was mad and did not care so I let up even more and he pulled with all his might and I just watched him struggle.

If lifters bounced the bar too hard off their chest, I wouldn't give the lift to them because bouncing leads to injuries. When it comes to arching, sometimes the lifter would arch so much that their butt came off the bench. At competitions, the butt must stay on the bench at all times, but I would allow it if they lifted their butt off the bench a little. If they moved their feet or head, it was no big deal. I also allowed bench shirts and wraps on their elbows. All powerlifters were allowed to wear wraps on their knees but not on the elbows for their bench. For me, my elbows are my knees. Wraps support your knees when squatting, keeping them tight and reducing the chance of injury. If something goes wrong with my elbow, I'm pretty much screwed since I won't be able push my chair around. But, for the bench press club, the rules were that pretty much anything goes.

The lifters got to max whenever they wanted and however many times they wanted. I wanted them to be able to go up and down weight at their own discretion. It is stressful only having three lifts to see what your max is. Some days you feel stronger than others. At some weight meets, I could have lifted more weight after my third lift, but I wasn't allowed to try and I always wondered what I could have lifted. The bench press club eliminated all excuses for not achieving a personal best.

■ ■ ■

That weekend, I finished designing the outline of the bench press club spreadsheet. Without giving the guys advance notice, I decided that we were going to max on Monday. I told them that we needed to max so we could get this bench press club started, that the weight did not have to be their max but just a weight so people could see how it was all going to be set up. I was going to post our results the next day and on Friday we were going to plan on actually maxing. I told Rocky and Jack that the bench press club was going to be based on ratios so they could watch their weight for Friday.

After talking to the guys, we started warming up with a set of 135 pounds and then 225 pounds for a few reps. From there, we increased the weight to 275 pounds and Rocky pressed it for one rep. We then changed to 315 pounds and Jack and I took turns pressing it one time. We dropped the weight back down to 290 and I wrapped Rocky's arms (Jack had never used wraps before and did not know how to do it). Rocky pressed 290 easily. After I got the wraps off him, we put on 350 pounds. I lifted it once (I can't start lifting a really heavy weight without warming up first) then Jack did the same.

From there we increased the weight to 375. I went first and had Rocky wrap my arms. I pushed 375 no problem. Jack was up and Rocky and I both wrapped his arms. This was the first time he had ever tried to max with wrapping his elbows. At the time, Rocky and I had been using wraps for over six years and loved to be wrapped as tightly as possible. But many people can't stand being wrapped on their elbows because it bothers them too much and the wraps can pinch your arms when you bend them or cut off your blood circulation.

We took it easy on Jack and didn't wrap him very tightly. He attempted 375 and couldn't get it. I was surprised, and you could tell he wasn't comfortable with the wraps. We dropped the weight to 370 and when he was ready, we wrapped him again and this time he got it. We were happy with what we'd lifted but we knew we could do more and that was the plan for Friday.

The next day I posted multiple sheets on the wall right behind and in between the bench press. As I was down at the gym, I would tell people about the bench press program, trying to get more members involved. It was a hit and more people started to max or tell me they wanted to do it in a couple weeks or a month. They liked the fact that they would get a free bench press shirt and be on the wall. That week I talked to forty or fifty different people, explaining the rules and ranking system.

I had rules posted beside the max sheets, but people liked to ask me. I didn't mind—whatever it took to get more people to want to max. A few other people ended up maxing that week and by Friday, Rocky, Jack and I were back at it. We maxed again and the results were etter than I expected:

Date	Lbs. Lifted	Lifter	Age	BW	Power Ratio
10/14/2002	290	Rocky Evans	22	198	1.4646
10/18/2002	315	Rocky Evans	22	191	1.6492
10/14/2002	370	Jack Gossard	42	238	1.5546
10/18/2002	375	Jack Gossard	42	230	1.6304
10/14/2002	375	Nick Scott	20	207	1.8115
10/18/2002	410	Nick Scott	20	193	2.1243

Rocky and I increased our maxes quite impressively. Jack increased his but I thought he would get more, though it still was impressive. Not only did we increase our maxes but we had also dropped weight. It wasn't just a little weight, either. Rocky had dropped seven pounds, Jack had lost eight pounds and I dropped fourteen pounds, all in four days. The funny thing was that I did not try to lose the weight.

Not only had I lost a bunch of weight, this was also the first time I had ever benched over 400 pounds. Four hundred did not mean as much to me as 405 pounds, though, since that was four forty-five-pound plates on each side of the bar and that weight was the next barrier of bench pressing because of how it looked with all those plates. However, it was the greatest feeling in the world to know that I pressed up that much weight when I was only twenty!

As people maxed, I kept updating the records on the wall so it would draw interest. People liked the ideal of having a place on the wall and getting a bench press shirt—and, most off all, the challenge of trying to beat someone. Maybe they wanted to be the best in their age or weight bracket, or wanted to get a higher overall ranking. Every week I saw many people hover around the bench press charts, checking out the rankings.

Deep inside it was one of the best feelings to know I had started something that I was very proud of. Not only did it push me to get stronger, but it did the same for the other bench pressers in the gym. The bench press club resulted in the most bench press progress the Ottawa Nautilus has ever seen.

Before I knew it, though, a couple of people were complaining about the whole support thing. They called it cheating. They did not think it was fair that they had to go against people who wore supportive gear because they chose to do it raw. I could see their point because, in powerlifting competitions, if you don't have supportive gear and someone else does then they have an advantage over you. Since I wanted everyone to be happy with the club, I split it up to a raw and support category and there were no more complaints.

Rocky, Jack and I kept training together and that is when I began looking for bench press workouts. I had come across EAS's seven-week, fourteen-workout program that is guaranteed to increase your bench press by fifty pounds. At first I laughed and was skeptical but thought I'd give it a shot. I liked the idea of low reps with a heavy weight and the more I looked at it, the more excited I got. Once you knew what your max was, all the weight and reps were laid out for you, which I liked very much. You could see what weight you would be attempting every workout, which was extremely intimidating because towards the middle and end, the workouts call for a weight you've never lifted before. There were also failure days and test days to determine if you moved up the chart. That week I had Rocky and Jack maxing with me without supports because we did not want to wrap every time we did a set.

We started the bench press workout the following week, without all the other stuff. There were very few exercises and sets that we were supposed to do and I did not like that. It was a lot less than what I was used to so I did my own thing and Rocky and Jack followed along. Those seven weeks were insanely intense given the weight we lifted. Seeing the weight on paper and actually doing it were way different. We couldn't do all the reps with the weight the sheet called for. In the beginning it wasn't bad but toward the end it all went south.

Regardless, in the end, Rocky and I increased our max by twenty-five to thirty-five pounds, which was awesome (Jack's bench max increase would be delayed for a couple of weeks). Even though I could lift over 400 pounds when wrapped, my raw max was always much lower. Before the workout, my max was around 350 or 360 and about ten weeks later I pushed up to 380, which was the most I have ever benched raw.

■ ■ ■

The last time I maxed down at the gym was May 17, 2004. There was a guy there who was the strongest bench presser at the Ottawa Nautilus. His max at the club was 445 pounds raw, and he weighed 258 pounds. Before May 2004, the last time I had maxed was in 2002, at 410 pounds.

I wanted to beat him, but I would only attempt it using supports. I didn't want to beat him to show people I was the best. I had another reason instead. Even though I still lifted a lot of weight, I had to prepare for this. After a month or so I was ready. I was about to attempt something no one had ever done: beat Big Jim at the bench press.

Jim was going to be gone the week I was attempting this and before he left, I told him I was going to beat his max. Jim had never had anyone come close to his max. He didn't compete at powerlifting meets; he just loved to work out. He had the potential to push a lot more weight if he wanted. In my attempt to beat him, I only hoped that he would want to push himself harder. That was the real reason I wanted to do this.

I hated the fact that he was going to be gone that week because I wanted him to see me lift, so I decided to do it that same week. I needed Rocky's help to wrap my arms. I did not trust anyone else to wrap me because I needed them to be extremely tight. The only bad thing was he would wrap me one arm at a time. That means while he was wrapping my second arm, the one that was already wrapped would be numb, and the blood circulation would be cut off that much longer. I did not want Rocky to rush wrapping my arms, though. I sat through the pain, mentally blocking out what few people can even think about doing.

After warming up, I started my first lift with 405 pounds. I had to start with a heavy weight if I were to beat the 445 pounds. The next weight I pushed up was 425 pounds, and I lifted it easily. This was awesome! Everyone in the gym was watching me. They stopped lifting to cheer me on. There were a couple of hot Latino girls my age on the second floor looking down and cheering me on. Now that really helped! I did not want to waste any more energy so I went straight to 450 pounds.

This was it! Jack held my wheelchair while Rocky started wrapping my arm. Everyone gathered to watch and cheer me on. I had Rocky spot me from the back, with Jack and another guy on each side of the bar for extra spotters. As I laid down, all I could think was, "Don't fail." I lowered the bar, and I felt the wraps pulling my flesh apart.

As the bar touched my chest, I started to push and all of a sudden the bar started to move toward my neck. I yelled, "Grab it!" Rocky saw it, too, and immediately grabbed the bar and yelled at the other spotter to get it as well. It was freaky and I don't know what happened, but I do know I was glad Rocky was behind me.

Even though I could have been decapitated, I was not going to end on that note. My arms were hurting from Rocky wrapping me so tightly. They were multi-colored and the colors were not fading. I had bad-looking, long blood spots under my skin but I asked Rocky if he had enough energy to wrap me once more, and he said he would. I wanted to attempt the weight again.

I knew that if I couldn't get it this time, I was done. My arms couldn't take it that much longer. Being wrapped three times is a lot, and a fourth time that tight was too much. It did not matter, though; I would sacrifice my body to achieve what others thought was impossible. Being wrapped the fourth time hurt like hell. My skin was sensitive but I showed no emotion. I had to block it out for this last attempt.

This was it. I lay back under that massive weight for the fourth and final time. Again Rocky gave me a lift-off as everyone was cheering. After that last attempt, I knew people had doubts that I could lift it. When that bar touched my chest, I pushed as hard as I could. It was going up, up, up. Then the bar got stuck under the left clip at the top. I had my right arm locked out and the left side was going nowhere. I tried to move it but it didn't budge. I was not about to rotate the bar sideways to get it out of the clip. If I lost control of the bar, I could put myself in serious danger. Dropping 450 pounds on myself would definitely hurt.

After holding the bar for ten seconds, I told them to grab it. As I sat up, people were amazed at what I had done. Even though I did not lock out the left side, in my heart I knew I lifted 450 pounds that day. It was fulfilling and a great feeling. Soon afterwards, they weighed me and I officially weighed 199, which they put on the chart. Despite what had happened, it was a success.

When Jim came back, he was surprised at what he heard. The funny thing was that a week later he maxed and pushed up 455. It was a great feeling knowing I had helped push him to the next level. Even though I did not succeed at lifting 450 pounds, I ultimately accomplished what I had intended in the first place.

Words cannot explain the chills I get from pushing people to their absolute max.

CHAPTER 45

Finding a Way

Working out was everything to me. It just didn't feel right if I missed a day, even when I was sick. Lifting was in my blood and I knew that my purpose in life was going to revolve around fitness. I did not choose it; it just seemed to have chosen me. Everybody is meant to do something in life and there is a reason for everything; sometimes it makes sense when you least expect it. But I understand that lifting is meant to be part of my life and no matter what the challenge, I face the gym with exercises. There is always a way!

Finding ways to perform certain exercises took me years. Experimenting and trying different angles was key. Yes, there were certain exercises that I could not perform but there was always an alternative with which I could still perform the same type of movement. In a way, everything depends on how open-minded you are and your willingness to try new things.

There were times people would look at me funny while I lay on the floor, working my biceps, but I did not care. It was something that I just had to try to see if it benefited me. Finding what works for you is the key to success in the gym, and the weird exercises I did helped me to evolve into the beast I am today!

CHAPTER 46
Ottawa University

I had the whole summer off from school. It was nice not having to take classes for a change. Now all the worries I had were about going to the gym. School was stressful when I tried to get good grades. I really had to put in the time and effort if I wanted to have a high GPA; I could get by if I tried, but having a good GPA was something I took pride in.

I was debating where I would go back to school in August; it was either Kansas University (KU) or Ottawa University. KU is about thirty minutes from where I lived and is a huge university with hills that are insanely steep, whereas Ottawa University is much smaller, three minutes away from where I lived, and very compact.

I really wanted to go to KU because there was so much more there—and so many more women. On the other hand, I did not want to have to drive back and forth if my classes were a couple of hours apart and I did not want to sit around all day.

Many people said that at KU, you could take a bus to get to the other side of campus just to get to your class. I did not like that one bit. Hills are horrible for people in wheelchairs; it's fun to go down hills super fast, but uneven cement, someone or something in your way, or something stuck in the cement could easily make you catapult out of your wheelchair if you weren't able to control how fast you were going. When you grabbed the wheels to slow down or tried to stop, they rubbed the skin off your hands or it turned into blisters later.

Going down the hill is only part of it, because what goes

down must go back up. Pushing uphill is hundred times harder than going downhill. Depending on how steep the hill is, it may be impossible to go back up it. There were times I tried to go up certain hills and when I tried pushing up them, I would have to lean all the way forward in my lap—and every time I pushed, I popped a wheelie. If I had pushed too hard, I could have rolled over backwards.

People said that it sometimes took twenty minutes to walk from class to class. If I had to do that type pushing in a wheelchair, it wouldn't be too bad. Pushing myself did not bother me; all the other factors I had to take into consideration did. If it were hot outside, my butt would be cooking on that cushion and there was a good chance I would develop an ulcer sore; same thing if it rained. Here in Kansas, snow and sleet are bad sometimes. If it snowed or sleeted and there was a layer of ice on the cement, it would be extremely hard to maneuver, and adding hills to that equation would not be a fun time.

Overall, it was just best for me to go to Ottawa University. It cost quite a bit more but my parents did not care. They were paying for my tuition and wanted me to go to Ottawa in the first place.

Going the full two years at Neosho and receiving my associate's degree paid off when I transferred to a university. Another student transferred to Ottawa University before graduating and was set back a year. He was so close to being a junior and all of a sudden he was a lower sophomore needing a lot more credits. Since I had my associate's, I was guaranteed to be a junior when I transferred.

It was weird realizing I was about to go to a different college as an upperclassman, not knowing anyone. I had never transferred to a different school. I was one of the few true Pomona students who had gone to the same school their entire life, from kindergarten to twelfth grade. Thirteen years! This was going to be brand new for me and I kind of liked the fact that I was going in with two years under my belt. The only thing I wondered about was how people were going to react to my wheelchair.

Before school actually began, all new and transferring students were required to show up for college orientation one Friday, Saturday and Sunday. We were supposed to meet in the lunchroom at ten in the morning on the Friday. I had no clue where that was, so my plan was to get there early and follow the crowd or ask someone. As I headed to the campus in my Blazer, I thought I should drive around the campus one time to scope things out. I been there before and the entire campus sat on two by two blocks.

As I drove into the main entrance, I saw that they had a couple of handicap parking spots, which gave me a good vibe, even though I knew they were required to have them. As I unloaded my chair from the back of my Blazer, the first thing I saw was buildings spread out but not that far apart. Three of the main buildings where classes actually took place were about seventy-five to a hundred feet apart from each other. The three dorms were spread out from one another but were all still within a five-minute walking or rolling distance.

After a few seconds, I could tell where everyone was going so I just followed. As I got closer to the building, I began to notice signs that said "Welcome" in black and yellow. Rolling closer, all I saw was about five stairs and a ramp close by. I headed up the ramp to the front door where there were a few people going in and out. As I approached, people made an effort to open the door for me. It's no problem for me to open doors, but it makes people feel better to help a person in a wheelchair. Women don't get the door held open for them nearly as much as I do!

There was a help desk about thirty feet ahead as I went in. The snack bar was to the left and the cafeteria off to the right. This place was so simple and it was very easy to go from one place to another. Everyone was heading to the cafeteria and when I rolled in there, it was packed. There were a dozen or so big round tables spread out, and I sat by one of the outer ones. I could tell there was a good mix of transfer students versus first-time students. The parents were with the younger kids and the others just looked around.

Orientation began with the whole welcome speech, telling us how there was only a certain percentage of students in the United States going to college and an even smaller percentage finishing college, and that some students were going to find their true love, as many students had in the past.

After about fifteen or twenty minutes of that, they broke everyone into groups. Multiple orientation leaders (students in bright-colored shirts) went to the front. Once everyone had been assigned a specific orientation leader, we went up to them and they led us to another building. It was over ninety degrees outside and when we went into a big, tin building, it was even hotter.

They had a platform stage set up with a microphone and speakers. Once everybody was in the building with his or her group, a man got on stage. He was there to break the ice. He had us go meet ten new people quickly, just saying "hi" and introducing ourselves. Then he made us do some games. It did work and I met people—but it was just so miserable sitting in that oven.

Afterwards, we took a break to eat lunch in the cafeteria and were supposed to meet back out front in an hour. I went home to eat because I did not want to eat there. Going back there after lunch felt weird. I was the only person in the entire school in a wheelchair and people were looking at me.

If being in the tin building wasn't uncomfortable enough, we next headed to the football bleachers. Some bleachers have ramps, but these did not. I wanted to leave so badly but I stayed because I had just gotten there. While everyone was sitting in the bleachers, I rolled off to the side to find an opening in the fence to get on the football field. After finding one, I wheeled in front of the base of the bleachers, about fifteen feet below everybody, and sat there alone and uncomfortable while we waited for a few minutes because others were still showing up.

I felt like such an outcast but, at the same time, I saw where I could intimidate them with my looks: I was a big, bald-headed guy who looked like Vin Diesel. One guy went through the railing and hopped down to where I was. You could tell he felt bad for me and I was glad for his company. I greeted him and he just smiled, asked me how it was going, and asked if it was okay if he sat down there with me. It was really nice of him to do that, but I still did not feel like one of them.

Once everybody showed up, the group played a little game while we just sat there and watched at the bottom. It did not last that long and soon everything was almost finished for the day and I was glad for that. I went home thankful the day was over.

■ ■ ■

School started that following Monday. Nervous and excited, I wondered how everything was set up, who the teachers were and how many students were in each class. Going from Neosho to Ottawa University was a big transition and when it came to the classes, it was like day and night. For the past two years, I had been going once a week for almost three hours. Now I had to go Monday, Wednesday and Friday each week for fifty minutes or Tuesday and Thursday for one hour and fifteen minutes. This was a walk in the park—well, for me a roll in the park!

As I sat in class, I saw others staring at their watches, doodling or doing something to make the time go by faster. But for me, it seemed like nothing.

My major was business and all the business classes were held in the administration building. The only problem was that building wasn't wheelchair accessible. They had to move all the classes I took into another building that was accessible.

As always, I showed up to class early and could tell the university did not give the students a lot of notice that the classes had been moved because some of them complained about the school moving classes around. Hearing comments like that made me feel horrible, but I couldn't do anything about it. It wasn't just one student who said it, either, but many of them. Some noticed that I was in a wheelchair and caught on as to why the class had moved, but others did not even notice.

The worst was when I went to class and no one showed up. I did not know what was going on; I thought the class might have been cancelled so I went outside, rolled over to the administration building and used my cell phone to call the registrar, which was in the administration building. I asked the woman about the class, and she said it should be in the room I had gone to. Then she told me that they might not have seen the sign and might still be in the original classroom. She said she would check and asked where I was.

I hoped they were not in that room because I did not want them to have to move just for me. After a minute, the woman came down to talk to me and said that they were all going over to the other building now. My heart dropped when she said that because I knew when they saw me they would know I was the reason they had moved. I hated that with a passion. I was sitting in the classroom as they entered and couldn't help but think they were all looking at me, thinking, *It was because of him that we had to move.* Dealing with things like that really made me feel terrible.

Another thing to deal with was the weather, which is unpredictable in Kansas. The worst of it was dealing with different seasons while being wheelchair-bound. There were many times the rain soaked me as I took my wheelchair out of the back of my Blazer. Not much I could do, and even if I had an umbrella, I needed both hands to push myself in the chair. In fact, even if I could use an umbrella, I wouldn't; it would just be another object I'd have to mess with.

Rain was nothing compared to the wintry snow, however. Snow itself is not bad; sleet, on the other hand, is awful. The blood circulation in my legs is bad and I have a hard time keeping my feet warm even in the summer; in the winter I have to wear a couple pairs of socks to make sure they are warm. Even with multiple layers of socks, my feet always seem to be freezing cold, but I have no way of telling if they are cold unless I feel them with my hands.

Many times in winter I would just about fall as I walked around the side of my Blazer, trying to get my wheelchair out the back. Falling on your butt for most people would be funny, but for me it is very serious. Ever since my wreck, my coccyx curved and I had very little muscle where it stuck out. If I did fall and land on my butt, I would easily break my coccyx, and if that happened it would affect what little walking I could do. I would be bedridden for months, unable go to school, unable to work out. My GPA would go down and my muscles would get smaller. Everything that I worked so hard for would all be in vain, so I got myself some chain booties that slipped on to the bottom of my shoes.

However, even after I was sitting in the chair, my worries were far from being over. I still had to get to class. After a few ice storms, the staff couldn't clear the parking lot and part of the walkways fast enough; having class at 8 a.m. didn't give the workers much time. Pushing through inches of snow is one thing, but when there is ice underneath the snow, it is a whole new ballgame.

Overall, it wasn't easy for me to go to college in a wheelchair. But I wouldn't let the difficulties stand in my way.

CHAPTER 47

Football

After a few days of going to school at Ottawa, one of the aerobic instructors from the gym approached me and told me that her husband was the football strength and conditioning coach at the university and he was looking for someone to help him out. She thought I might be interested since she knew what I'd done in the past and how I was always down at the gym. I said yes instantly and was so excited to possibly have the opportunity to help with the football team. The way I saw it, it was a chance to gain more experience working with a wider range of people.

A day later, the football coach called and asked if helping with the football team in the weight room would be something I would be interested in doing. I told him I was all for it. We set up a time to meet in person so he could ask me a few questions and get to know me.

He was a nice guy and very friendly. We got down to business and he began asking me questions like how long I had been lifting, what experience I had and other issues along that path. I told him I had been lifting since 1995, had done multiple powerlifting competitions and even competed in a World Cup two years in a row, and I was in the process of getting my personal trainer certificate. After a few minutes of questioning, he was all for taking me on to help him. He told me to stop by the football office later that day to meet the head coach.

I went to the building later on and when I tried to open the door, it was locked. I saw a guy walking toward me from the left and asked if he knew when the doors would be open. He said he was opening them now. Then he said, "You must be Nick," and stuck out his hand for me to shake. As I shook his hand, I was startled and said, "Oh, hi. You're the one I'm here to see." I was expecting an older guy.

As we talked, he told me that the other coach was impressed with me and that he could tell I'd been lifting a while. He asked me if I could show up the next day where they practiced so he could introduce me to the guys.

The next day I showed up in the middle of their practice. I got out of my Blazer and wheeled over to the head coach to let him know I was there. I shook his hand and talked for a bit then headed over to some shade by the trainers. After about thirty minutes, the practice was over and the coach got everyone together down on one knee. The strength coach waved for me and I rolled over to where he was gathering everyone. After he gave the team a little talk, he introduced me as "Coach Scott" and told them that I would be helping in the weight room. He said he expected everyone to listen to me and do what I said. That totally caught me off-guard—even more so when he said "Coach Scott." That just sounded weird but I liked it.

Afterwards, the strength coach told me that weights were at 6 a.m. I told him I would be there.

That night I had so many thoughts running through my head that it was so difficult to go to bed. I got up at four-thirty to do my morning routine and headed out by five-thirty. Wide awake from excitement, wondering how it was going to be, I pulled into the school. I knew where the weight room was but realized I had no clue what equipment they had.

As I opened the doors and rolled in the building, there wasn't much room. There was enough room to wheel around a bit but all I saw was a door to my right and stairs. The door to the right was like a closet door, but locked. I figured that wasn't the gym; the damn gym was upstairs.

All I thought was how can I get up the stairs, and after a few minutes it hit me. The stairs had a wooden rail that I could hold on to. I would take a few steps up the stairs and pull my wheelchair up then take a couple more steps. First I tried grabbing the front of the wheelchair but once I pulled on it, it just wanted to go back down, not giving me any support to take more steps. That did not work so I tried pulling the wheelchair up from the back, grabbing on the bar that's in the middle of the back support.

After taking my first couple of steps and dragging it up the steps, the front of the wheelchair where I place my feet rested on the steps, stopping it from falling forward. However, that alone did not give me the support I needed to move further up the stairs. Then I got an idea!

I needed to use my wheelchair like a cane. Instead of just dragging it, I had to drag and lift the wheelchair so the front footrest would dig into the stair and no wheels would touch the stairs. In doing this, I could actually use my wheelchair as support. I felt sturdy with the rail in my left hand and the wheelchair in my right. I then took two more steps, dragged and lifted. This was working and I got to the top. A chill came over my body and the hairs on my arm stood up.

After getting up the flight of stairs, there was another flight of stairs and I could see the open door at the top. Starting up again, I moved more quickly, getting to the top of the second flight in a little over a minute.

I could have waited for the guys to help me but I wanted my options to be unlimited as to where I could go. No matter what type of situation, there is always a way to overcome it. Many people don't believe this, but it's true; they just don't stick with the problem long enough to figure out the most efficient answer.

There was the gym and it was big, a lot bigger than where I lifted; it was more spacious than anything. There was a desk to the left as I came in but everything was set out on an old basketball court. There was open space in the middle, treadmills to the left and dumbbells beside them. To the right were wooden plate forms with rubber padding to do power clean and straight ahead were all the benches and machines. I just sat in my wheelchair by the desk, waiting for everyone to show up.

Around five-fifty, the football players slowly started coming in and the strength coach came around that time, too. I wasn't nervous because weight lifting was my life, and my passion for fitness burned with an eternal flame.

The coach smiled at me and said he would come talk to me once he'd gotten the guys going. Most of them had arrived by six but some were still wandering in later. You could tell they were tired and did not want to be there. The coach had them stretch as a team and then split them into groups of three and four.

Each group was assigned to a specific lift and then switched after a set period of time. After they'd started, the coach came over to me and asked what I thought. It was totally different than what I was used to. Most of the football guys had been lifting since high school. Since I'd been around weight so much, I could tell most of them had never been taught proper techniques. It wasn't their fault, though; they could only do what they'd been taught.

The coach sat down and began telling me he wanted me to watch the guys to make sure they were doing the exercises right. After I had been doing this for a while, when he thought I was ready, he would let me be in charge of them, which made me feel great.

He got the workout and went over some of the things with me to let me know why he did what he did. Looking at some of the names, I had no clue what they were and asked him to explain. I wasn't shy about asking because I wanted to know. Different exercises and movements fascinate me. Learning movements

and which muscles they worked interested me, and I'd even gone
so far as to research the best technique and form to perform the
movement.

The first day I just observed everyone. I wanted them to get
used to my presence before I started making comments and suggestions. I wondered how the guys were going to take it since I was
about the same age as them, if not younger; some of them were
even in some of my classes. At the same time I figured they would
listen to me because I was more muscular than they were.

At about six-fifty, the second batch of guys started coming in.
The coach had split the team by offense and defense. The guys did
the same workout and left around ten to eight. Those who had an
8 a.m. class lifted with the 6 a.m. team so they had enough time to
clean up and get ready.

When practice had finished, I started to head out and they
helped carry my wheelchair down. I got out of it and held on to
the railing with both hands as I walked down the stairs sideways.

It felt good knowing I could go upstairs not having to depend
on others for help, but I had no clue about how to go downstairs,
and that bothered me. So the next time I went to the gym, I tried to
figure out how to go down the stairs on my own. As I sat at the top
of the twenty steps, it hit me. I would walk down about four stairs
on my right side holding on to the railing. Then, with the back of
my wheelchair facing me, I would grab the back support bar with
my left hand and pull the wheelchair to me slowly while holding
the rail with my right hand.

Once the back tires hit the first step, I would push the wheelchair forward and upwards by supporting the back tires on the
step. The wheelchair did not move and felt sturdy unless I pushed
down. Feeling supported with my wheelchair in that position, I
took two more steps down and pulled the wheelchair down two
steps as well. Using this process, it took some time to reach the

bottom, but it did not matter how long it took; it was a blessing that I could even do it in the first place. For that alone, I was grateful.

On my second visit to the gym with the team, I began correcting some of their form to make sure they were doing the exercises correctly. Along with my suggestions, I always explained to them why they should do it as I said. Knowing the reason they were doing it in the first place gave them comfort and some of them felt a big difference with my suggestions.

Lifting weights is an art. Every exercise has a certain technique, and if performed correctly, you will feel more emphasis in the muscle you are supposed to be working. The guys warmed up to me very quickly and some came to me to ask questions. They began to believe in me, and that made me feel good.

■ ■ ■

Every morning it was the same routine until they "red shirted" some of the guys; the ones who made the team continued to work out at the same time in the morning and the red shirts lifted later in the afternoons.

This really took a toll on my workouts with Rocky and Jack down at the gym because I had to change my schedule to make sure I was with the team for both the morning and afternoon. It was hard to make the change. My emotions were like a roller coaster. I felt bad for Rocky and Jack because I was working out with them less, but helping with the football team was a great experience and made me a well-rounded trainer.

Rocky, Jack and I had lifted religiously, even when I had school, but I saw this as a chance of a lifetime. So my workouts began to revolve around the football team. Most of the time I still met up with Rocky and Jack, but I began to work out on my own. I did not mind it, though. I was always motivated to work out regardless of who I was training with. Training is my passion and I am committed to that.

Rocky and Jack knew it was a good opportunity and were happy for me. I still worked out with them as much as I could, but helping with the football team meant a lot to me, and I took it to heart. I wanted to be there for the guys so they would have someone to count on if they had questions and to make sure they got their lifts in.

As time went on, I tried to help motivate these guys even more. Every once in a while I would break out a joke, and the one that they all fell for was:

"Did you hear about me almost getting arrested last night?" I said this with a serious look on my face.

"For what!" they'd ask.

I raised my arms and flexed my biceps in a front double bicep pose and, with a smile on my face, said, "For carrying these guns."

There were other jokes I told, too, and they would always laugh, especially when I caught them off-guard. Lifting for years in a gym, you hear all sorts of jokes. Some of the football players would tell me jokes, too, and there were a few guys who opened up to me more than others. They were the ones who always came to me with questions while the others just did their own thing.

I felt that I was having a positive impact on all the players, however. And, for me, it felt good to be part of the team again.

CHAPTER 48

The Talk

Throughout the season, one member of the coaching staff and I were both present at the morning weight sessions. The night weight sessions were different, though. I was the only coach there to help the red shirts. I got an attendance log from the strength coach and kept track of who showed up.

The head coach and strength coach knew they could count on me because I didn't like when the players missed weight training. If they did, I would always make them do something extra as soon as they got in the door the next time.

The coaches gave me the kinds of shirts, jackets and other clothing that they all wore to weight training and games, and the head coach asked if I was going to be able to make it to the games. I said, "Sure," without thinking—but that totally caught me off-guard because I wasn't expecting to go to the actual games. Deep down, I wondered if it was going to bother me to watch these guys play the sport that I loved.

When the time came for the first game, it was an interesting feeling. I sat in my wheelchair on the sidelines with pride. Even though I had no role during the game, I knew that everything the players had done in the weight room affected their performance on the field. The difference between a good player and an elite player is the quality of their training. The more explosive, conditioned and stronger a player, the more he will exceed and excel in his position during a game. That is what I cared about.

Being on the sidelines did not make me feel uncomfortable

or sad. Instead, I felt like I was a part of the team. I pushed myself up and down the sideline or the team helped push me. I enjoyed myself, but there were some disadvantages. For instance, I did not realize how cold it was going to be when I got to the first game. I wore khakis, an OU coach shirt and an OU jacket. By the end, I was happy it was over because I was so damn cold. My head was just about frozen because it was freshly shaved that morning, and my hands were numb as well. Worst of all, my legs felt like ice cubes, especially my calves and feet, then my quads. Even though I couldn't feel them, I still had to make sure they stayed warm enough.

The next game felt like it was going to be a cold one again, but I was prepared so I could actually enjoy the game instead of freezing on the sidelines. I wore two pairs of thick socks, two pairs of sweatpants with a windbreaker on top of them, a shirt, a sweatshirt, a jacket, a wool cap and a pair of gloves. Sitting on that sideline felt good—and I could devote all of my attention to enjoying the game, yelling and supporting the team.

Sometimes sitting on the sideline got really interesting. OU's field is not that great, and they schedule all their games in the early afternoon because they don't have any lights. The sideline was pretty much dirt, so it turned out to be one of the worst things about the field, at least for me. Not so much because of the dirt—but because of what happens to that dirt when it rains. Mud is the worst, and the players had to help push me around through it. My wheels were covered and my pants had mud all down the sides from the tires had flung it. My hands were also a mess from using the area of my pants near my knees to wipe off the damp dirt.

Some of the players messed with me and threw mud at me, while others snuck up behind me and slapped some on my back or the back of my head. People laughed at me because I was covered in mud, but I couldn't help but laugh myself, too. The whole thing cracked me up and I had a good time. Afterwards I just found a water hose and sprayed the chair and myself down.

■ ■ ■

I ended up going to all their games that season. It was a great experience, but the one thing that felt weird was riding to the games in the coaches' van. Here I was, the same age as these players—and younger than some—and I was one of their coaches. Because once I was in that van, it really sunk in.

The different places that we went varied in wheelchair accessibility. I couldn't go into most of the locker rooms to hear the coach speak, so I just sat on the sideline at the beginning and half-time, even at home games.

Overall, 2003 was an awesome season; the players just worked well together. We had a couple NAIA All-Americans, seven First Team All-Conference, two Second Team All-Conference, and fourteen Honorable Mentions. One of the running backs was especially phenomenal. Not only did he break the record for the most yards rushing in a single season (2,951), but he also had the record for most yards rushing in a single game (315) and most touchdowns in a season (28). He was drafted in the NFL and turned professional. This was a great experience and I was so glad I was a part of it.

Once that season was over, the head coach switched to another school and he pretty much took the other coaches with him. By the time summer arrived, OU had a new head coach and strength program. I ended up asking them if I could help in the weight room, and they were more than happy to have me help, but this time was a lot different. There wasn't actually a summer program and they were debating about purchasing some expensive software, in which they could enter data and other maxes, and the machine would give specific weights throughout fifteen weeks. Each week would have different percentages.

OTTAWA UNIVERSITY—2003 FOOTBALL RECORD

Date	Location	Opponent	Score	W/L	League	Overall
09/13/03	Ottawa, Kan.	Mid-America Nazarence University Pioneers	27-34	L	0-0-0	0-1-0
09/20/03	Lindsborg, Kan.	Bethany College Swedes	16-14	W	1-0-0	1-1-0
09/27/03	Lansing, Kan.	Saint Mary Spires	45-7	W	2-0-0	2-1-0
10/04/03	Ottawa, Kan.	Southwestern College Moundbuilders	48-21	W	3-0-0	3-1-0
10/11/03	Ottawa, Kan.	Sterling College Warriors	37-12	W	4-0-0	4-1-0
10/18/03	Salina, Kan.	Kansas Wesleyan University Coyotes	49-14	W	5-0-0	5-1-0
10/25/03	Ottawa, Kan.	Friends University Falcons	55-0	W	6-0-0	6-1-0
11/01/03	Hillsboro, Kan.	Tabor College Bluejays	27-3	W	7-0-0	7-1-0
11/08/03	Ottawa, Kan.	McPherson College Bulldogs	39-23	W	8-0-0	8-1-0
11/15/03	Athletic Park, Newton, Kan.	Bethel College Threshers	51-3	W	9-0-0	9-1-0
11/22/03	Orange City, Iowa	Northwestern College Red Raiders	33-36	L	9-0-0	9-2-0

Well, I loved Excel on the computer and could easily do what they wanted, so I told them to tell me the specifics and I could design that program. The coach liked that a lot. Once he told me exactly what he wanted and gave me guidelines for the layout, I had the program ready for him in less than a week. I spent hours just trying to make the layout and design look nice. They were impressed and all we had to do was get the maxes for all the football players who were still around.

Once school was out, the players were pretty much on their own, but when school started again, things started to piss me off. For the past year, the school had been in the process of building a new weight facility. I got in touch with the coach and he told me when they were lifting—but when I showed up at the gym, there were no stairs and it was so much smaller, although it had nicer equipment.

When the guys arrived, some faces were familiar and others were new. Some of the new guys looked at me like, "Who are you?" The coach never told them who I was or what I was there for, and that made me feel uncomfortable. The next time I showed up, no one else was there. So I gave the coach a call and he apologized for not telling me the correct time.

I decided right then that if he wasn't going to make an effort to tell me when they were lifting, I wasn't going to waste my time anymore. So that was the end of my helping with the football team.

CHAPTER 49

Mr. Brave

Every year, Ottawa University had a male comedian pageant called Mr. Brave. It was held at the chapel one evening in the middle of the fall semester. To become Mr. Brave, you must represent your club, performing four parts: club wear, swimwear, lip sync and formal. Not only do you have to perform all this in front of three main judges, but everybody who shows up from school.

I had transferred to the school, had been helping with the football team for a couple months, and had just joined the SAF (Student Activate Force) club. I thought this was a great opportunity for people to see who I really was—not just some serious weight-lifting guy in a wheelchair. So I told myself I would do it!

Instantly I grew nervous because when I asked other people if they were going to compete, they responded, "NO WAY!" Apparently, there were some really funny people who had entered in the past and were going to participate this year, but the past winners were not allowed to enter it again. On top of that, most of the school showed up to watch.

Well, that was just great—but I still was going to do it! If that many people were going to show up, I had to make it good. I asked SAF if I could represent the club and they were all for it because no one else wanted to. That worked out great—now all I had to do was figure out what was I was going to perform for each part. I had less than a month, but I was already going through my collection of music and doing research.

After hour and hours of listening, I finally picked my music. For club wear, I chose "What Is Love" from the *Saturday Night*

Live sketch. I asked David, who had been crowned Mr. Brave the previous year, for help and he was just hilarious, with the stuff he did during school. He was a chubby fellow and was proud of it, often wearing a shirt that said, "I Beat Anorexia."

The plan was to set up a table like a bar and have signs saying, "Root Beer Drinking Contest" while David and I wore red and blue suits and stood at the bar. But I couldn't find anything close to what they actually wore in the TV skit, so I spray-painted jean jackets and jeans red and blue. The whole root beer drinking contest was perfect because, earlier in that week, SAF actually had the contest—which I won, by the way, beating over a dozen men and women.

The rules were simple: Whoever drank six cans of root beer the fastest won. This took place after the powder puff football game outside, on the ledge of the main union building. I had asked the woman in charge of SAF if I could enter—then I asked if it was all right if I puked afterwards because I didn't want the carbohydrates in me. She laughed and said that was fine.

So after the powder puff football game, everybody who wanted to participate in the contest lined up and they brought out the root beer. Some people were trying to talk to me and I told them that I was trying to focus because I had to win. I had been talking crap the whole week, telling people to enter because I wanted to beat them, so I couldn't lose or I'd hear it from them later.

After all the sodas were lined up and everybody was in place, we began. I wasted no time! I just drank without taking breaths, sucking down the pop as fast as I could. In between drinks, the gas in my stomach would build up and I would burp quickly and really loudly to release it as quickly as possible so I could hurry up and drink another root beer. The more I drank, the louder and longer my burps were. I didn't focus on the people around me—instead, I focused on my six sodas.

Before I knew it, I was done and I had won! It was the best

feeling in the world and you could tell I shocked everyone. People assumed that the bigger guys would win and gave me little chance. After I won, I asked if it was all right if I puked now and they told me to go ahead. Without hesitation, I got out of my wheelchair and stood over the ledge. I stuck my finger down my throat and instantly started puking. All the other contestants were still close by me and all of the spectators stood on the grass, watching us. After about ten seconds of listening to my loud, heaving noises, the other contestants began puking over the ledge as well.

After I finished, people came up and told me that I had made them puke as well—not only the contestants, but also some people out on the grass, too. And the girl that was beside me during the contest said she couldn't drink her root beer because I was freaking her out every time I belched. That was so funny and I had a great time—but now I was focused on just one thing: becoming Mr. Brave.

■ ■ ■

The club wear we had for the contest was perfect! The way I had it set up was based on the root beer drinking contest earlier in the week. I would wear the blue outfit and David would wear the red, and we'd stand there drinking from root beer bottles, shaking our heads to the rhythm, like on SNL. I would have people on stage dancing, just the way they did it in the dance club scene on TV. Then we'd both turn around at once, I would sit in my wheelchair and we'd go over to a friend of ours. David would dance crazily up on her and front-bump her until she fell into my lap. Then I'd move my arm in a big circle, grab her butt and she would slap me, turning my head to the audience. I'd pause for a second and after that dramatic moment, David and I would both yell, "SCORE!"

Next, for the swimwear stage, I picked the song "Kokomo" by the Beach Boys. The plan was to come out dressed in a girl's top with a wig and a pair of shorts, and make a scene out of putting on suntan lotion.

For the final lip sync portion, I chose "Baby Got Back!" and would have some girls come out on stage with me. Finally, for the formal stage, I chose "What the World Needs Now."

Everything was set! It was Thursday night and the show began at 7:00 p.m. All the contestants had showed up early and I remembered to bring all my props. We also had to come the night before so they could explain everything to us and pick our order; I was set to go last. The stage was not wheelchair accessible, so I had someone carry my wheelchair up there as I lifted myself on stage. I was going to have to stay in the back of the stage, off in the corner, and hide behind the piano. I had to change there and stay there for the whole show.

The closer it got for my turn on stage, the harder my heart started to beat. David and I were both back there, already changed and ready to put up the sign. When it was my turn, the organizers knew not to play the music until I stood and our backs faced the audience. We were cracking up the whole time and then the music started. The audience laughed so hard, knowing what scene we were performing. After I grabbed my friend's butt and she slapped me, everybody got even louder. They wanted entertainment and that is what I gave them.

The swimwear portion was a pretty good success but the lip sync bit just flopped. All the girls backed out on me and I was up there alone with the "big butt" song.

The audience loved the formal portion. All the other guys came out in suits, tuxedos, or some nice outfit. I, on the other hand, came out dressed like a Chippendale's dancer and threw flowers to the audience. Before we finished the formal portion, we had to answer one question. While the judges were tallying to see who had won, everybody got back on stage and entertained the audience by dancing to "YMCA" and "Macho Man."

The votes were in. I ended up taking second. The guy that took first had an awesome routine but his lip sync set him apart. He memorized the dance moves and lyrics, and taped a clothes hanger wire to his face, performing the song "Bye, Bye, Bye" by NSYNC—perfectly, too. In the back of my mind I knew that he was going to win from how crazy the audience was when he finished his routine. But for my first time, I thought I did pretty well.

That night, I made a commitment to myself to do the contest again next year and win it—and, within a month, I had already thought of a couple of songs to which I could perform. When I lost the first time, something inside clicked; I wanted to prepare far in advance to make the next one turn out so much better. Plus, it gave me time to find better songs, since I would be able to feel the music from within and visualize myself performing to it.

■ ■ ■

The fall of 2004 arrived and the Mr. Brave contest was coming up again. I was still in the SAF club and asked if I could represent them for another year. But I waited a bit too long and another guy was already representing them. I was shocked because SAF was the only club I was in. Now what was I supposed to do? I really wanted to do Mr. Brave again; not doing it was not an option. Then it hit me—I had to join another club: THE MATH CLUB! I knew the president pretty well and when I went to talk to her, she said I could represent them. So for just a few weeks, I joined the math club.

The day of the contest, not only did I change in the back of the stage, but I got the closet as well. The favorites to win the Mr. Brave title were me and another guy, who had been putting a lot of work into his routine. Everybody told me how good it was and that he was going to be extremely hard to beat. I never said anything to anyone about my routine except the people that were going to help me.

This time, I wasn't performing last, though I was near the end. The guy who was the favorite to win would be going last.

Before my routine this time, I wasn't nervous at all. I focused more on not messing up rather than on what people thought of me. Since I was representing the math club, I dressed up like the stereotypical nerd: pocket protector, black glasses with white tape in the middle, white shirt and black pants. To top off the club wear, I told a riddle—not just any riddle, but the Missing Dollar Pizza Riddle. It went like this:

Three guys order a pizza and it comes to thirty dollars. They decide to split it three ways, so each pays ten dollars. The delivery guy comes, drops off the pizza, takes the money, and goes back to the pizza place. But when he gets back, the boss says, "No, the pizza only cost twenty-five dollars." So the delivery guy tells his boss that he will take the money back.

As he's driving, he realizes that the guys didn't tip him. So he decides to pocket two dollars and gives them three dollars back. They each got one dollar back, so then each of them actually only paid nine dollars (since ten minus one equals nine). But if nine times three is twenty-seven, and the delivery guy pocketed two dollars, the total is twenty-nine dollars. Where's the missing dollar?

Afterwards, I told them that some people are verbal learners and others are visual learners, so I had a special surprise for the visual learners. As soon as I said that, David came strutting his stuff from the back of the stage, dressed exactly like I was, and the audience went crazy. I already had poster boards with the numbers set up on three different music stands, with the back of the posters facing the crowd.

After David came out, we got into place and turned our backs to the audience; he stood by the far right music stand and I stood by the far left one. That was the cue to start the music. The song I chose was "It's Raining Men" by the Weather Girls. I had them start it about twelve seconds before the song really kicked in. So as the music got going, David and I threw off our glasses, started to unbutton our sleeves and shook our bodies like male dancers. When the song said, "It's raining men," we instantly turned around and ripped off our shirts. Then the math club president, Sharlynn, and one member, Stacy, popped up from behind the stage wearing ponchos and holding big water guns. They started spraying us down as we took off our shirts.

Under the shirts we both wore bow ties and shiny cuff bands around our wrists, like Chippendale's dancers. The crowd got loud and crazy, especially the women. Then we displayed the riddle with the poster boards, as David walked around and handed me the poster like he was the delivery guy. When we went backstage, we still heard the crowd going nuts.

For the swimwear portion, I came out to Aqua's "Barbie Girl" wearing a bikini top stuffed with a whole roll of toilet paper. As I bent over, a roll of toilet paper popped out and I threw it out into the audience. My lip sync song was "She Thinks My Tractor's Sexy" by Kenny Chesney. After a bit of the music playing, I came out popping a wheelie. Not just any wheelie, though—my family and I had built the front of a tractor out of a cardboard box and I had attached it to my wheelchair, transforming it into a tractor. When I popped that wheelie, the crowd went crazy! Sharlynn soon came out in her little country girl outfit with some crazy Halloween teeth and helped me out.

Finally, for the formal portion, I came out like a male dancer, except I added suspenders; as soon as the girls heard "Truly, Madly, Deeply" by Savage Garden, I won their hearts. I came out with a big batch of flowers and rolled to the edge of the stage, tossing them to everybody. Some girls even ran to the stage to get them.

Soon after, I got my question and answered it really well. Then the rest of the guys finished up. Overall I felt good, but I didn't know if I was going to win. The other guy who was favored had a strong routine all the way through. When he did his lip sync, I could tell he had practiced for many weeks, with four other girls trying to get the dance moves down to Michael Jackson's "Thriller."

As we lined up to see who was going to be that year's Mr. Brave, they started giving out other awards. This year they were not going to place first, second and third; instead, they were just going to crown the new Mr. Brave.

As the announcement was about to be made, all I thought was, *Please be me!* The announcer said, "Mr. Brave for 2004 is…NICK SCOTT!" That was an instant relief and the previous Mr. Brave crowned me to cheers from the audience.

The next day, people told me they thought it was close and, over the next few weeks, they kept coming up to congratulate me. It was awesome and a lot of fun to participate, but winning made it even sweeter.

Not winning bothers the crap out of me, no matter what I'm doing. I train hard, work hard, become dedicated and motivated, and do everything in my power to win! To me, that's what being Mr. Brave is all about.

CHAPTER 50

Diveheart 2004

Everything at OU was going great. I had finished my contract at the college, which was an outline of all the classes I needed to take the following year to make sure I had all the requirements to graduate on time.

Then, early in the spring of 2004, I got a phone call from Sara. Oh, yeah—I was going scuba diving for the third time! She called to tell me that Diveheart was having an alumni trip and she wondered if I wanted to go. This was awesome: three years in a row! The timing was perfect, too, since I wasn't taking any summer classes.

This trip was scheduled in the middle of August, about a week or so before my senior year of college started. So I told my mom and we planned everything out. It was exciting to know that I was going to see almost everyone in the program again.

This time my mom and I took an early flight and flew straight into Chicago on the same day. It was great seeing everybody I knew and to meet all the new people. Everything was the same as usual, but this trip was going to be one that we would never forget.

■ ■ ■

We were scheduled to stay at the HoJo hotel and dive in the same places as before, but things quickly changed. As we arrived at the hotel, everybody was evacuating to the north. There was a hurricane coming but it wasn't going to hit that night. It was already late and had been a long day so the trip organizers talked the hotel staff into letting us stay the night and heading out in the morning.

That next morning, we all rounded up and headed out. The plan was to go to Orlando, so we'd be away from the ocean. The drive from Key Largo to Orlando was almost five hours long and I was so happy when we arrived. After getting to the hotel, we scoped it out for a bit then all voted on where we should go out to eat.

Well, as we were heading to the hotel, I just happened to notice a Hooter's a few blocks down. So I said, "We should go to Hooter's since it's so close." Instantly, some of the girls exhaled and said, "Oh, God." But ten minutes later, we were at Hooter's.

I had told a couple of the guys that ninety-five percent of the girls working at Hooter's have boyfriends and they just play it off like they don't. Right away, the guys did not believe me. I told them that back in Kansas, there was a girl at my gym who I helped off and on, and she worked at Hooter's. She was the one who had told me that.

Just so I could convince the guys, I asked one of the waitresses if what I'd been told was true. She agreed right away and said that all the girls who were working right then had boyfriends. I started laughing and the guys were just floored—and possibly disappointed. After we ate, I had to get a couple of Hooter's shirts for me and Rocky.

When we got back to the hotel, the weather really started to change. The sky grew dark-gray and it began raining. I went outside with three of the guys who were in high school and one of the other guys in a wheelchair; we just headed out into the rain and ran or raced for a while, for no reason.

The hurricane had shifted and was heading our way; it was going to hit that night. I called my mom soon after I got back in. She was worried sick and her nerves were getting the best of her.

I could sense it in her voice. My father was also worried about me and was working in Florida just a few hours away. They were both watching the weather on the news. Yes, the hurricane was going to hit, but it did not bother me. I didn't think I was going to die or anything like that. Instead, I was going to have a good time.

■ ■ ■

After talking to my parents, I went out to mingle with everyone. The youngest of the three guys on the trip was shy around women. He got nervous just thinking about asking a girl for her number. So I took him under my wing as my apprentice and taught him how to conquer this fear. I told him women were attracted to confidence more than anything. It does help if you are good-looking and have a great personality, but confidence is key. Then I said I would show him. I told him to pick any girl and I would get her number. So he chose this beautiful Latino girl who was about my age.

I told him to come with me as I strolled up close to her, so she knew we were there. Then I waited a few seconds and started talking to her. I introduced us then began asking her questions—where she was from, why she was down there—just to keep the focus on her. After talking for neither too long or short a time, I said that a group of us were going to the bar in the hotel later on and suggested that she join us. Then I asked if I could get her number so I could call her later on. Instantly, she wrote it down for me and then we said our goodbyes.

As my apprentice and I left the hotel, he was so excited. He thought what I had just done and how I went about it was so awesome. I told him it was simple: If you stick to the basics, you will get more numbers than you can handle. 1) Be confident; 2) Ask her questions that keep the conversation about her; 3) Smile and joke a little with her if the context permits; 4) Don't overstay the initial conversation; let her know you're interested but leave her wanting more. If you stick with this, you will succeed.

He was excited and ready to talk to some other girls, so we scoped out the area and I spotted this cute girl about his age. I talked him into going over to her, but before he did, I told him to just be confident and keep asking questions about her. About five minutes later, he came back with her number. As we left, I gave him five and told him he had done an awesome job. He said he couldn't believe how easy that was and thanked me again. After that, he got even more numbers and made me proud.

■ ■ ■

Later on, we headed into the hotel bar/lounge with everyone. There were a lot of people already there. But soon the storm came and the lights flickered on and off. You could hear the wind pick up and the heavy rain on the roof; it was wicked, but I liked it.

My apprentice and I were sitting at the table with a few other people. Out of the blue came the woman whose number I'd gotten earlier, along with some of her family; they sat at a high table right beside ours.

Off and on, I would catch her staring at me and I would stare back; I kept catching her eye. After about ten minutes, I couldn't take it anymore and asked if she wanted to join us. Instantly, she came and sat by me. We hit it off and everybody was laughing and having a good time. I did not even think about the storm with her presence beside me. She made me feel good and I liked the feeling.

As the time passed, people started to leave one by one. It was getting late and she was leaving first thing in the morning with her family, who was giving her the eye to go, but she didn't care.

Her family finally called it a night and began getting up as if they were about to leave. She had to go with them but she wanted a picture taken with me. As her sister took a photo of us, I had my apprentice take a picture with my camera phone, too. She kneeled by me but then ended up on my lap—and it ended with me lifting her up. After that night, though, I never saw her again.

The storm kept going throughout the night and, the next morning, many things were destroyed. Trees and branches littered the ground—and they were not little trees, either. A tollbooth was also torn to shreds, but that's about all the damage I saw where we were. I couldn't believe all that had happened the night before. I was so focused on that girl that I had blocked out everything else.

After hanging out at the hotel for a couple days, we talked about going to Walt Disney World. I was down for that! I had never been there in my life and was very excited about going.

When we arrived at Disney World, we split up. Those who wanted to do nothing but go on rides went in one group and the others did their things. I went with the riders, but our group of thrill-seekers was not that big; there were only about six of us.

Being in a wheelchair always comes in handy at an amusement park. We were basically rolling VIPs. Every single ride we went on, we went straight to the front of the line. Later, we caught up with everybody else and rode together. Walt Disney World was a blast and my favorite ride was Spiderman, which was a 3D ride. The 3D graphics were amazing and I had never experienced anything like it.

■ ■ ■

The next day, Jim had scheduled us to go scuba diving in their waters. That would be awesome because they had so many sea creatures—but it didn't happen. The park was having problems because of the hurricane, and they did not allow us to dive. They felt bad for us, though, and gave us a tour in the back, where very few people were allowed.

Even though we did not dive, it still was an interesting trip. During every Diveheart trip I have been on, something crazy always happens—and, this time, I couldn't believe we went through a hurricane. But the trip was at an end and, before I knew it, we were back at the airport again—only I was not going back with everybody else. I had a straight flight to Kansas City, so I said my farewells in Florida then headed home.

Halfway home, I did not feel right. I sensed something was wrong with me but I did not know what. When I arrived, my uncle was waiting outside my gate. Before we left the airport, I had to use the bathroom, and as I was in the stall, I still did not feel right: either something was tight on my feet or I had been sitting on my butt too long.

So I stood up, holding the railing on the wall, and felt my butt to make sure I did not have pressure sore lumps. Back there, I felt something seriously wrong. The skin by the tip of my tailbone felt like loose meat, and it was a pretty big area, too. My heart dropped as I felt it—it was moist and, when I looked at my hand, I could see that the moistness was blood mixed with my own flesh. I couldn't believe I hadn't noticed it before. I had just changed in the hotel without looking.

All I wanted to do was go home, get my mom and go straight to the emergency room. As I got out of the bathroom, though, I played it off like nothing was wrong. Then, about halfway home, I told my uncle I had a bad sore near my tailbone and needed to go to the emergency room, but we needed to pick up my mom first. He was shocked and asked me how bad it was and I told him it was really bad, but that I did not want to call and tell my mom over the phone because she had enough worries with the hurricane.

As soon I got home, I greeted my mother and wasted no time

telling her I had to show her something. I told her what it was and how bad it was, and as I showed her the sore, she said, "Oh, my God…we're going to the emergency room!"

My doctor was on vacation in Florida and wouldn't be back until the next week, so the doctor in the emergency room said I would have to wait for him and sent me home. My mother went around looking for saline solution to clean out my sore. This was not the first time I'd had one and we knew what we had to do until I saw my doctor.

The sore was huge for an ulcer. The affected area was about ten inches in diameter and the sore itself was about an inch and a half in diameter. I could tell it was deep since fatty tissue was coming out of it. There was not much I could do, however, but lie on my stomach and wait, while my mother cleaned the sore multiple times a day.

I was devastated! I only sat on my butt if I absolutely had to. This was horrible! I couldn't work out, but, worst of all, school was starting in a few days and there was no way I could go to class.

I just began to cry.

CHAPTER 51

Ups and Downs

I had my ups and downs at OU, especially because I experienced that first ulcer sore right before going back to school for my final year. Getting an ulcer sore turned out to hurt more than I expected—but what was worse was that I didn't know if I was going to be able to take classes that semester. Everything revolved around how my sore was healing.

I stopped working out and laid on my stomach and sides to take pressure off the sore as much as I could. Feeling worthless and worried, I had no clue what was going to happen to me. If the sore did not heal well enough, I would have to drop my classes and push everything back—including graduation that year.

It was a rough time for me. I had worked so hard to graduate on time, but now that was something that might not happen. There was nothing I could do except wait and see.

Unfortunately, my sore hadn't healed enough by the time classes began. The truth hit me hard and tears started to run down my face. It was as if I were reliving the past. Graduating was not just for me but also for my family. I am the baby of the family and the only one who was actually going to graduate from university.

On top of all that, not being able to train was the worst. Lifting weights made me feel free. It was the one thing that kept me sane after my wreck—and now I was stuck again in a bed.

My mother felt my pain. She knew how much school and working out meant to me; they were my livelihoods. She hated that fact that I worked so hard and that things like this always seemed to happen to me. I knew I had to stay strong for her.

■ ■ ■

The doctor scheduled me to go to wound care at rehab. We asked him if there was any way that I could go to school. My sore had healed some, but it was still about an inch and a half deep and pretty close to the bone. The fatty tissue had dried up and now it was a huge hole in my back; it was the worst type of ulcer you could possibly have. My doctor told me that attending school depended on how the sore looked. That at least gave me hope.

I went to the wound care center in rehab, which had moved to a brand-new facility. One of the therapists that I used to do rehab with ended up taking care of me. He measured the sore to keep track of the healing progress. Because it was such a deep sore, he stuffed it with gauze to ensure that it did not heal over the top without healing from the inside first. I had to see him multiple times a week, but if the wound healed well, I could see him less often. So my mother also took care of the sore so we could speed up the healing process.

I called OU's registration department, explained my situation and could tell that the administrator felt bad for me. I asked her if there was any way I could miss the first two weeks to let the sore heal up some more before returning to classes full-time, and she said there shouldn't be any problems—except with senior Core. Senior Core was the only class that I had to show up for during the first few days of that week, since that was when they picked the groups for the whole semester. But there was no way I could show up; it would risk the sore getting worse since it was hot outside and my butt would be sweaty from sitting on the black wheelchair cushion. So I was out of that class for the semester.

■ ■ ■

Before too long, however, my sore was healing fast—mainly because I was in such great physical shape and took in large quantities of protein. We finally decided that I was fine to go to school as long as I went there and came home immediately to get off my butt. That was fine by me! A huge relief came over me; I thanked God that my sore was getting better.

Even though I was healing, I was still taking a risk by going to class, but as long as I did pressure releases more often and came home right after school, I figured I would be fine. After going to class a couple of times, that turned out to be the case.

My sore was healing up and I was so grateful to be taking classes that semester. The only thing that made me mad, though, was not being able to take senior core. I knew there was a purpose for everything, but that just frustrated me.

In our junior year, we had to fill out our contracts, which meant making sure we had all the right classes and credentials to graduate on time. Senior Core is the pinnacle class at Ottawa University and a requirement in order to graduate, regardless of your major.

Since I couldn't take the class during my fall semester, I had to see if they would allow me to take it in the spring—but the registration department wouldn't allow that because of the classes I was taking the following semester. My spring semester was full the way it was; I had Comprehensives, Christian Thought I and Gospels. Since Ottawa University is a Christian school, both Christian Thought I and Gospels were required, but that wasn't the problem. The problem was that I was taking both religious classes at the same time with a tough teacher.

Everyday Tuesday and Thursday we had to turn in a two-page paper about the assigned readings. Since I was taking both at once, that was twice as much work. Along with that, I had to attend eight chapels and write a one-page paper on each of them, as well as two eight-page papers for each class and many other assignments.

Eight pages wouldn't be bad, but I had to do it for both classes! Sixteen freaking pages! Twice in one semester! Those two classes were tons of bookwork and my Comprehensive turned out to be a fifty-plus page business plan for a gym.

At first I didn't understand why they wouldn't allow me to take Senior Core, but while taking those classes, I grew to understand the reasoning. In fact, it turned out to be a blessing!

CHAPTER 52
Melissa

It was my senior year at OU and the semester had just begun. I got to class early, like always, and watched as people filed in the door, filling up the back of the room first, as they always do. A part of me so desperately wanted to take a seat in the back of the room; however, because of my condition, I was limited to only the most mobile areas, which, unfortunately, happen to be at the front of the classroom nearest the door, making me the center of attention as other students enter.

I watched as, one by one, the students strolled through the doorway. Everything was familiar about this scene, like a recurring dream that had been repeating itself over the last four years. I lowered my head only for a moment as the sound of footsteps outside the door began to multiply. Then I looked up slightly and everything began to disappear as a single person captivated my attention. Time seemed to stop as all other objects in the background became motionless. The air grew silent until the only sound registering itself in my brain was the rapid beating of my own heart, which was increasing in speed and strength with every breath.

She had a tall, athletically slender figure, each curve toned and perfectly molded. Long, dark hair fell neatly to her shoulders, giving off a luminescent deep-red hue, as the light seemed to embrace each strand. As I found myself completely paralyzed in a trance-like gaze, my mind became my only active part, and I had to remind myself not to stare. It was no use. Her beauty was so captivating that my body simply refused my brain's commands to look away.

Sensing my drawn-out stare, she turned toward me and we locked eyes. In a desperate maneuver to hide my obvious gaze, I quickly turned away, but continued to watch her from the corner of my eye. Still in view, she broke her stride and changed direction. With each step, she drew closer and my heart began to beat faster, until each beat began to echo throughout my body. Before I knew it, she was sitting right next to me.

As long as I had been going to OU, this was the first time someone sat next to me on the first day; I was taken aback for a moment at the whole situation and desperately searched for something to say. This was the first time in my life I found myself hanging speechless and dumbfounded. On the exterior, I tried to project a calm and cool image, but inside I was a wreck.

At the peak of my tension, she spoke and, in one instant, the mood changed. My nerves began to soothe at the gentle sound of her soft and kind voice. As the tension melted away, we found ourselves deep in conversation, talking as if we had been friends for many years. Our personalities clicked instantly and this felt like it would be the start of a very good relationship.

■ ■ ■

In the beginning, Melissa and I only really talked during classes and the occasional hangout after school. We both led very busy and active social lives. She was always at softball practice while I was always in the gym. Although we both had very demanding schedules, we managed to find time to just talk and hang out.

Melissa had a very unique personality, different from that of any other woman I had ever met. She was fun and had a charismatic way about her that always left me wanting to spend more time with her.

As the relationship became more comfortable, we even found ourselves teasing each other the way old friends and close family members do. Melissa had a wonderful smile, one of those smiles at which you can't help but smile back. When you really made her laugh, her smile widened so that it pushed her soft cheeks up to form an adorable chipmunk-like expression. I used to playfully tease her about her wonderful smile, until she began trying to hide her smiles in my presence. Her lips tightened and puckered together, quivering with every muscle to keep from smiling, but she could never hold back for long.

I will always carry that cute, chipmunk smile with me. No matter what, its memory always makes me laugh.

CHAPTER 53

Rock's Wedding

Not too long after that semester began, Rocky told me he was going to propose to Tiffany. They had been dating since June of 2000, for over four years. He told me he loved her with all of his heart and could not see himself with any other woman. She was the one.

We talked about how he was going to propose, because the best proposals are when you catch the woman off-guard. Tiffany worked at the local country radio station and he knew her family would be listening, so he wanted to propose to her on air. After getting the ring and setting it up with her boss, everything was in place. I was listening to the radio and recording it. Tiffany was live on-air.

At that time on the radio, people could call in to sell or trade items. So Rocky was in the building and called in. Tiffany had no clue as Rocky started to talk about the ring and how he was willing to trade it for a wife, but not just any wife—she had to be loving, caring, and he kept on going for a bit.

Tiffany was asking who that was, and you could hear the emotion in her voice. Then she lost connection to the caller and kept saying, "Hello…hello?" She had to try to keep her focus by moving on to the next subject but then, over the radio, I could hear Rocky enter the room and there was a pause as he kneeled and said, "Tiff, will you marry me?" She answered, "Oh, my God…YES!"

After a few weeks, Rocky asked me to be one of the best men in his wedding. It was an honor; after everything we had been through together, I was proud to stand up there by his side.

After all the planning, October 9, 2004, finally arrived. Of the five weddings I'd been in and the few others I'd attended as a guest, Rocky's was the best. His was not too long or short; it was perfect. This was the first wedding I was in that had three best men because Rocky didn't want to hurt anybody's feelings by leaving them out. But he asked me to stay closest to him—and that was a great moment in my life.

The reception was a blast and I got down with my bad self! Everything was perfect and they made a great couple. I wish them the best and may God bless them!

CHAPTER 54
OU Oscars

The Student Activity Force (SAF) that I was a part of at OU planned and put on all of the events for the school. In my senior year, the club decided to do something new; students could vote for whomever they thought was the best-suited to specific categories. It was called the OU Oscars.

At the awards ceremony, they ended up announcing my name for the "2004/2005 Body Guard—Most Physically Fit" award. I was totally blown away.

This award really got to me and meant more to me than anything I had won in the past. Not that it was a fancy piece of paper or award, but the majority of the students chose me, out of all the other athletes at the school. That alone was such an honor; I did not realize, over the two years I had been there, that I made that much of an impact without even playing one single sport at that school.

That truly was one of my greatest accomplishments.

CHAPTER 55

College Graduation

During the spring semester of 2005, a problem arose. Graduation was in May and I still had one class left to take…Senior Core! I didn't even know if graduating was still an option. With only one class left, would they at least let me graduate and go through the ceremony?

I did not want to wait until May 2006 to do the ceremony and have my friends and family put it off another year. I could see if it was my fault and I had put my own graduation in jeopardy, but I couldn't do anything about getting a sore, and the school did not allow me to take the required class.

While talking to other students about my situation, I learned that, in the past, students had still walked at graduation and finished their classes in the summer. I instantly started to see hope again! So I called registration and the woman there told me I needed to write a letter of intent to graduate to another woman, who would have to give me permission to graduate with the class of 2005. She added that I would have no problem, since I only had one class left, I lived in Ottawa and there was no reason I wouldn't be capable of taking that class. Enthusiastic, I wrote the letter that week.

The next day I got a phone call from the woman who gave me permission to graduate with my class. Excitement overcame me upon hearing those words! There was so much to do in so little time. Graduation was just a couple of months away and I needed to get invitations out to everyone—though I did not want to make it extravagant. That's just how I am.

■ ■ ■

With only a few months left, it was also time to do the unthinkable. I wanted to walk across the stage at my college graduation. Not just walk with forearm crutches like at my high school graduation, but *without* them! I wanted to just get on stage and walk with my AFOs to get my diploma. My whole family and closest friends were going to be there and this was going to be for them.

This would be something that few have ever witnessed. And, frankly, I wondered, *Can I even do it? Walk for the first time again?* I had walked with forearm crutches and, at the gym, I could walk a step or two, but then I had to hold on to something. Deep down in my heart, the passion burned for me to do this.

■ ■ ■

On top of my workouts, I went down to the gym every day for a second time leading up to my graduation ceremony. I spent an hour working on my walking and cardio. I went to the gym either early in the morning or late at night, depending on what was going on with school. I wore the new braces and worked in the aerobics room, which wasn't enclosed; people upstairs on the treadmills could see me and people walking by could just glance in the door. The aerobics room was in the middle of the gym but that did not bother me because I was focused.

I had my iPod around my neck, cranked all the way up, while listening to the *Rocky IV* soundtrack, repeating "Eye of the Tiger" or "No Easy Way Out" or any other type of music that motivated me; I gave myself chills that way.

On one side of the room, I tried to stand up without touching the wheelchair with my hands—using just my legs. As I tried to stand, I lost balance and began to fall forward on my face, but I would catch myself with my hands. Trying to stand up and keep my balance, I felt my muscles in my back start to shake. This was going to be difficult, but I was going to walk at graduation. Nothing would stop me.

I had practiced walking at my house, but I normally held on to something or took only a few steps before grabbing something for balance. This was different. I took a step and it was not smooth, so then I took a step with the other foot. As I took my third step, I lost my balance and fell face-first, but caught myself just in time.

It took me a few seconds, but then I got back up from the ground. I continued taking steps. The aerobics room was about fifty feet in length, more than enough room to practice. After falling more than a dozen times, I eventually got to the wall, turned around and began to head back to my wheelchair. On my way back, I lost balance again and again, falling completely to the floor; sometimes I even fell sideways.

When falling, it's not a fast movement, but like slow-motion, because I resist the fall and it never hurts me; it's more frustrating than anything. All I could do was stay focused, take my time and follow through with my steps. The more I practiced, the easier it got and the less I fell.

Working out at the gym forced me to get up and move around a lot, which actually helped me get where I was. Leg training gave me the foundation, which is why my legs were strong. Over the years, I just kept training the muscles that could be worked in my legs; I could leg press over 700 pounds and do leg extensions with the whole stack of weights for reps of ten. But I could barely lift ten pounds with my hamstring muscles, no matter how hard I trained them.

After walking back and forth multiple times, I really got into the rhythm and fell less often. I pushed myself to the next level by getting in my wheelchair and setting eight of those square blocks

that go under aerobic steps on the floor to my right and left. I
spaced them three feet apart so that, as I walked, I bent down and
touched the block on the right with my right hand, and reverse on
the left. This action trained me to bend down and be able to stand
back up.

After a few repetitions, I spread the blocks even farther apart
so I had to walk more. Then I switched the square boxes for medicine balls, but this time I picked the ball up and set it back down
or carried it with me.

There were multiple things I did to try to better my balance.
In the process, I fell so many times, but never once did it hurt me.
During that time, different people came up to me and told me how
shocked they were to see what I was doing. They had no clue I had
that much mobility and were happy for me, telling me to keep up
the good work. And I did.

■ ■ ■

With months of practice behind me, everything was set. School
was out and all I had left was the rehearsal. This rehearsal was
much different from my high school graduation; the ceremony
was going to be held at a church.

At the rehearsal, they told us where we were going to be sitting once we arrived, and everyone sat in their spots. They also
told us how we were going to enter, how we went about going to
our seats, and when to sit and stand. After that, we went through
the walk just once. There were only one problem…the stage was
not wheelchair accessible. It was wide and there were doors on
each side through which you could access the hallway. From the
hallway, stairs led up to the stage.

People entered the right door, went up the stairs, walked across
stage, shook hands, exited the stairs on the opposite side of the

stage and headed back to their seats. When everyone did his or her walk-through, I did not practice walking; instead, I went through practice sitting in the wheelchair. They did not know I was going to walk, but if I hadn't known I could do it, it would have been awful.

If I were not going to walk, graduating wouldn't have had the same feeling. I would receive my diploma on the floor-level, where no one could see me, and I wouldn't get the same type of ceremony; either they would have bent down and handed me the diploma while they stood on stage or they would send someone down there to shake my hand because I was "special."

But just because I am in a wheelchair doesn't mean I need to be treated like a second-class citizen. Even though I planned to walk, that burned me because I knew what others would have to go through at future graduations if they were wheelchair-bound.

After practice was over, the organizer told us the time to meet in the library the next day. When everyone left, I stayed behind to talk to the guy in charge. I told him that I wanted to walk tomorrow and asked him if there was any way I could practice later that day because I had to go get my other braces. With a surprised and happy look, he said that the church was going to be open for a few more hours and asked if I needed any help. I grinned and told him that I wouldn't need any help and that I'd be back in about twenty minutes.

After getting my braces and something to eat, I was ready to take on this challenge. As I entered the church, I rolled down to the stairs on the right. The organizer came to talk to me again. At first, what I'd said to him earlier didn't sink in, so he asked now what I was going to need. I asked him if there was any way they could take my wheelchair to the other side tomorrow without people seeing it because I did not want my family to see my wheelchair. He told me that the hallway went all the way around and he could have a couple of people wait with the wheelchair on the other side for when I walked down the stairs.

I showed him that my wheelchair wouldn't fit unless they took it apart. We then tested it, so I got out of my wheelchair, taking off the tires to be sure that it fit. It did fit easily through the hallway like that, which was a huge relief. If that hadn't worked, they would have to push my wheelchair to the other side along the bottom of the stage, giving away the surprise of what I was going to do.

The organizer was very enthusiastic, telling me how great this was going to be. He added that I should make sure to let him know if I needed anything else.

Right then, I didn't need anything but practice. I left my wheelchair by the wall and stood up, holding on to the walls in the hall. I made my way to the stairs and climbed them with ease. At the top, there was a wall to the left and people couldn't really see you until you took a few steps out.

The stage was huge and I knew the path I had to walk. The stairs were already set up but then I saw a problem: an inch-high board I had to step over. Walking was one thing, but having to step over an obstacle was another story. Deep down in my stomach, I knew that little board was going to cause me big problems.

Even so, it felt good letting go of the railing and taking steps. After months of practice, I was in my zone as I analyzed the stage with my senses, zeroing in on my surroundings. It was as if everything was so much more detailed.

On approaching that board, I did my best to try to step over it—and it wasn't that hard with my slouched walk. Once I'd passed that, it went smoothly. I walked calmly across that stage back and forth multiple times, taking breaks in between as I sat on the chairs.

Teachers and some classmates appeared and were amazed at what they had just seen. They never knew I had that much mobility and, with shocked looks, they told me how awesome that was.

They asked me if I was going to walk at graduation the next day, and I replied that I was. Again, they repeated how amazing that was and I thanked everyone for the support.

I was pretty much done at that point. I walked back to the stairs on the right and left the church. Tomorrow was the big day.

CHAPTER 56

This Is It!

O n the day of my college graduation, my family was excited for me, especially my mother. Her emotions got the best of her and tears came easily. During the last few days, she hugged me over and over with a smile on her face, telling me I was her baby boy. I love my family and that is why I did what I did. They motivated me to be the best I possibly could be.

I left my house early that morning to making sure I was at the library with plenty of time. As I left, my mother was an emotional wreck, trying to find the perfect outfit.

When I arrived, the school had flags out all over the campus from the previous years, which looked nice. Last year, they did the same thing and it's a reality check when you see those flags, especially on your graduation day. It's gratifying to know you're done with college and about to embrace a new adventure in your life.

■ ■ ■

Even with the wind blowing, the sun's heat in the cloudless sky really cooked me under my black gown. Heading to the library felt good; it was as if the end were here, even though I had one more class to complete.

Time went by so slowly while sitting in that library. It got crowded quickly, packed with black and red gowns. People sorted themselves into different lines based on alphabetical order by last name. We knew who we had to be behind from the previous day's practice.

Everyone got quiet as we started to leave the library. I stayed with the class until we got to the main parking lot. They were planning to go down the sidewalk and take a left that led directly to the main entrance of the chapel.

The problem was that there was no ramp to the main entrance, so instead of following everyone else, I had to go in through the back entrance, as I always did. Once inside, I headed to the main entrance and waited for everyone else to enter. When they started coming through the main doors, they just kept going and walked into the chapel where the guests were seated. All I was trying to do was find the person I was supposed to be walking with so I could get back in line—and as she finally entered, I hurried to get beside her.

Heading to my seat, I gazed at everyone in attendance, trying to find my family and friends. Before I knew it, familiar voices caught my attention and I saw everyone with smiles of joy on their faces as they waved at me. It had been a long time since I was this happy.

Once I was settled in my spot, I couldn't help but think about how much of a blessing it was to see them all there, and I continued to look back at them and wave. They were all such a big part of my life and had been there for all of the ups and downs I'd been through.

As I sat there, I thought about the past. I got flashbacks, reliving my wreck and seeing that sky for the first time, and my mom and dad in the hospital as I lay in bed, helpless.

More visions from my life—from past to present—filled my head. Time passed very quickly and it seemed like all of a sudden, they were ready for us to walk. The rows of graduates started to stand up. Chills came over my body and my hands instantly got cold. I shook inside and could feel my bottom lip starting to tremble. The girl who sat next to me saw how nervous I was and was worried about me. Taking my hand to comfort me, she told me it was going to be alright.

The feeling was awful but the rows kept getting shorter. My row was up! As we lined up in the hall, I could see two people waiting for me. I quickly got out of my wheelchair and kneeled down on one knee to show them how to take it apart. It took about fifteen seconds then I stood up and entered the hall, following my chair. My classmates who hadn't seen me practicing the day before were stunned and asked me if I was going to walk. I told them I was. They were amazed, telling me: "That's awesome!" It made me feel better.

As the line got shorter, I stood in the stairs and couldn't help but think that I only had one chance. Up until it was my turn, all I did was ask the Lord over and over not to let me fall. Seeing the audience didn't help. There were so many people there and all eyes were going to be on me.

As my fellow classmate shook hands, that was the sign for me to walk. This was it! I started up the steps. Before I knew it, they called my name and all I heard was screams from the crowd. It felt good hearing others yell for me but I was focused on that little board I had to step over.

Wasting no time, I just went for it and that was a big mistake. As I did that, I just about fell forward but, thankfully, there was a table right by my side. I grabbed it, using it for support, and stood up. The dean was right in front of me when I almost fell and as I stood up, he shook my hand, telling me how proud he was of me.

As I slowly walked to the center to get my diploma, I could see all of my classmates start to stand up and clap their hands. Chills shot all through my body as I moved forward. When I stopped to receive my diploma, I could hear the cheers and screams growing louder. After shaking the last pair of hands, I took a couple of steps, looked for my family and pointed to where they were seated. That was my way of saying, "This was for you."

Focused on my walking, I headed for the stairs on the other side of the stage. Before exiting, I lifted my arm and waved, showing everyone I was appreciative of the support.

Walking down the stairs, I was so happy. I knew deep down that I wasn't going to fall; it felt as if someone or something was watching out for me.

A person was waiting at the end of the hall with my wheelchair; I got in and headed back to my seat. It was a great feeling.

■ ■ ■

When the graduation ceremony was over, I had to take the back way out to leave the chapel. Outside, people started coming up to me, shaking my hand, congratulating me and telling me how awesome it was that I walked. Some of the women who had known me for years hugged me, and I could tell that they'd been crying by their bloodshot eyes and red cheeks.

After a couple of minutes, my family found me and they were in tears. My mother, father, and sister especially, but I could tell everyone was emotional. They all gave me hugs but when my mother and father leaned down, they held me tight, telling me how proud they were of me and that they loved me. When I looked into their eyes, I could see pure happiness. Everyone was shocked at what they'd just seen; they knew I could stand and walk a little, but not as far as I had just shown them.

Lucus, Rocky and Tiffany were there, too. After so many years, they were still by my side. Lucus and I had been friend since the sixth grade, and Rocky and I had been friends since the ninth. They stuck by me when my world came crashing down. When I hit rock bottom, they were the first ones I saw: Lucus at my wreck and Rocky at the hospital. They were there for me through thick and thin, and now they were by my side at my graduation.

Once high school is over, most friends go their separate ways—not us, though. The only other person I wished was there was Zack, but he was graduating with his bachelor's degree the same day I was. I wanted him to be at my graduation as much as he wanted me to be at his.

■ ■ ■

After talking for a while, all of us headed to my house for the reception. I stayed around to say goodbye to some of my classmates then, about thirty minutes later, I loaded up and headed home.

At home, everyone was happy to see me. Others had shown up, including Lucus's mom and stepdad, and Jack. My mother cooked a feast that could feed an army, plus snacks, deserts and everything in between. They had streamers, balloons and the whole works set up inside the house.

Everyone was asking me what I had done to be able to walk on stage. That's when I revealed the work I had been doing down at the gym. They were impressed at what I had achieved and told me the drive I had was like no other.

It is a blessing to have so many people that love and care for me. The support they give me is one-of-a-kind and I am so fortunate. Over the years, I have had many challenges and it has not been an easy road. But quitting was never an option and I always strived to be the best at whatever task was at hand.

I learned that it takes patience, but if you believe—and believe in yourself—you will go far.

CHAPTER 57

What's Next?

As time passed after graduation, I finally understood what I was supposed to do. While I was trying to find out what I was meant to do for the rest of my life, it found me.

Even though I graduated with a BS in Business Administration, my true passion has always been fitness. Over the years of training and studying fitness, my love for it only seemed to grow deeper. I love helping people and helping them succeed in becoming the best they can possibly be. The most rewarding part of it all is seeing them get results and continue to make a lifestyle of it.

After receiving the Most Physically Fit award at Ottawa University, something inside of me changed. I really didn't care about how much I could bench press anymore. Instead, I had a growing passion for doing bodybuilding competitions, and my workouts began to change. (Heavy bench-pressing still led my workouts, however, since the roots of my workouts were too hard to change.)

■ ■ ■

When the fall of 2005 came, I decided to write this book you are reading at the moment. So I went full-force on working on this book. It's funny how things turn out in life. I hated writing in school and told myself I would stop writing once I was done with it. Now, here I am today, telling you my story.

So what's next? I competed in my first wheelchair bodybuilding competition in March 2006 at Palm Beach Gardens, Florida, and placed second in the heavy weight division. I want to keep participating in wheelchair bodybuilding competitions and really get more people who have physical challenges involved through leading by example.

In fact, I want to become the best wheelchair bodybuilder in the world. If you set your mind to it, you can achieve great things.

I have also designed a website specifically for wheelchair body-building, www.wheelchair-bodybuilding.com. If you or someone you know is wheelchair-bound and thinking about competing, please visit the site. I will help you achieve more than you ever thought possible!

I do believe this isn't the last you will be hearing from me. Thank you and God bless!

Powerlifting Achievements

I competed against all non-chair athletes

2005 Bench Press - Ottawa University, Light Weight Overall Champion

2005 Bench Press - Ottawa University, 1st - 198 WT Class

2005 Bench Press - Ottawa University, 2nd - Partners

2002 World Cup Championships, Bench Press - NASA, 1st - Open - 187 WT Class

2002 World Cup Championships, Bench Press - NASA, 1st - Pure - 187 WT Class

2002 World Cup Championships, Bench Press - NASA, 1st - Novice - 187 WT Class

2002 World Cup Championships, Bench Press - NASA, 1st - Teenage - 187 WT Class

2002 World Cup Championships, Bench Press - NASA, 1st - Junior - 187 WT Class

2002 World Cup Championships, Curl - NASA, 1st - Open - 187 WT Class

2002 World Cup Championships, Curl - NASA, 1st - Pure - 187 WT Class

2002 World Cup Championships, Curl - NASA, 1st - Pure Novice - 187 WT Class

2002 World Cup Championships, Curl - NASA, 1st - Teenage - 187 WT Class

2002 World Cup Championships, Curl - NASA, 1st - Junior - 187 WT Class

2002 State Championships, Bench Press - NASA, 1st - Open - 187 WT Class

2002 State Championships, Bench Press - NASA, 1st - Pure - 187 WT Class

2002 State Championships, Bench Press - NASA, 1st - Pure Novice - 187 WT Class

2002 State Championships, Bench Press - NASA, 1st - Teenage - 187 WT Class

2002 State Championships, Bench Press - NASA, 1st - Junior - 187 WT Class

2002 State Championships, Bench Press - NASA, 1st - 187 WT Class

2002 State Championships, Curl - NASA, 1st - Open - 187 WT Class

2002 State Championships, Curl - NASA, 1st - Pure - 187 WT Class

2002 State Championships, Curl - NASA, 1st - Pure Novice - 187 WT Class

2002 State Championships, Curl - NASA, 1st - Teenage - 187 WT Class

2002 State Championships, Curl - NASA, 1st - Junior - 187 WT Class

2002 State Championships, Curl - NASA, 1st - 187 WT Class

2002 State Championships, Curl - NASA, *BEST CURLER

2001 World Cup Championships, Bench Press - NASA, 2nd - Open - 187 WT Class

2001 World Cup Championships, Bench Press - NASA, 3rd - Pure - 187 WT Class

2001 World Cup Championships, Bench Press - NASA, 2nd - Novice - 187 WT Class

2001 World Cup Championships, Bench Press - NASA, 1st - Teenage - 187 WT Class

2001 World Cup Championships, Bench Press - NASA, 1st - Junior - 187 WT Class

2001 World Cup Championships, Curl - NASA, 1st - Open - 187 WT Class

2001 World Cup Championships, Curl - NASA, 1st - Pure - 187 WT Class

2001 World Cup Championships, Curl - NASA, 1st - Pure Novice - 187 WT Class
2001 World Cup Championships, Curl - NASA, 1st - Teenage - 187 WT Class
2001 World Cup Championships, Curl - NASA, 1st - Junior - 187 WT Class
2001 State Championships, Bench Press - NASA, 1st - Open - 187 WT Class
2001 State Championships, Bench Press - NASA, 1st - Pure - 187 WT Class
2001 State Championships, Bench Press - NASA, 1st - Pure Novice - 187 WT Class
2001 State Championships, Bench Press - NASA, 1st - Teenage - 187 WT Class
2001 State Championships, Bench Press - NASA, 1st - Junior - 187 WT Class
2001 State Championships, Curl - NASA, 1st - Open - 187 WT Class
2001 State Championships, Curl - NASA, 1st - Pure - 187 WT Class
2001 State Championships, Curl - NASA, 1st - Pure Novice - 187 WT Class
2001 State Championships, Curl - NASA, 1st - Teenage - 187 WT Class
2001 State Championships, Curl - NASA, 1st - Junior - 187 WT Class
2001 State Championships, Bench Press - NASA, *STATE RECORD - Open - 187 WT Class
2001 State Championships, Bench Press - NASA, *STATE RECORD - Teenage - 187 WT Class
2001 State Championships, Bench Press - NASA, *STATE RECORD - Junior - 187 WT Class
2001 State Championships, Curl - NASA, *STATE RECORD - Open - 187 WT Class
2001 State Championships, Curl - NASA, *STATE RECORD - Pure - 187 WT Class
2001 State Championships, Curl - NASA, *STATE RECORD - Pure Novice - 187 WT Class
2001 State Championships, Curl - NASA, *STATE RECORD - Teenage - 187 WT Class
2001 State Championships, Curl - NASA, *STATE RECORD - Junior - 187 WT Class

www.nickfitness.com